HAMPTON

From the Sea to the Stars
1610-1985

James T. Stensvaag
General Editor

Design by Jamie Backus Raynor
The Donning Company/Publishers
Norfolk/Virginia Beach

*Dedicated
to
the people
of Hampton*

The Donning Company/Publishers
5659 Virginia Beach Boulevard
Norfolk, Virginia 23502

In-House Editor: Richard A. Horwege

Library of Congress Cataloging-in-Publication Data
Main entry under title:

Hampton: from the sea to the stars, 1610-1985.

   Bibliography: p.
   Includes index.
   1. Hampton (Va.)—History. 2. Hampton (Va.)—Description.
I. Stensvaag, James T.
F234.H23H35   1985   975.5'412   85-20470
ISBN 0-89865-427-0 (special ed.)
ISBN 0-89865-428-9 (pbk.)

Printed in the United States of America

Contents

Hampton waterfront looked like this
from the 9th floor of City Hall in
1980. Courtesy of the Planning
Department, city of Hampton; photo
by Barbara Dorr

Foreword

Publication of this pictorial history culminates a year-long celebration of Hampton's 375th Anniversary. Through this unique glimpse at Hampton's past, the authors provide a perspective for us to recognize and appreciate our city's potential for the future.

In planning the birthday observance, Hampton City Council established the framework for marking an anniversary which has significance not only for our city, but for the state and the nation as well. As the oldest continuously-occupied English-speaking settlement in the country, Hampton holds a special place in history. City Council's goals were to promote a sense of pride among Hamptonians, to recognize properly the city's historical heritage, and to encourage economic development and tourism.

Through the efforts of many citizens the 375th anniversary celebration has been a tremendous success. A number of special events and programs have been sponsored. These included our celebration premiere in February, "In Pursuit of Hampton," an anniversary concert, birthday party, and parade. Fort Monroe, Langley Air Force Base and NASA reserved special days to commemorate our anniversary, and several area businesses contributed funds and facilities to sponsor sporting events, lecture series, exhibits, and receptions in our honor. The entire community was actively involved in this celebration.

The purpose of this pictorial history is to establish a visual link with our past. Several rare photographs and sketches complement the text. Research tapped many area resources, including libraries, archives, private collections, museums, and even personal interviews. The committee that prepared this volume selected a topical format to make the book more readable. But in doing so, they also underscored how important those topics were—and are—to the history of Hampton.

Thanks in large measure to the efforts of this committee, a bit more of our history has been preserved and recorded for thousands to read and enjoy. We are very proud of our city and its past 375 years. Hampton has a great history, and we are confident that our future will be just as great.

James L. Eason
Mayor

Acknowledgments

This book is a labor of love by volunteer authors and the many people who helped them. Elizabeth Brauer, co-chairman of Hampton's 375th Anniversary Committee, suggested the project as a legacy of the city's birthday celebration year. She established the Historical Committee which produced this book and appointed its membership. Organizational work was begun by Cody Phillips. Carolyn Hawkins co-ordinated writing the text and assembling the photographs in addition to serving as an author. Kathleen Anderson supervised the production of the book.

The production committee was made up of Rick Piester, Bo Parker, Elizabeth Brauer, Martha Steppe, Cathy Mercer, and Erika Page. The manuscript was read by Rufus Easter, Jane Martin, Beverly Gundry, Elizabeth Brauer and Dr. Mary Christian. Through it all, Dr. James Stensvaag, general editor, provided wise and skillful guidance. With its sponsorship, Old Point National Bank made the book a reality.

Their work would not have been possible without the generous assistance of Hampton General Hospital's Department of Public Relations, the Archives of Hampton University, and the printing and graphics departments of NASA.

Additional acknowledgments from the authors appear at the end of each chapter.

Introduction

James T. Stensvaag, General Editor

This book is a labor of love, and we associated with it acknowledge that bias from the beginning. The people who wrote these chapters did so because they enjoy living, working, and playing in Hampton, Virginia, and because they want others to know why they enjoy it. But the authors share another bias as well. They are all dedicated to truth, accuracy, and completeness, the three virtues of well-conceived history. They have written for the love of the subject and in the sincere belief that what they do is of value to their community.

Each of the authors has made a contribution which is as true, as accurate, and as complete as the sources and time would allow. Considering the amount of time they were given, a year or less from inception to publication, the results are remarkable. Even so, readers should consider this collection of essays and pictures as a stepping-off point rather than as a culmination of historical research. The authors do not consider their images and words to be an exhaustive treatment of any of the subjects. In fact, as with any first attempt at building a history, these essays raise as many questions as they answer. While we hope that the book stands on its own merits as a mirror of Hampton's past, we also hope that it stimulates other minds to explore the richness of local history in general, and Hampton's history in particular. Perhaps by the time of Hampton's 400th Anniversary Celebration 2010, this book will be remembered as the first in a series of ventures into Hampton's history which have contributed to a better understanding of the community.

The authors present glimpses of the city's past which are available in no other way. Film and word recall people and places that the passage of time has taken from us. These writers try to sort out for us the confusion of names and locations, no small task over nearly four hundred years. The English settlers of 1607 landed on this particular shore by accident, or perhaps fate, but not by design. No particular glory surrounds the founding of Kecoughtan in 1610—just human drama. No overwhelming destiny drove the development of Elizabeth City, Elizabeth City County, Hampton, Phoebus, or the rest—just the individual destinies of the tens of thousands who have called the area home. This is the stuff of which real history is made, and out of which civic pride is born.

From the Sea to the Stars is a collection of pictures and essays; it is not a "history" in the classic sense. It presents images of a locality, drawn from the authors' viewpoints and from the availability of illustrations. Each author has an individual style and point of view, and you may find the same topic treated differently in two or more chapters. Here, then, is a bit of totally unsolicited advice on how to approach the book. Don't hurry. Browse through the pictures, reading a caption or two as it strikes your interest. Then pick a chapter, any chapter, and read it through, associating the pictures with the text. Each of the chapters stands on its own, which is the advantage of a subjective rather than a chronological approach. Lay it down and come back to it later for another chapter. When you have gone through it all, go through the images again with a closer eye for detail. Finally, if you have the opportunity, take book in hand and prowl the city's streets, associating then with now. Go by car when you must and on foot when you can. At the end of this process, you will be amazed at how much your appreciation for and understanding of Hampton will have grown, and how many questions have occurred to you which have yet to be answered.

When I was chosen to serve as general editor of this book, those who sat in judgment (many of them the authors) made it clear that they selected me because of my erstwhile editorial skills. Their politeness prevented them from saying that they chose me in spite of my complete ignorance of Hampton's history. The authors proceeded over the next eight months to relieve me of at least that portion of my ignorance, for which I am very grateful. My wish for you, dear readers, is that you learn as much from these pictures and words as I have. The authors and I could have no greater reward.

THE PORTRAICTUER OF CAPTAYNE JOHN SMITH, ADMIRALL OF NEW ENGLAND.

Æta: 37.
A°: 1616.

These are the Lines that shew thy Face; but those
That shew thy Grace and Glory, brighter bee:
Thy Faire-Discoueries and Fowle-Overthrowes
Of Salvages, much Cibilliz'd by thee
Best shew thy Spirit; and to it Glory Wyn;
So, thou art Brasse without, but Golde within.

1

Chapter

From the Sea to a City

by Joe Frankoski and Judith Milteer

The earliest history of the area which would become Hampton is obscure. Its first known inhabitants were members of the Algonquin Indian nation. Evidence indicates that in 1570 a band of Spanish Jesuit missionaries arrived at the Virginia Peninsula and established a mission in today's York County hoping to Christianize the Indians. However, the missionaries were massacred by those whom they had hoped to convert.

A survivor of the massacre, a boy named Alonso de Olmos, took refuge with the Indians in the Hampton area. The chief of those Indians protected him and treated him like a son. The local Indians were agriculturists and according to a Spanish eyewitness, they had fine vineyards as well as plum, cherry, and persimmon trees. Powhatan, famed emperor of the Powhatan Confederacy and father of Pocahontas, claimed to have defeated the local or Kecoughtan Indians in about 1596 or 1597. Therefore, the Indians who farmed the lower peninsula may or may not have been members of the original tribe.

On the European side of the Atlantic, strong forces moved Englishmen westward. King James I of England, following his ascension to the throne in 1603, ended the war with Spain and the associated English privateering ventures in the West Indies. His action forced merchants to seek new ways of earning profits on their own. Almost immediately, "Virginia Fever" raced across England. Tales from a previous unsuccessful expedition surfaced, recalling the rumor of fabulous gold mines which no one yet had been able to find. A new colony would certainly discover the gold, and in addition, the passage to the Pacific just beyond the mountains. Meanwhile, settlers could live at ease with the great plenty of natural resources described so graphically by the earlier adventurers. So grand were the dreams that a popular play of 1605, *Eastward Ho*, mocked these great expectations. Reporting of Virginia, one of the characters stated:

I tell thee gold is more plentiful there than copper is with us; and for as much red copper as I can bring I'll have thrice the weight in gold. Why man, all their dripping pans and chamber pots are pure gold; and all the chains with which they chain up their streets are massy gold, all the prisoners they take fettered in gold, and for rubies and diamonds they go forth on holidays and gather 'em by the seashore to hang on their children's coats....

Capt. John Smith is believed to be the first Englishman to draw a map of what would become the town of Kecoughtan. Courtesy of the Casemate Museum

On April 30, 1607, English settlers landed at the Kecoughtan Indian village, where they were entertained and fed. Several days later they left the village and continued on their journey to found the first permanent settlement at Jamestown. Drawing by Jackie Johnson

So heightened were the expectations and spirit of the English voyagers and their supporters that, on December 20, 1606, a poem was read which had been written expressly for the historic and profound journey to Virginia.

Britains, you stay too long,
Quickly aboord bestow you

And cheerefully at sea,
Successe you still intice,
To get the pearle and gold,
and ours to hold,

VIRGINIA,
Earth's only Paradise,

Where nature hath in store
Fowle, venison, and Fish;
And the fruitful'st soyle,
Without your toyle,
Three harvests more,
All greater than you wish.

In 1607, under the command of Capt. Christopher Newport, the famous ships, *Susan Constant* (or *Sarah Constant*), *Godspeed* (or *Goodspeed*), and *Discovery*, sailed from England after the promise, across the Atlantic and through the broad water channel between Cape Charles and Cape Henry, named for the sons of James I, into the Chesapeake Bay. On April 30, 1607, the would-be settlers anchored their ships off a long sandy point of land which they called Cape Comfort because of the deep water which allowed navigators the "good Comfort" of being able to pass into the safe harbor beyond. Captain Newport put a boat ashore where he saw the Kecoughtan village of eighteen wigwams. A map prepared by John Smith, and other contemporary evidence, suggests that the site of the Indian village was very near the spot on which the Veteran's Administration Hospital was later built. George Percy wrote of this encounter:

When we came first a land they made a doleful noise, laying their faces to the ground, scratching the earth with nails. We did thinke they had beene at the Idolatry. When they had ended their Ceremonies, they went into their houses and brought out mats and laid upon the ground; The chiefest of them sate all in a rank; the meanest sort brought such dainties as they had, and of their bread which they make of the Maiz or Gennea wheat. They would not suffer us to eat unless we sate down, which we did on a mat right against them. After we were well satisfied they gave us of their tobacco, which they tooke in a pipe made artificaly of earth as ours are, but far bigger, with the bowle fashioned together with a piece of fine copper. After they had feasted us, they showed us, in welcome, their manner of dancing, which was in this fashion. One of the savages standing in the midst singing, beating one hand against another, all the rest dancing about him, shouting, howling, and stamping against the ground, with many Anticks, tricks and faces,

This monument, erected to commemorate the landing of the English settlers in 1607, is on the traditional site of the Kecoughtan Indian Village at what is now the Veterans Administration Medical Center. Photo by Joe Frankoski

John White, the second governor of the settlement at Roanoke Island, painted scenes of local Indian life in the 1580s. His paintings were the first true view of North American life. Courtesy of Charles H. Taylor Memorial Library

making noise like so many Wolves or Devils. One thing of them I observed; when they were in their dance they kept stroke with their feet just one with another, but with their hands, heads, faces, and bodies, every one of them had a severall gesture; so they continued for the space of halfe an houre. When they had ended their dance, the Captain gave them Beades and other trifling jewells.

The Algonquin Indians, of which these Kecoughtans were part, believed in a great number of devils who were to be warded off by pow-wows, tricks, and deceptions, and they were inclined to believe that Percy and his friends, if not devils, were messengers sent by devils.

The Englishmen indicated that these Indians had between two and three thousand acres of cleared land and that their gardens were "peninsularized." This is taken to mean that the cultivated areas ran along the various streams and inlets along the shoreline of the Chesapeake Bay and the Hampton Roads. Probably the cultivated area included the lands from the James River into the Buckroe Beach of today. These Indians were also characterized as being excellent farmers.

13

After spending several days with the inhabitants of the Kecoughtan village, the settlers reboarded their three ships, proceeded up the James River, and eventually settled on an island, naming their village Jamestown.

In October 1609, Capt. John Ratcliffe (Radcliffe) wrote that he "was raysing a fort" at Old Point Comfort. The purpose of this fort was for protection not from the Indians, but rather from the Spanish. Named Fort Algernourne, this fortification was the first of several at strategic Point Comfort. During the winter of 1609-10 the Jamestown colonists endured the "Starving Time." This period was a nightmare of horrors, and when spring finally arrived only sixty of the almost five hundred settlers who had started the winter were left alive. The tragedy changed the lives of the colonists in many ways, not the least of which was their relationship with their neighbors. On July 6, 1610, Gov. Thomas Gates was en route down the James River when he noticed the longboat belonging to Fort Algernourne beached for unknown reasons in what later became the Hidenwood area of Newport News. He sent Humphrey Blount to retrieve the boat. However, Blount was seized by Indians there and put to death. No one knew at the time which tribe was responsible, though there is considerable evidence now that Blount was killed by the Nansemond tribe. This is especially likely since the traditional location of his death would have been eleven-and-a-half miles as the crow flies from the Kecoughtan Village, but just across the river from the Nansemond.

Gates apparently continued his river voyage to Fort Algernourne. He may have blamed the Kecoughtans or perhaps he used the incident to the settlers' advantage. Whatever the reason, on the morning of July 9, he attacked the Kecoughtan Village. It appears that fourteen or fifteen Indian warriors were slain and the remainder of the tribe driven away. Shortly thereafter, Englishmen began farming Kecoughtan plots. This event is of considerable significance in American history as it marks the first time in the English Colonies that the Indians were driven from their lands to make way for English settlement. That July date has traditionally been used as the time from which there have been English-speaking persons permanently settled in what is now Hampton, Virginia.

The Spanish did eventually arrive; in 1611 a Spanish vessel came to Fort Algernourne under the

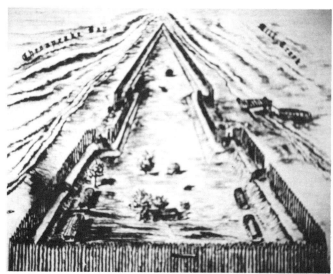

Fort Algernourne, first English fortification at Point Comfort (Fort Monroe). Courtesy of Syms-Eaton Museum

pretext of searching for a missing ship. The captain of the fort sent a navigator, John Clarke, to the Spanish vessel to lure it within range of the fort's guns. Meanwhile the captain seized three men who had come ashore. Unfortunately for Clarke the Spanish vessel sailed away to Cuba. Clarke was later released and served on the *Mayflower*, the ship which brought the Pilgrims to Massachusetts.

Of the three captured Spaniards, one died in captivity on shore. The other two were placed on the ship which took Pocahontas, her husband John Rolfe, and their son to England. No doubt the vessel stopped at Fort Algernourne to take dispatches to the mother country. One of the two remaining "Spaniards" was Francis Lymbry, an Englishman serving Spain as a spy. En route to England, Lymbry was hanged.

The justices were the most influential men in Elizabeth City County. Service as a justice was considered a political stepping stone to the much coveted position of a membership in the House of Burgesses. Colonial law stated that two burgesses were elected from each county in the colony of Virginia and that law remained in effect through the entire Colonial Period. The Elizabeth City County burgesses were required to attend legislative sessions, at the request of the royal governor, first in Jamestown and later in Williamsburg. This long and arduous journey was certainly not viewed with favor; however, arrival in eighteenth century Williamsburg must have been an enriching experience for Elizabeth City County representatives, allowing them new heights in political and cultural exposure.

With the exception of the presiding justice, the most important single official in the county was the high sheriff. He performed many functions of the court, from the collection of taxes to the execution of hangings and floggings. He also conducted elections for the House of Burgesses. From the written record we know that Elizabeth City County had a jail and a courthouse by 1640 and that the courthouse was approximately twenty paces from the jail site. There is no existing evidence to suggest where they were located, perhaps near the parish church which at that time stood near the Strawberry Banks. Generally, the jail served as a holding facility for individuals awaiting trial. Never during the Colonial Period was a convicted felon sentenced to long periods of incarceration because it was felt taxpayers should not be forced to pay for criminal's provisions. Minor offenses such as abusive language, disorderly conduct in taverns or other public locations, endangering the safety of others by riding one's horse too fast, forgery, and malicious gossip were punishable through public humiliation—generally by being placed in the stocks. Major crimes, murder, rape, grand larceny, treason, piracy, and counterfeiting, were tried in an appeals court in the General Court in the capital of the colony and were punishable by hanging, banishment from

COURT and COUNTRY DANCES.

the colony or, in the case of mercy from the court, branding on one's hand.

Court days attracted large crowds that created capacity-filled conditions in local taverns. Regulated by the county court, tavern owners were required by law to secure a license and to post prices for food and lodging.

Gambling was a favorite form of entertainment and was considered a gentleman's privilege. Among the many sources of wagering was Loo (a Colonial card game), Royal Game of Goose, dice, cock fights, and cribbage.

Taverns provided a forum for political discussions, and debates, as well as dances and dinner parties in abundance while merchants were actively engaged in selling. In addition, various forms of correspondence were left in the hands of tavern owners in hopes the letters would be directed to the proper source. Messages of interest to the general public were posted on the walls. An announcement could communicate news of runaway slaves or runaway wives. It could advertise new medical treatments, or announce names of ship captains seeking cargo destined for England. Hampton's leading tavern, the King's Arms, was situated on South King Street. In celebration of the Stamp Act repeal in 1766, townspeople gathered there in great numbers. That same year, the King's birthnight prompted lively toasts (14 in all), bonfires, and a formal ball. The tavern played host to George Washington and other prominent guests during their sojurn in this port city. At the time of the Revolutionary War, the inn was still being operated by a member of the Brough family whose ancestor, Coleman Brough first established the inn here in the 1680s. Several times during its existence, King's Arms was managed by a female member of the Brough family following the death of her husband. At that time, it was sometimes necessary for a widow to take over her late husband's occupation to provide a family income. Obviously, taverns were a central part of the politics, economy, and culture of colonial Hampton.

In 1619 another event of extraordinary importance occurred when a ship discharged about twenty black persons at Fort Point Comfort. (Fort Algernourne burned in 1612. No record exists of subsequent fortifications on Point Comfort with that name.) This marks the first known entry of blacks into the English Colonies. Five years later in a census, Capt. William Tucker, commander of the fort, reported that Antonio and Isabella, a black couple, and their son William, who had been baptized, were members of his plantation. It is probable that Antonio and Isabella were part of the first group of black persons to enter the English Colonies. It is also likely that their son was baptized in the second church of Kecoughtan, the site of which is near Hampton University. Certainly Antonio and Isabella were not slaves—rather they were among the many indentured servants, both black and white, who were transported from England.

Taverns were lively and festive scenes of gala dances and dinner parties and also provided a forum for politicians. Courtesy of Colonial Williamsburg

Chesterville, early home of lawyer George Wythe, was part of the Lamington tract in Elizabeth City County. It burned in 1911. Courtesy of Charles H. Taylor Memorial Library

The same year, 1619, representative self-government was born in Virginia. The London Company, financial backers of the Virginia expedition, authorized the settlers to summon at Jamestown an assembly known as the House of Burgesses. Kecoughtan's first two representatives were Capt. William Tucker and William Capps. One of the first acts of the initial session of the Assembly, July 31, 1619, was to address a petition to the Virginia Company requesting a change in the name Kecoughtan. The request was granted. Accordingly, records state that on May 17, 1620, by order of the council, "the ancient (former) Borough of Kicowtan hereafter shall be called Elizabeth City by the name of His Majesties [sic] most vertuous and renowned daughter." Even so, the name *Kecoughtan* and variants remained as an informal designation for the area, as witnesses a 1683 letter written by Nathaniel Bacon from "Kiketan."

In an effort to provide financial support, the Assembly tried the device of taxing the ships which were to be protected by the guns of the fort. Each ship was required to halt at Point Comfort and pay castle duties of powder and shot to the captain of the fort, as well as a new arrival fee for each man on board at the rate of six pence each. Lack of proper management and funding and further complications caused by a severe thunderstorm forced the General Assembly to legislate the closing of the fort. The abandonment of the fort at Point Comfort marked at least a temporary end of Elizabeth City's role as gateway to the colony.

Elizabeth City County was created by the House of Burgesses in 1634 along with the seven other original counties of Virginia. This elevated status required the establishment of county government to include eight justices, a sheriff, constables, town patrols, surveyors, inspectors, and the clerk or secretary of the court. The royal governor, direct representative of the king in Virginia, appointed all the important county officials. All local government was in the hands

17

These ruins are all that remain of Chesterville, the family home of George Wythe. Wythe was a signer of the Declaration of Independence and taught law to Thomas Jefferson and to John Marshall, who is considered by many to be the most famous Chief Justice of the United States Supreme Court. The ruins are located at NASA Langley. Photo by Joe Frankoski

of the justices and since it was left to them to nominate their successors and name each other in rotation for sheriff, clearly the government was in the hands of the chosen few. The most complex of their duties was the hearing of both civil and criminal cases. Since none of them had legal training until 1746, when a young attorney from Hampton named George Wythe became a justice, it is remarkable how well they functioned. All public works came under their jurisdiction, the building of highways and bridges, the maintenance of public wharfs, the courthouse, the tobacco warehouses, and the construction of a prison. They were also required to supervise county weights, measures, and ferries, license ordinaries (taverns and inns) and set their rates.

In 1677 a small squadron of Dutch ships arrived and succeeded in capturing a number of English vessels that they knew would be laden with tobacco, already by then a staple of Virginia's economy. Col. Miles Cary of Warwick County is believed to have received mortal wounds in action on Point Comfort with these Dutch raiders, and died within a few days at his plantation. John Rolfe, perhaps best known for marrying Pocahontas, was more importantly the introducer of commercial tobacco planting. Enormous quantities of tobacco were being sent to England by mid-seventeenth century. This commerce required ports, and in 1691 the colony's governor ordered that a port be constructed south of the Southampton River. The port was officially established in October 1705 in

an act of the House of Burgesses which stated: "That the places hereinafter named, shall be the ports meant and intended by this act, and none other place or places whatsoever. On James River, Hampton, James City, Flower de Hundred." Hampton replaced Old Point Comfort as the port of debarkation and would play an important role in the development of Virginia and the country. (Point Comfort became *Old* Point Comfort in the latter years of the seventeenth century when a spit of land on Mobjack Bay became *New* Point Comfort.)

In 1705 the General Assembly attempted to make Hampton more accessible by establishing ferries across Hampton Roads and over the bay to the Eastern Shore. This reflected the growing importance of Hampton as a commercial center, and the town's gradually acquiring a more urban appearance.

The seventeenth century art of town planning reached Hampton in 1692 when trustees, Thomas Allamby, William Marshall, and Pascho Curle, laid out the town. According to the second town act, a simple street pattern was designed with elementary cross roads. King Street ran northward from the water and Queen Street crossed it not quite at right angles. Half-acre lots were surveyed and the following year twenty-six of these had been sold. When John Fontaine visited Hampton in 1716 he found it, "a place of the greatest trade in all Virginia, and all the men-of-war commonly lie before this arm of the river. It is not navigable for large ships, by reason of a bar of land, which lies between the mouth, or coming in, and the main

George Wythe, gifted teacher and professor of law, was a Hampton native son. Courtesy of Colonial Williamsburg

channel, but sloops and small ships can come up to the town. This is the best outlet in all Virginia and Maryland, and when there is any fleet made, they fit out here, and can go to sea with the first start of wind. The town contains one hundred houses, but few of them of any note."

In 1729 more streets were laid off to provide for new houses, and three years later the court ordered all wooden chimneys pulled down as a menace to the public safety, to be replaced by brick. The abundance of trees in the area provided building materials for the construction of homes and public buildings. The availability of sand and pits of clay created the necessary ingredients for the making of bricks. Sand mixed with burned oyster and clam shells provided lime that resulted in mortar. Local natural resources and the skill of craftsmen allowed steady progress in the continued development of Hampton.

Although little is known about education in the early years of Hampton, there were obviously literate people as evidenced by wills, deeds, and other legal documents. In 1634, Benjamin Syms marked his will (he himself could not write his name) which bequeathed land and cattle for the founding of a free school, "to Educate & teach the Children of the adjoining Parrishes of Elizb. City & Poquoson...." Further in the will, Syms specified that the school was to educate poor children. The will of Benjamin Syms is one of the most significant documents in American history and education. It provided for the first of the

so-called charity schools, but more important, it created the concept that education was not just for those who could afford it, but for all including the children of poor parents.

Literacy was crucial for early Hamptonians, since the population of a port town had to be literate to handle commercial transactions, such as preparing and reading bills of lading. Probably tutors were used to educate some children while other parents sent their children to England for education. Court records show that orphans were placed under guardians who were required to ensure that the children learned to read and write. Poor orphans were apprenticed not only to learn a trade, but also to become literate.

As noted above, the lucrative Virginia-England tobacco trade attracted privateers and pirates. The situation became so serious that a convoy system was established in which English warships would escort the tobacco-laden merchant ships into the Atlantic en route to England. One of the most notorious pirates was William Teach, better known as "Blackbeard." He began his somewhat brief, certainly infamous, career about 1716. During May 1717, Blackbeard and other pirates forced tribute from ships passing through the Virginia Capes. He plundered the coast of North Carolina to the extent that the North Carolinians asked Gov. Alexander Spotswood of Virginia to rid them of this scourge. Spotswood hired two sloops at his own expense. In November 1718, these sloops, manned by British sailors and commanded by Lt.

This small Virginia house is similar to those which were built on the shores of Harris Creek. Courtesy of Colonial Williamsburg

Eager to emulate English high fashion, wealthy residents donned elegant clothing made of imported silk and velvet. Gentlemen purchased padding to be inserted in their stockings to give the appearance of a full, firm calf. Courtesy of Colonial Williamsburg

In 1634, Benjamin Syms marked his will bequeathing land and cattle for the founding of a free school. Courtesy of Charles H. Taylor Memorial Library

In 1659, Dr. Thomas Eaton left five hundred acres of Elizabeth City County for the support of a second free school. Courtesy of Charles H. Taylor Memorial Library

Blackbeard was a notorious pirate whose treasure was reportedly buried near the mouth of the Hampton River. Courtesy of Charles H. Taylor Memorial Library

Robert Maynard, departed Hampton to hunt down Blackbeard. Four days later they found the blackguard's vessel at Ocracoke Inlet in North Carolina. In writing about the action, Governor Spotswood stated:

> As soon as Teach perceived the King's men intended to board him he took up a bowl of liquor and calling out to the officers of the other sloops, drank damnation to anyone that should give or ask quarter and then discharged his great guns loaded with partridge shot, which killed and wounded twenty of the King's men....

A hand-to-hand encounter took place between Maynard and Blackbeard. Blackbeard finally fell to the deck with twenty sword and five pistol wounds. The head of Blackbeard was severed and brought to Hampton. There, it was placed on a pole and displayed for all to see—close to the mouth of the Hampton River near the end of what later became Ivy Home Road.

Although the tobacco which drew the pirates remained the most important product raised in Virginia, it exhausted the soil quite rapidly. Elizabeth City County remained largely agricultural and its chief products were grains, although animal husbandry was also important. There were some early

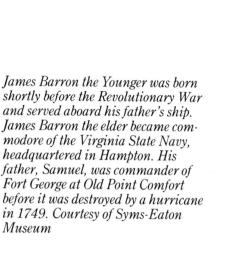

James Barron the Younger was born shortly before the Revolutionary War and served aboard his father's ship. James Barron the elder became commodore of the Virginia State Navy, headquartered in Hampton. His father, Samuel, was commander of Fort George at Old Point Comfort before it was destroyed by a hurricane in 1749. Courtesy of Syms-Eaton Museum

efforts to cultivate grapes, probably the white grapes which are native to this part of Virginia, but they appear to have failed. The system of indentured service gave way to slavery. There are no reliable estimates on the number of slaves—Indian or black—during the seventeenth century. In 1700 the white population of the County numbered 1,188 according to John Oldmixon's *British Empire in America*. He listed 460 males, 719 females and children. Of the 196 men in the militia, 54 were cavalry and 142 were foot and dragoons.

In 1728 another fortification was raised at Old Point Comfort to replace previously abandoned fortifications. It was named Fort George, and was considered to be a substantial strongpoint. It consisted of two brick walls, one twenty-seven inches thick, and the other sixteen inches, about sixteen feet apart. Cross-compartments between the two walls were filled with sand. Since the fort had been built on private property, the owner, Robert Beverly, had to be reimbursed. Although Fort George was deemed so strong that "no ship could pass it without running great risk" it fell to the wrath of nature. In 1749, a great hurricane occurred and the winds blew with such force that Fort George was destroyed. The garrison, however, was saved through the efforts of its commander, Capt. Samuel Barron, who had the men of the garrison and their families carry furniture and heavy articles to the second floors of the buildings. The weight kept the buildings on their foundations and perhaps saved the lives of the inhabitants. Barron and his family later moved across Mill Creek (formerly Point Comfort Creek) and took up residence in the settlement there.

A description of Hampton in 1755 was provided by a Mrs. Browne who accompanied the newly appointed chief of British forces in America, Gen. Edward Braddock, to the port. She wrote in her diary:

My Brother and self went on shore to Hampton in the Pilots Boat. Gave 7s, 6d for rowing 2 Miles. Went to the King's Arms and breakfasted. Walk'd till Dinner. A very agreeable Place, and all the Houses extreemly neat. Had for Dinner a Ham & Turkey, a Breast of Veal & Oysters, to drink Madeira Wine, Punch, and Cyder. Stay'd till 4 in the Afternoon and then went on Board....

Glimpses of life and activities of young ladies of the gentry during the second half of the eighteenth century appear in the following letter, written by Anne Blair (b. 1746), daughter of lawyer John Blair, Jr., and granddaughter of John Blair, Sr., who served as president of the Council and acting governor before Botetourt arrived in Virginia.

It is an age since writing to my Dr. Sist. nothing but the want of an opportunity should have occasion'd

The Braddock Monument is located at the intersection of Bridge Street and Victoria Boulevard. While it is not known whether General Braddock came ashore at this location, his army did stop at Hampton before marching to their defeat near Fort Duquesne during the French and Indian War. Photo by Joe Frankoski

this long silence; I have been in Hampton ever since the first day of the Court, and to have sent a Letter to our House in order to be forwarded I knew would be vain for they generally toss about till lost. Hampton is now more gay then the Metropolis, the Rippon, the Lancester, & the Magdelane are all in Harbour here; Ball's both by Land and by Water in abundance: the Gentlemen of the Rippon are I think the most agreable, affable set I have ever met with, and realy it is charming to go on Board; the Drum & Fife, pleasing Countenances, such polite, yet easy Behaviour all bespeak a hearty welcome: this Family receive a great many Civility's from all the Gentlemen, presents' on presents; if there happen's a day without seeing them there is so many Compts. to enquire after our Health's, that indeed to be people of consequence is vastly Clever. how stands yr. hea[rts] Girls I hear you ask? why I will tell you; mine seem's to be roving amidst Dear Variety; and notwithstanding there is such variety, do you think Betsy Blair & Sally Swendy [did] not contend for one. Betsy gave for her Toast at Supper Mr. Sharp (a Lieut: on Board ye Rippon) Miss Sally for a while disputed it with her at length it was agread between them to decide it with Pistoles when they should go to Bed; no sooner had they got upstairs then they advanced up close to each other, then turning short round Back to Back marched three steps forward & Fired so great was ye explosions so suffocating the smell of ye Powder that I quited ye Room, till by Betsey's repeated Shouts I soon learn[ed] she had

got ye better of her Antagonist: dont be alarm'd at the name of Pistol—they were themselves the Pistol's, and their Ammunition nother more then Wind—the perfume of which was ye exact fragrance of a—Sir Reverance.

Nothing my Dr. Sisr. (a Husband excepted) could give a more additional satisfaction to ye Happiness we now enjoy then yr. good Company; do come, and resolve with us, Since Life is no more then a passage at the best to strew the way over with Flowers...My Sisr. Cary is writing. I therefore submit to her abler pen to do justice to the present amusements, and that i may be inducement enough to bring you to us is wish'd by all but none more earnest in it then

Yr. truely Affec. Sisr:
A. Blair

June 14th 1769

....adieu—I am going to Dinner, after which we have a desert of fine Rasberry's & Cream, I wish you with yr. little Woman (to whom present my Love) & a few other chosen acquaintances were here to partake with us, and with truth I assure you there is as much sincerity in this wish, as may be conceiv'd in the Heart of her, who without further delay stiles herself

Yr. Affec. Friend
A. Blair

P.S. A Line a Line a Kingdom for a line.

Mary Jemima Balfour was the wife of James. Her portrait and that of her husband and son were painted in 1773 by Matthew Pratt.

James Balfour lived with his family in Little England outside the town of Hampton. Balfour represented the English mercantile company of Hanbury and Company. He also testified in the Stamp Act debates in London in 1766 and it appears he played a role in their repeal. Packets of correspondence and a quill pen indicate literacy in Colonial Hampton and Elizabeth City County. Balfour, who died in 1775, is shown with his son, George. The painting is in Battle Abbey, Virginia Historical Society in Richmond.

Twenty years later, in 1775, Lord Dunmore, the last royal governor of Virginia, fled his capital of Williamsburg. He issued the *first* emancipation proclamation in that he declared all slaves who joined his forces to be free. His forces raided the little settlement at Mill Creek in October, and shortly thereafter made an attack on Hampton. The populace had sunk some boats in the Hampton River to impede passage and appealed to Williamsburg for help. On October 24, British forces under Captain Squiers bombarded the town from their vessels. St. John's Church and several other buildings were damaged, but the townspeople returned the fire from the wharf and buildings with such effect that the British were forced to withdraw. The next morning, reinforcements from Williamsburg arrived under the command of Colonel Woodord. Again, Squiers bombarded the town and again he was driven away by the effective fire of the patriots.

The county had been instructed to raise a company of fifty men for the patriot's army. The appointed officers were John Cary, captain; John King, lieutenant; and Joseph Selden, Jr., ensign. During the Revolutionary War Hampton served as homeport for the Virginia State Navy. Several war vessels were constructed there. Many of the county men served in the Virginia Navy, including one of seven licensed navigators named Cesar Tarrant. Tarrant was considered to be one of the great war heroes of Virginia. The unusual nature of his status was that besides being a pilot and war hero, Tarrant was also a slave. When the war was over Tarrant was freed by a special act of the Virginia Assembly in November 1789:

WHEREAS, it is represented to this Assembly, that Mary Tarrant of the county of Elizabeth City, hath her life in a negro named Cesar, who entered very early into the service of his country, and continued to pilot the armed vessels of this state during the late war, in consideration of which meritorious services it is judged expedient to purchase the freedom of the said Cesar; Be it therefore enacted by the General Assembly, that the executive shall appoint a proper person to contract with the said Mary Tarrant for the purchase of the said Cesar, and if they should agree, the person so appointed by the executive shall deliver to the said Mary Tarrant a certificate to the auditor of accounts, he shall issue a warrant for the same to the treasurer to be by him paid out of the lighthouse fund. And be it further enacted, that from and after the execution of a certificate aforesaid, the said Cesar shall be manumitted and set free to all intents and purposes.

It should be noted that the act placed no ceiling or limit on the purchase price.

Throughout the war the Virginia Navy battled the British. However, British land forces did not arrive in strength on the Virginia Peninsula until 1781. On New Year's Eve 1780, several hundred British landed at Newport News Point and marched on Hampton. Along the way they rousted the inhabitants from their houses and forced them to march with them. This was done so that no alarm could be given. At about midnight the British entered the little town. Hoping to capture Virginia Navy vessels, they looked for pilots who knew the local waters. After interrogating the townspeople for two hours, the British marched back to their boats. By now, the militia had been alerted and fired on the rear of the British column. Several of the Queen's Rangers were wounded and several soldiers were missing—probably having deserted.

On January 3, 1781, a force of about one hundred Royal Marines and sailors moved into the center of the county on a foraging expedition, seizing livestock and poultry. There seems to have been some minor action as the British commander reported a slight bayonet wound in his foot when chasing a "rebel."

The relative ease and success of this foraging expedition, however, would lead to a disaster on the next. On the sixth of January, a party of forty Royal Marines under a Lieutenant Brown moved into Warwick County on a similar expedition. They were observed, the alarm was given, and Capt. Edward Mallory gathered thirty Elizabeth City County mounted militiamen who galloped to intercept the marauding party. Towards evening, the Marines were returning to the James River with the results of their foraging when they sighted Mallory's men. They deployed to protect the livestock. Only fifteen patriots had effective muskets, and Mallory ordered them to open fire. The other fifteen men were given the best horses and ordered to charge with swords and pistols. Lieutenant Brown and nine of his Marines were killed or mortally wounded and eleven were captured. Only one Elizabeth City militiaman was killed, and the foraged property was returned to the owners.

Several months later, another decisive engagement took place—the first Battle of Big Bethel. On the same site would later occur the first planned, formal land engagement of the War Between the States in June 1861. Preliminaries to the first Battle of Big Bethel began early on the morning of March 8, 1781, when between two and three hundred British landed in York County and marched on the Halfway House and ordinary (tavern), on another foraging expedition. The alarm was given and Col. Francis Mallory and Jonathan Curle led a small body of Elizabeth City County militia to intercept the enemy column. Apparently they planned to reach Tompkin's Bridge (near the site of today's Big Bethel Bridge) and engage the British there. However, the enemy reached the bridge first and in what was probably a meeting engagement, ran into the company of forty militiamen, who were overwhelmed by the substantially larger British force. Various accounts and casualties were reported—the British reported that they killed seventeen of the militiamen including Colonel Mallory and captured eleven including Colonel Curle. The British suffered at least one officer killed and another wounded, and a number of soldiers wounded. Even though the county militia lost the battle, because of their resistance the British were forced to leave the

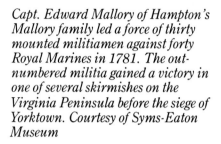

Capt. Edward Mallory of Hampton's Mallory family led a force of thirty mounted militiamen against forty Royal Marines in 1781. The outnumbered militia gained a victory in one of several skirmishes on the Virginia Peninsula before the siege of Yorktown. Courtesy of Syms-Eaton Museum

supplies that they had foraged.

Nevertheless, the security situation in the county was considered very poor as evidenced by the March 27, 1781, letter from Miles King in Hampton to the governor. An extract follows:

> Must not our situation be deplorable. The only protection is a Guard of six men below Old Point Comfort, and a guard of twelve men at Newport News, which suffered 17 Boats full of Troops to land and make about fifty Fires, and let them go off without their discovering of them. How sorry I am that we should have only such men to trust to. Our County men is as willing as ever to step forth when assisted. The number of the Enemy don't discourage us, but what we want is men to stand by us. The late unfortunate affair in this County will I hope sufficiently prove the Courage of our County men. In that Action many Guns were lost, and what Small quantity of Ammunition the men had, was nearly Expended. We are now in want of about sixty stand of arms, flints, powder & Ball, and some men to assist us, and then our County here will turn out as much cheerfulness as ever.
>
> Light Horse are very necessary for this part of the Country tho' we have only Three. I was Just now informed that forty five sail of Vessells were counted in the Bay this morning, Including the Line of Battle Ships.
>
> P.S.—Since writing, 3 more large ships is coming up, which appears to be Transports.

Elizabeth City County and Hampton also played roles in the Battle of Yorktown. Col. James Innes notified Gov. Thomas Nelson on July 14, 1781, that "four hundred British landed at Hampton old fort yesterday, where they remained until the evening surveying the Grounds. They have said it is their interest to rebuild Fort George." This interest in Old Point Comfort was brought about by a directive from Sir Henry Clinton, British commander in New York, to Lord Charles Cornwallis to look into the possibility of fortifying that place. For several reasons General Cornwallis found it to be unsuitable and chose to fortify Yorktown instead. Rather than a British fortification, a French artillery position was constructed at strategic Old Point. Adm. Comte De Grasse asked Gen. George Washington to send soldiers to help in the construction of a naval battery at Old Point. De Grasse also asked for a hosptial to be established in the town of Hampton to treat a large number of sick men in his fleet. Public buildings such as the county courthouse were used to house the men. After the great victory at Yorktown, part of the French Army used Hampton as

winter quarters.

The men and women of Elizabeth City County and Hampton made other significant contributions as well during the Revolutionary War. Ships of the Virginia State Navy were manned by the local sailors. The county met all of its requirements to send men to serve in the Virginia Continental regiments from the start of the war until 1781—one of relatively few Virginia counties that did so. The county fought against overwhelming numerical odds in 1781 against an enemy who commanded the waters around the Virginia Peninsula.

At the end of the war, Hampton found that it had lost its place as an important port to Norfolk, largely because of the decline in trade with the British West Indies. The county remained agricultural, producing grains and livestock. Both the Syms Free School and the Eaton Free School continued to educate poor children.

But, peace and calm were not to last for long. Soon the town was again invaded by the British—this time during the War of 1812. In 1813 British forces arrived in the Chesapeake Bay. Their purpose was to bring the war home to the Americans and the first target was Norfolk. On June 22, 1813, the British attempted to land forces at Craney Island; however, they were repulsed by the American forces there. The British commanders, Adm. Boarlase Warren, Adm. George Cockburn, and Gen. Sidney Beckwith turned their attention instead to the little town of Hampton.

Maj. Stapleton Crutchfield commanded a force of 436 militiamen who had gathered to defend Hampton. Part of his force was made up of men from the local 115th Virginia Militia Regiment as well as men from the James City County Regiment. The remainder of the 115th Regiment was posted in various parts of the Virginia Peninsula. Crutchfield placed four twelve-pounder and three six-pounder guns in position to defend the Hampton River entrance to the town. He had previously requested reinforcements as he knew he would be greatly outnumbered, but he apparently received none.

During the night of June 24, a large force of British infantry and marines landed near Indian River. They were not discovered until the next day, and Captain Servant's rifle company was sent to

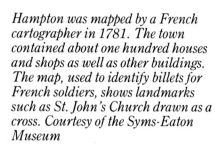

Hampton was mapped by a French cartographer in 1781. The town contained about one hundred houses and shops as well as other buildings. The map, used to identify billets for French soldiers, shows landmarks such as St. John's Church drawn as a cross. Courtesy of the Syms-Eaton Museum

engage them. Servant's small force caused a number of casualties among the enemy, but the British advanced on Hampton. Crutchfield ordered his command to engage the enemy and later wrote:

We advanced in columns of platoons thro' lane and an open cornfield which led from our encampment to the enemy. We were fired upon by the enemy's musketry from a thick wood at the upper end of a field immediately bordering on the road. Upon this discharge, orders were given to wheel to the left into line and march upon the enemy...the enemy opened upon us two 6-pound field pieces loaded with grape and canister shot, and his machines filled with rockets of a small size. Upon this sudden and unexpected attack with ordinance, I deemed it necessary to wheel again into column and gain if possible a passage through the gate....

The total British force, estimated to number about twenty-five hundred, continued to advance. The militia broke and fell back in disorder. Hampton, now undefended, was seized by the British. Captain Pryor's artillery unit defending the Hampton River was now in danger from the overland force of the enemy, so the artillerymen spiked their cannon and threw them into the river. As the British approached, the Americans swam across the river with, apparently, no casualties. The enemy turned full attention to Hampton and its

inhabitants. There were reports of rape, murder and looting, and Lt. Col. Charles Napier of the British Army wrote, "Beckwith ought to have hanged several villains at little Hampton. Every horror was committed with impunity—rape, murder, pillage and not a man punished." Beckwith placed blame for these outrages upon French soldiers who had been captured during the Napoleonic Wars and were serving in the British force. The British remained in Hampton for several days. A party of Royal Marines occupied Old Point Comfort and it is believed that they used the lighthouse there as an observation post.

This attack and pillage of Hampton seems to have had the effect of unifying American opinion about the War of 1812. Newspapers nationwide lashed out against the British Admiral Cockburn who became a hated personage and identified with "incendiaries and murders."

The first two centuries of Hampton's existence held great significance for the development of Virginia and the nation. Hampton was the scene of the first coastal fortifications in Virginia. The driving of the Indians from their lands began a process which would continue on for the next two-and-a-half centuries. The will of Benjamin Syms was a cornerstone in the growth of public education in the country. Although by the 1800s most of the dramatic action of the Revolution and the governing of the United States had moved from the Virginia Peninsula, Hampton's resi-

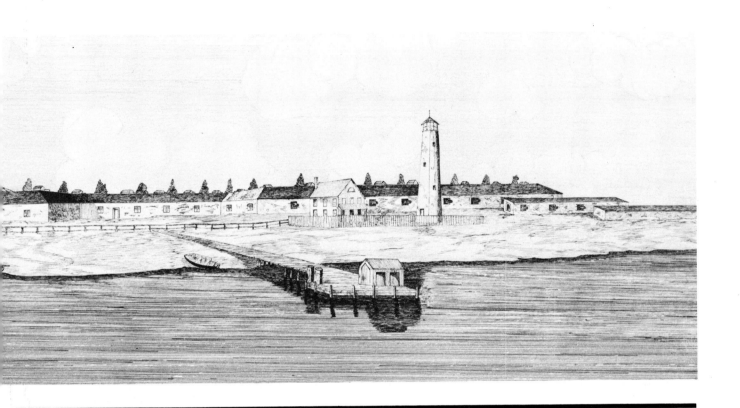

dents during the community's first two hundred years laid a firm foundation for future generations.

Fort Monroe and the Old Point Comfort Lighthouse are shown as they appeared in 1850. The lighthouse, built in 1802, was the oldest structure remaining at Old Point Comfort and was still in operation in 1985. Courtesy of the Casemate Museum

Acknowledgments

We would like to thank the staffs of the archives of the Colonial Williamsburg Foundation, the Mariners Museum, the Virginia Historical Society, Charles H. Taylor Memorial Library, Hampton Center for the Arts and Humanities, and the Royal Marines Historical Society for their assistance in researching this chapter.

The Old Point Comfort Lighthouse, built in 1802, was the oldest structure remaining on Old Point Comfort and was still in operation in 1985. Courtesy of the Planning Department of the City of Hampton

2

Chapter

Hampton and the Military

by Richard P. Weinert, Jr.

Hampton has a long and rich military tradition, as old as the city itself. The first settlements of the English colonists in what is now Hampton were military posts. Fort Algernourne was built in 1609 at Old Point Comfort and the city dates its claim to continuous settlement from the establishment of Fort Charles and Fort Henry in 1610. While sporadic attempts were made at maintaining fortifications at Old Point Comfort and the town had been the scene of military activity in both the Revolution and the War of 1812, a permanent military presence did not come until the second decade of the nineteenth century.

The disasters which took place along the American coast during the War of 1812, including the sacking of Hampton, resulted in a complete reappraisal of national coastal fortification policy. Simon Bernard, a distinguished French military engineer and former aide to Napoleon, was appointed to design a new system of fortifications in 1816. After a complete survey of the American coast by Bernard and a board of American engineers, preliminary work started at Old Point Comfort in 1818 and actual construction of a fort began in 1819. At the same time, work began at the Rip Raps on a supporting work to provide cross fire at the mouth of Hampton Roads. The large fort was named after President James Monroe and the fort on the Rip Raps was named for John C. Calhoun, his secretary of war.

Fort Monroe is by far the largest masonry fort ever built in the United States. The circumference of the walls is about a mile. The fort covers sixty-three acres and was designed to mount 412 guns with a wartime garrison of 2,625. Fort Monroe has seven bastioned fronts surrounded by a moat eight feet deep. The moat varies in width from 60 feet at the East Gate to 150 feet at the Main Sallyport. Extensive outworks, including a redoubt and a redan, were built opposite the north face to cover the only land approach to the fort. A detached water battery of 40 guns was constructed opposite the East Gate.

The work on the fort was done with military prisoners, augmented by civilian artisans from the North and some hired slaves. To control the prisoners, the first garrison of Fort Monroe—Company G, Third United States Artillery—transferred from Fort Nelson in Portsmouth on July 25, 1823. Since 1823, Fort Monroe has been continuously garrisoned as a post of the United States Army. Work continued on the fort until 1834, but even by the time of the Civil War it was not really completed.

In 1824, Fort Monroe was selected as the location of the Artillery School of Practice. This was the first

Second Lieutenant Robert E. Lee of the Corps of Engineers assisted in the construction of Fort Monroe and Fort Calhoun from 1831 to 1834. Courtesy of the Casemate Museum

Army service school. From the little school established in 1824 has grown the far-flung system of Army service schools which is still directed from Fort Monroe.

Because of the importance of the school, the large garrison, and its central location, Fort Monroe had many prominent residents and visitors during the first half of the century. In 1824, the Marquis de Lafayette came to participate in a ceremony at Yorktown and to visit the Rip Raps. From 1828 to 1829, Edgar Allan Poe served as sergeant major at the fort. President Andrew Jackson used the uncompleted Fort Calhoun as a summer White House in 1829, 1831, 1833, and 1835. Robert E. Lee, a young second lieutenant assigned as assistant constructing engineer, arrived at Fort Monroe in 1832 and remained until he was briefly transferred to Fort Calhoun in 1834. Most of the prominent officers who served on both sides during the Civil War were stationed at the fort or passed through it during the following years. President John Tyler, who owned a summer home in Hampton, was a frequent visitor to the fort. Following the death of his first wife in 1842, Tyler used the Rip Raps as a retreat.

The garrison of Fort Monroe was called out during the Nat Turner Rebellion in Southampton County in 1831 and for the Black Hawk War in Illinois in 1832. The outbreak of Seminole disturbances in Florida brought an end to the Artillery School and the departure of most of the artillery garrison in 1834.

For the duration of the Seminole War, Fort Monroe was used as an assembly, training, and shipment site while the engineers went back to work on the fort. Early in the 1840s the garrison returned and Fort Monroe served during the Mexican War as an embarkation site for units destined for Mexico.

The years following the Mexican War were peaceful at Fort Monroe despite increasing national tension. The Artillery School was reestablished in 1858. Construction of Fort Calhoun, which had been stopped in 1830 because the artificial island on which the fort stood was settling, also resumed in that year. The Hygeia Hotel at Old Point Comfort became one of the major resorts of the country. All this ended in April 1861 when Virginia seceded from the Union leaving Fort Monroe an isolated Federal outpost.

Fort Monroe was one of only four Federal posts in the South which remained in Union hands throughout the Civil War. At the outbreak of hostilities, there were seven full companies of regular artillery at the fort and about half of its heavy armament had been mounted. By the end of May, the Federal strength had risen to 4,451 troops at Fort Monroe and the newly established Camp Hamilton in what is now Phoebus.

While the Federals were reinforcing Fort Monroe, the Confederates had begun organizing an army to defend the lower Peninsula and approaches to Richmond. The political sympathies of the Hampton area had been generally opposed to secession, but once

Confederate troops advanced along Queen Street in Hampton in May of 1861. Courtesy of the Casemate Museum

Virginia withdrew from the Union, the majority of local citizens rallied to the defense of their state. Lt. Col. Benjamin S. Ewell, the president of the College of William and Mary, had been ordered by Gen. Robert E. Lee to prepare the defense of the lower Peninsula and to organize the volunteers in the area. The only armed and equipped units at the time were the Williamsburg Junior Guards and the Wythe Rifles of Hampton, both of which had been organized during the John Brown raid of 1859.

Maj. John B. Cary, who had been the principal of the Hampton Military Institute, commanded the 130 Confederate volunteers in Hampton. On May 14, Ewell was in Hampton and upon learning of apparent movement by the troops at Fort Monroe, he went to see Col. Justin Dimick, the post commander. Dimick informed Ewell that he had taken possession of a spring west of Mill Creek to get water for the garrison, but he had no immediate idea of aggressive movements and they agreed to keep their pickets apart. Ewell ordered Cary to hold his men one-half mile from the fort and form a camp of instruction for some eight hundred men, but there were only three hundred muskets available, half of them obsolete flintlocks.

Cary reported to Ewell on May 21 that Dimick appeared ready to advance. Ewell considered this likely and prohibited Cary from any useless resistance unless the Federals moved beyond the range of the fort's guns. Ewell continued: "It is difficult to manage Hampton. The people are excitable and brave even to rashness and are unwilling to give way. It (Hampton) might, on the approach in force of Federal troops, be evacuated by the military, and the remaining citizens ought to make terms, unless, indeed, it is made a second Saragossa. I doubt if, from the nature of the buildings, this could be done."

At this early date, the war still had an unreal and darkly comical quality. On the afternoon of May 23, most of the First Vermont Infantry advanced on Hampton. As the troops neared the town, Major Cary was vainly trying to burn the bridge across Hampton Creek. Cary sent a lieutenant over to Colonel Phelps, the Union commander, to demand the reason for this approach with so large a force. Phelps replied that he had no hostile purpose, but Maj. Gen. Benjamin Butler, who had been assigned as the senior officer at Fort Monroe, had sent him to reconnoiter. Receiving assurances that the people and property of the town would not be molested, Cary, with some of the citizens and the Vermonters, put out the fire on the bridge. The First Vermont then marched into Hampton, remained a short while, and then returned to their camp.

Lieutenant Colonel Ewell hurried forward to find out what was happening. Cary had meanwhile gone to Fort Monroe to learn from General Butler "how far he intended to take possession of Virginia soil, in order that I might act in such a manner as to avoid collision between our scouts." Butler informed Cary that it was

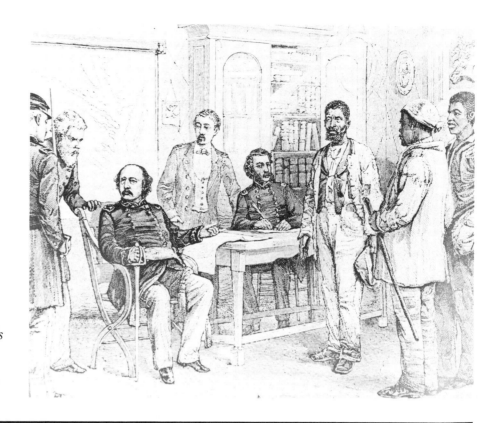

Maj. Gen. Benjamin Butler interviewed the escaped slaves of Col. Charles Mallory of Hampton. Butler's decision to classify runaway slaves as "contraband of war" was to have far-reaching effects during the Civil War. Courtesy of the Casemate Museum

a military necessity for him to occupy land for an encampment, referring to the establishment of Camp Hamilton, but if he was not interfered with he would molest no one. By this time Ewell had been unceremoniously captured. After a protest by Cary, Colonel Dimick presently released Ewell. Not amused by the entire affair, Ewell immediately ordered Cary to complete the destruction of the bridge across the Hampton River.

That same night three slaves of Col. Charles Mallory of Hampton managed to escape to Fort Monroe. The following morning Major Cary was back to see General Butler to demand return of the slaves under the terms of the Fugitive Slave Law. Butler told Cary that he would take possession of anything necessary to meet his own requirements or that might be an aide to the enemy. He refused to give up any Negroes who came to the fort, stating in effect that they were property and "contraband of war." This policy was to have a far reaching impact on the war as it was adopted by other commanders and supported by the federal government.

As a result of the contrabrand policy, escaped blacks flocked to Fort Monroe, which soon became known as the "Freedom Fort." The refugees were a great assistance to the Union military and naval forces in the Hampton Roads area. They served as cooks, servants, stevedores, carpenters, and laborers, receiving rations and a small monthly wage. A few served as guides for the Union troops, but the government was slow to accept blacks into the Army. It was not until much later in the war that the Union began to accept black troops, including the First and Second United States Colored Cavalry and Battery B, Second United States Colored Light Artillery, which were organized at Fort Monroe and Camp Hamilton.

On May 30, 1861, Federal forces occupied the unfinished Fort Calhoun on the Rip Raps. Troops from Fort Monroe also occupied Newport News and established Camp Butler there. Confederate strength had been slowly increasing and Brig. Gen. John B. Magruder, the Southern commander, ordered fortifications erected on the road from Hampton to Yorktown at Big Bethel.

Learning of the Confederate activity in the Big Bethel area, General Butler determined to drive them back and destroy their camp. He ordered one force from Camp Butler to demonstrate in front of Little Bethel while another column from Camp Hamilton attempted to get in the rear of the enemy between Little Bethel and Big Bethel. The two columns marched on the night of June 9 and were supposed to effect a junction about a mile and a half from Bethel Church in time to make an attack at dawn on June 10. The troops wore white armbands as distinguishing marks in the dark. The column from Camp Hamilton crossed Hampton Creek and brushed aside a few Confederate pickets, who apparently gave warning to Magruder of the Union advance. Everything went well until the two columns approached the fork in the road where they were scheduled to meet. Unable to see the white armbands in the dark, the column from Camp Butler fired into the one from Camp Hamilton. Two

The Battle of Big Bethel was the first significant land engagement of the Civil War. Here, guns of Lt. John Greble from Fort Monroe support the Union attack on Confederate defenses. Courtesy of the Casemate Museum

Camp Hamilton, in what is now Phoebus, is seen from Fort Monroe in 1861. This large camp was established for the overflow of troops from Fort Monroe. Courtesy of the Casemate Museum

Escaping slaves fled to safety at Fort Monroe in 1861. Fort Monroe became known as "freedom's fortress" to many blacks who sought shelter there during the Civil War. Courtesy of the Casemate Museum

men were killed and sixteen wounded and some of the units began to fall back before the mistake was recognized. The firing alerted the Confederates, who withdrew to their entrenchments beyond the bridge of Brick Kiln Creek. Information about the Union advance reached the Confederates from retreating pickets and Hannah Nicholson Tunnell, a local citizen. Brig. Gen. Ebenezer W. Pierce, the Union commander, decided to proceed with the attack despite the loss of surprise.

The Confederate force at Big Bethel consisted of the First North Carolina Infantry under Col. D. H. Hill, the Richmond Howitzer Battalion, a battalion of the Third Virginia Infantry, and a number of separate Virginia units including the Old Dominion Dragoons, a Hampton cavalry company attached to the 115th Virginia Militia Regiment of Elizabeth City County.

After a delay caused by the confusion of the collision in the dark, the Fifth New York Zouaves drove in the Confederate advanced pickets about 9 A.M. and arrived before the Confederate position covering the bridge. Lt. John Greble from Fort Monroe brought his battery up and opened fire as the Federal force deployed. About 11 A.M., the Federals attacked and carried the Confederate position south of the creek. A counterattack drove them back and the Third New York Infantry, mistaking one of its own units for an enemy flank force, fell back. This ended the action on the right and center of the Confederate line, but at about this time a volunteer force under Maj. Theodore Winthrop, one of General Butler's aides, attacked the Confederate left. Crossing the creek, the men charged and were met with withering fire. Winthrop was killed and Pierce decided to break off the engagement and withdraw to Hampton. Lieutenant Greble was killed covering the retreat. He was the first regular army officer and West Point graduate to die in the war.

The Federal force had lost, including the affair at the road junction, eighteen killed, fifty-three wounded, and five captured. Confederate casualties were only Pvt. Henry L. Wyatt of the First North Carolina killed, seven wounded, and three captured. This was a very small battle compared to the devastation of the next four years, but it was the first significant action of the war and it caused an immediate sensation in both the North and the South. As a result, both sides overestimated the importance of the Confederate victory.

Following the Battle of Big Bethel, the Confederates continued to fortify Yorktown and the Warwick River line while the Federal forces consolidated their position in the Hampton-Newport News area. Meanwhile, General Butler had managed to mount a rifled gun on the Rip Raps and on June 15 opened fire on the Confederate position at Sewells Point guarding the approach to Norfolk. Intermittent fire from the Rip Raps continued for the remainder of the summer. On July 3, the Third and Fifth Massachusetts Regiments occupied Hampton. Skirmishing continued in the area until the Union defeat at the Battle of First Manassas in northern Virginia on July 21. A large part of General Butler's command was ordered north to protect Washington and the Union troops departed from Hampton on July 26.

The Confederates under Magruder immediately became more aggressive, pushing patrols toward Hampton and Newport News. A copy of the *New York Herald* stating that Butler intended to quarter his troops and runaway blacks in Hampton fell into Magruder's hands. The story in the newspaper was not true, but Magruder acting on this information decided to burn the town. Magruder ordered Capt. Jefferson C. Phillips of the Old Dominion Dragoons to destroy the town on the night of August 7. Phillips took with him his company, the Mecklenburgh Cavalry, the Warwick Beauregards, and the York Rangers, which also contained many men from the Hampton area.

Shortly after dark, Phillips crossed Newmarket Bridge and brought his command to St. John's churchyard. Leaving the horses there and posting a detachment to cover the Hampton River bridge, Phillips then notified the citizens that he would have to burn the town. Each of the companies was assigned a quarter of the town to destroy. Firing broke out at the bridge, but the entire town was quickly a mass of flames. As soon as Phillips was sure that the destruction was complete, he withdrew his command by the way they had come.

No lives, military or civilian, were lost, but the historic old Colonial town was in ashes. Only the gutted ruins of St. John's Church remained standing. The Federal authorities, having no idea of the reason for the destruction of the town, were shocked by the burning of Hampton. General Butler reported, "A more wanton and unnecessary act than the burning, as it seems to

Capt. Jefferson Curle Phillips of Hampton led the Confederate forces which burned the town on August 7, 1861. Courtesy of the Syms-Eaton Museum

This shows Confederate troops of Capt. Jefferson C. Phillips setting fire to the town on August 7, 1861. Courtesy of Charles H. Taylor Memorial Library

me, could not have been committed. There was not the slightest attempt to make any resistance on our part to the possession of the town. . . . There was no attempt to interfere with them there, as we only repelled an attempt to burn the bridge."

Also in 1861, Hampton was the location of an early experiment in aerial reconnaissance. General Butler invited John LaMountain to bring two balloons to Fort Monroe and he made ascensions on July 25 and July 30. On August 3, LaMountain made what could be considered the first flight from an aircraft carrier when he raised his balloon from the deck of the tugboat *Fanny* to observe a Confederate camp some six miles northeast of Hampton.

During this first year of the war, Fort Monroe's main importance to the Union cause was as a base for amphibious expeditions against coastal points farther south. On August 26, an expedition sailed from Fort Monroe which captured Cape Hatteras. This was followed at the end of October by an expedition which captured Port Royal Sound in South Carolina, in January 1862 by an expedition which captured Roanoke Island, and in February by the expedition which eventually captured New Orleans.

Meanwhile, skirmishing continued in the Hampton area, most notably around Newmarket Bridge. The Confederate companies from Hampton became part of the Thirty-second Virginia Infantry and were to serve with the Army of Northern Virginia in most of its battles until the final surrender at Appomattox Court House. The Old Dominion Dragoons became part of the Third Virginia Cavalry and Jefferson C. Phillips rose to colonel of the Thirteenth Virginia Cavalry.

Early in 1862, Maj. Gen. George B. McClellan persuaded President Lincoln to attack Richmond from the Virginia Peninsula. The Confederates, however, still controlled Norfolk and the James River. They had been busy converting the former United States warship *Merrimack*, which had been scuttled when the Norfolk Navy Yard was abandoned, into the ironclad C.S.S. *Virginia*. On March 8, the *Virginia* steamed into Hampton Roads and in a few hours made wooden warships obsolete as it destroyed the frigates *Congress* and *Cumberland* off Newport News. Apparently Fort Monroe shot off a few of its guns in frustration, but the battle was too far away for the fort to be really involved. That night, the Union ironclad *Monitor*

arrived in Hampton Roads and took station to protect the remaining Federal ships. When the *Virginia* came out on the morning of March 9, the *Monitor* was there to meet her. The first battle between ironclad warships lasted four hours. Neither ship was able to do major injury to the other, but the *Monitor* prevented the *Virginia* from doing any more damage to the Union fleet.

In the days following the battle, General McClellan landed his Army of the Potomac consisting of over one hundred thousand men at Fort Monroe. McClellan pushed the Union lines up to Yorktown and the Warwick River. The cautious McClellan was slow to push his advance toward Richmond with the *Virginia* still threatening his supply lines. An aggravated President Lincoln came to Fort Monroe and directed Maj. Gen. John E. Wool to capture Norfolk and eliminate the threat of the Confederate ironclad. On May 9, Lincoln went to the Rip Raps to view the preparatory bombardment of Sewells Point. The unfinished fort at the Rip Raps had been renamed Fort Wool in honor of the senior officer at Fort Monroe following the battle between the *Monitor* and the *Virginia*. The following day, General Wool led an amphibious expedition across Hampton Roads which captured Norfolk without resistance. With its base gone and drawing too much water to retreat up the James River, the *Virginia* ceased to be useful and the Confederates blew it up.

With the advance of the Army of the Potomac toward Richmond and the fall of Norfolk, active military operations receded from the Hampton area. Fort Monroe remained the departmental headquarters for the area and for the remainder of the war provided direction to various small operations on the Peninsula and Eastern Shore and overall command of the Union troops around Suffolk during the Confederate siege of 1863. The post also served as a major supply base, transfer point for exchanged prisoners of war and mail between the lines, and headquarters of the Army of the James. In April 1864, Lt. Gen. Ulysses S. Grant came to Fort Monroe to direct General Butler, who again was in command, to move the Army of the James up the James River and attack Petersburg while Grant advanced on Richmond from the north. The movement of the Army of the James from Fort Monroe a month later was the last major military activity in the area

Ships of the expedition to capture Port Royal Sound, South Carolina, gather off Fort Monroe in late October of 1861. Fort Monroe served as the base for several amphibious expeditions against the coast of the South. Courtesy of the Casemate Museum

This engraving shows the battle between the USS Monitor and CSS Virginia (Merrimack) on March 9, 1862, in Hampton Roads. The first battle between ironclad warships ended in a draw, but revolutionized naval warfare. Courtesy of the Casemate Museum

The twelve-inch Union Gun, to the left, and the fifteen-inch Lincoln gun, in the distance to the right, were emplaced at Old Point Comfort to cover the mouth of Hampton Roads in March of 1862 to prevent the CSS Virginia from entering Chesapeake Bay. Courtesy of the Casemate Museum

Federal troops are seen moving through the ruins of Hampton on April 19, 1862. The town had been burned by Confederate forces on August 7, 1861. Courtesy of the Casemate Museum

during the war.

President Lincoln came to Fort Monroe in January 1865 on the steamer *River Queen* to meet Confederate commissioners in an attempt to end the war. This effort proved futile and the struggle continued until the spring. With the fall of Richmond, Confederate President Jefferson Davis attempted to make his way to Texas to continue the fight. He was captured by the Union army in Georgia and on May 19 was brought by steamer to Fort Monroe. Davis was confined in a casemate in the fort under very harsh circumstances until Lt. Col. John Craven, the post surgeon, managed to ameliorate his condition and after five months have him transferred to Carroll Hall inside the fort. Davis had been falsely accused of complicity in the assassination of President Lincoln and was held at Fort Monroe until May 1867. By that time the charges had been proven to be false and he was released on bail without ever coming to trial.

Although large masonry forts had been proven to be obsolete as strongholds during the Civil War, Fort Monroe remained one of the most important posts of the Army. While the engineers and ordnance experts strove to develop new types of fortifications and heavy armament to defend the coast, artillery instruction once more took place at Old Point Comfort. The Artillery School of the United States Army was reestablished at Fort Monroe in April 1868, but small military appropriations left the post cluttered with temporary wartime buildings. Repairs were few and replacement was entirely lacking for the next decade.

Following the Civil War, the United States for the first time made an effort to care for its former citizen soldiers. Three homes for disabled veterans were established in the North in 1866. General Butler had acquired the former Chesapeake Female College, established in 1854, which had served as a military hospital during the Civil War. Butler petitioned Congress to buy the property to make a fourth home for former Union soldiers and sailors in the South. The National Asylum for Disabled Volunteer Soldiers and Seamen was established in 1870 using the former college dormitory. The Rev. Charles A. Raymond, who had been president of the Chesapeake Female College, was named the first director of what was popularly called the Soldiers Home.

Because of the importance of the Artillery School, Fort Monroe finally began to acquire new barracks

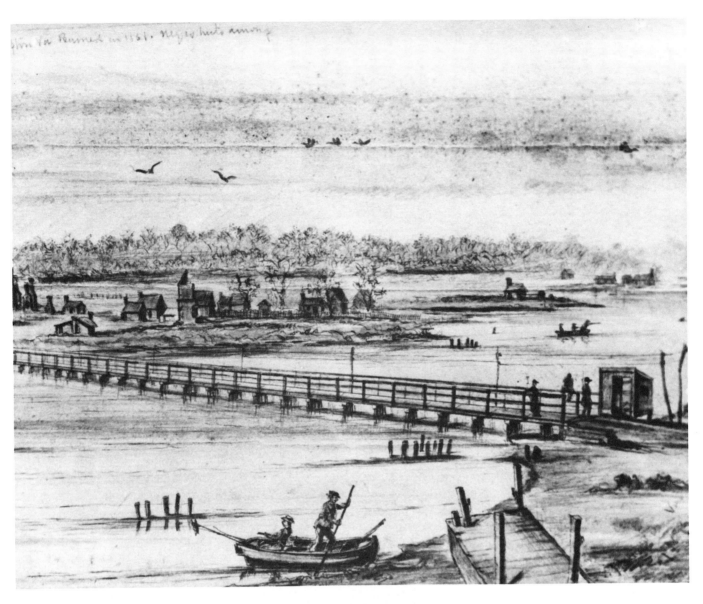

Houses of freed slaves are visible among the ruins of Hampton in this sketch of Hampton Creek in late 1863. Courtesy of the Casemate Museum

Col. Joseph Roberts, post commander of Fort Monroe, stands in front of a casemate door in the fort with officers and their families during the Civil War. Courtesy of the Casemate Museum

One hundred eighty-six thousand blacks served in the Union Army during the Civil War. This photo shows Company E, Fourth United States Colored Infantry. Black soldiers were stationed at Fort Monroe. Courtesy of Charles H. Taylor Memorial Library

and sets of family quarters. In 1886 the Endicott Board, chaired by Secretary of War William C. Endicott, recommended a new system of seacoast defense. Work began on the first of the new defenses at Fort Monroe in October 1891. During the following years, a series of massive detached batteries was built outside the old stone fort. The batteries, built of reinforced concrete protected by thick earth parapets, contained ten-inch and twelve-inch rifled disappearing guns and twelve-inch mortars. After the turn of the century the defenses of Hampton Roads were completed by the construction of batteries for three-inch and six-inch guns at Fort Monroe, and Fort Wool was entirely rebuilt to mount six-inch disappearing guns and three-inch rapid fire guns.

The Spanish-American War brought a brief flurry of excitement to the Hampton area. Agitation resulting from the Cuban revolution against Spain had caused increased tension in America. The sinking of the battleship *Maine* in Havana harbor on February 15, 1898, brought the crisis to a head and the United States declared war on Spain on April 25. In response to the federal call for volunteers, Hampton's Peninsula Guards rallied to the colors. The Peninsula Guards had been formed after the reorganization of the

Virginia Militia following the Civil War and was comprised of men from Hampton, Phoebus, and Newport News. The infantry company, consisting of eighty-seven men, left Hampton by train for Richmond on May 20, following a ceremony attended by three thousand people. In Richmond, the Peninsula Guards were mustered into service as Company D, Fourth Virginia Infantry Regiment. From Richmond, the Fourth Virginia went to Jacksonville, Florida, on June 6 and began training. However, the victory of the Army at Santiago, Cuba, on July 1 and the destruction of the Spanish fleet two days later, prevented the Peninsula Guards from seeing any active field service. Homesickness and boredom was the lot of the Fourth Virginia. The regiment finally received sailing orders for Cuba in December as part of the occupation force. The regiment returned to Savannah, Georgia, in February 1899, and was mustered out of federal service in April. The Peninsula Guards' only casualty during the war was one death from sickness. Despite having missed the actual fighting, the Peninsula Guards received a rousing welcome home and a banquet on their return to Hampton on April 28.

While the Peninsula Guards were waiting to fight in Cuba, Fort Monroe was hastily attempting to put

This was the view of Fort Monroe around the year 1880 as seen from the roof of the Hygeia Hotel. Courtesy of the Casemate Museum

Old Point Comfort and Fort Monroe looked like this around the year 1885. In the foreground are the Baltimore Dock and the second Hygeia Hotel, erected following the Civil War. Courtesy of the Casemate Museum

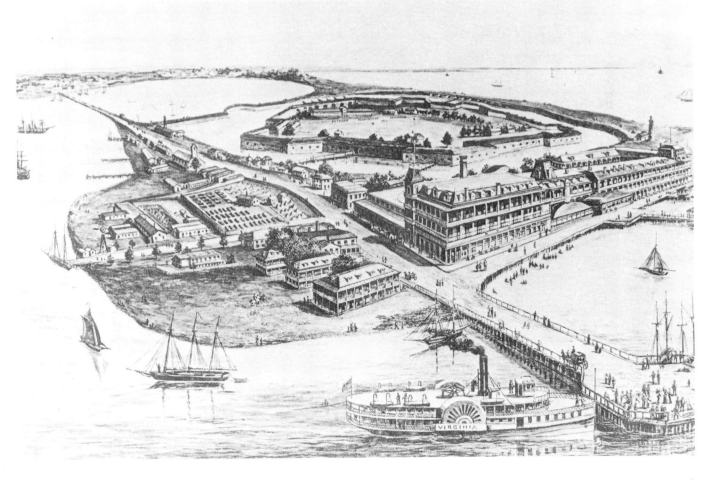

These large converted Rodman-rifled cannon and a fifteen-inch Rodman gun on the South Bastion of Fort Monroe in the 1890s are typical of the armament of the fort during the last half of the nineteenth century. Courtesy of the Casemate Museum

This shows the National Asylum for Disabled Volunteer Soldiers and Sailors, better known as the Soldiers Home, as it appeared in 1885. Courtesy of the Veterans Administration

the defenses of Hampton Roads in order. Work had begun on modernizing the defenses in 1891, but had proceeded slowly with limited appropriations until the war. There was a great fear along the Atlantic coast that the Spanish fleet would suddenly attack one of the defenseless ports. Work was pressed on completing the mortar battery at Fort Monroe, a battery of four modern rapid fire guns was mounted over the East Gate of the old fort, and an electrically-controlled minefield was laid across the entrance to Hampton Roads. Most of the regular garrison left the post to join the forces preparing to invade Cuba and Puerto Rico and the Artillery School temporarily ceased operations.

To replace the departed regulars, the First Maryland Infantry Regiment was assigned to Fort Monroe. The only real bloodshed of the war for Hampton came as the result of an altercation between some of the Maryland volunteers and the remaining regulars. On the night of June 14, 1898, about one hundred regulars encountered the same number of volunteers outside a house of entertainment in Phoebus and a bloody brawl soon took place. The Phoebus police were quickly swept aside by the combatants. The colonel of the Maryland regiment finally arrived with troops from the fort and quelled the riot. As a result of the riot, seventy-five soldiers ended up in the guard house and twenty more in the hospital with various minor injuries.

The outbreak of yellow fever at the Soldiers Home in the summer of 1899 caused a panic in the Hampton area. This dreaded disease had caused more deaths during the war than had the Spanish. Fort Monroe and the Soldiers Home were quarantined on July 30 and most of the fort's garrison was removed to Plum Island, New York, to avoid the dreaded disease. Twenty-two deaths occurred at the Soldiers Home

Company D, Fourth Virginia Infantry, from Hampton pose during their service in the Spanish-American War. Courtesy of Syms-Eaton Museum

Hampton's Company D, Seventy-first Virginia Infantry, is shown after returning from street car strike duty in Norfolk in 1900. Courtesy of Syms-Eaton Museum

A ten-inch disappearing gun of Battery Church is being loaded at Fort Monroe about 1910. This battery, begun in 1894, was one of the thirteen modern seacoast gun batteries built on the Fort Monroe reservation between 1891 and 1906. Courtesy of the Casemate Museum

The Basic Class of the Coast Artillery School poses on the steps of the YMCA at Fort Monroe in 1910. The expansion of the Coast Artillery Corps following the Spanish-American War resulted in rapid growth and modernization of the school. The YMCA was built in 1903 to meet the needs of the garrison. Courtesy of the Casemate Museum

before the quarantine was lifted on August 15, but the troops did not return to Fort Monroe until September.

The return of peace also marked the emergence of the United States as a world power. The resulting rapid expansion of the country's military forces had a profound impact on the Hampton Roads area. The modernization of the defenses of Fort Monroe and Fort Wool were rapidly pushed to completion. The Artillery School reopened in 1900 and soon greatly expanded to meet the increased needs of the numerous coastal defenses being erected along the American shore and overseas. In 1905 the Navy conducted extensive joint exercises with the Army in Chesapeake Bay and Hampton Roads. Both Fort Monroe and Fort Wool became training sites for the Virginia National Guard in the following years.

Between 1906 and 1912 a massive construction program took place at Fort Monroe to provide modern academic buildings, barracks, and quarters for the school. In 1907 the school was renamed the Coast Artillery School to reflect the new organization of the artillery and the importance of the coast defense role. Fort Monroe was the heart of the Coast Artillery Corps. Here was located the branch school, the Coast Artillery Board which was the focal point for the development of new materiel for seacoast defense, and the headquarters of one of the strongest harbor defenses in the country. All regular coast artillerymen sooner or later returned to Fort Monroe and there the spirit of the corps lived.

The Great White Fleet, President Theodore Roosevelt's demonstration of America's growing naval strength, steamed past the guns of Forts Monroe and Wool in October 1907 as it began its around-the-world

Battleships of the fleet steam past Fort Monroe in 1910. Courtesy of the Casemate Museum

cruise. The fleet returned on a rainy day in February 1909 to be greeted by a large crowd of spectators at Old Point Comfort.

In the early 1900s, just as it had happened half a century earlier, trouble in faraway Mexico was felt in Hampton. The Mexican Revolution of 1910 threatened violence along the frontier. On March 11, 1911, five companies from Fort Monroe sailed for Texas to become part of a provisional regiment protecting the border. The regulars returned to Old Point Comfort in July, but the violence along the Mexican border continued to increase. The Peninsula Guards had been disbanded following the Spanish-American War, but a new militia company of the same name was formed in Hampton during the summer of 1915. This unit was designated Battery D, First Virginia Field Artillery Regiment. Drilling began and the battery received its first shipment of artillery horses in January 1916. On March 9, 1916, Pancho Villa raided Columbus, New Mexico, and the United States sent a punitive expedition in pursuit into Mexico. Most of the National Guard was mobilized and Battery D was called into active service. A parade on Queen Street honored Battery D as its five officers and 197 men departed for Richmond on June 27. Battery D was mustered into federal service on July 5, but remained three months longer in Richmond. On October 2, orders finally arrived transferring the battery to Camp Wilson near San Antonio, Texas. The Hamptonians found the

Texas winter climate depressing and spent their active service fighting mud rather than Mexicans. The return of the Mexican Punitive Expedition under Brig. Gen. John J. Pershing quieted the crisis and on March 11, 1917, Battery D returned to Hampton.

Hampton played a large role in the advance of military operations in the air as well. The Army Appropriation Act of 1916 authorized the purchase of suitable land for an aviation research and experimentation facility to be used jointly by the National Advisory Committee for Aeronautics (NACA), the aviation section of the Army Signal Corps, and the Navy. After several months of investigation, a site four miles north of Hampton seemed suitable. Learning of the government's interest in the area, Harry H. Holt, H. R. Booker, and Nelson S. Groome of Hampton formed a citizen committee and acquired Moorefield, Bloomfield, Pools, Lamington, and Sherwood plantations immediately north of the southwest branch of Back River. The committee offered the 1,659.4 acres to the government, and the secretary of war agreed to its purchase for $290,000 on December 17, 1916. The headquarters of the Aviation Experimental Station and Proving Grounds opened in an office on the third floor of the Bank of Hampton on February 2, 1917. Architectural drawings were prepared, but actual work on the site did not begin until the end of April. The first Army detachment arrived in April and was quartered at Fort Monroe until facilities became available in November

Soldiers practice with three-inch rapid fire guns of Battery Irwin at Fort Monroe around 1910. The Old Point Comfort Lighthouse is in the background at right. Courtesy of the Casemate Museum

Soldiers fire twelve-inch mortars of Battery Anderson at Fort Monroe about 1910. Their high angle fire was intended to be directed against the lightly-armored decks of warships. Courtesy of the Casemate Museum

A Chesapeake and Ohio Railroad train enters Fort Monroe at the Mill Creek Guard House. The Zero milepost of the railroad was established at Fort Monroe in 1895 and passenger service continued from the post until the 1930s. Courtesy of the Casemate Museum

National Guardsmen of Hampton's Battery D, First Virginia Field Artillery, are shown at gun drill at Leon Springs, Texas, in 1916. Courtesy of Syms-Eaton Museum

At Fort Monroe's Battery Parrott during World War I, the massive twelve-inch disappearing guns were the largest armament on post. The gun in the foreground is lowered for loading while the gun in the background has been raised and is firing over the parapet. Courtesy of the Casemate Museum

at the airfield. On August 7, 1917, the airfield was officially named Langley Field in honor of American aviation pioneer Samuel Pierpont Langley.

By this time, the United States was again at war. As a result of German submarine operations, the United States declared war on April 6, 1917, and entered World War I on the side of the Allies. With the outbreak of war, Fort Wool was quickly garrisoned and the mine defenses and a submarine net laid to protect the entrance to Hampton Roads. Additional seacoast guns also were mounted at Fisherman Island at the mouth of Chesapeake Bay and Fort Story, the new army post at Cape Henry. Unlike in previous wars, the Coast Artillery School did not close its doors during World War I. Fort Monroe, in addition to its responsibilities for the coast defenses of Chesapeake Bay, became the headquarters of the Coast Artillery

Training Center. In addition to the school, the Coast Artillery Training Center comprised a series of officer candidate training camps at Fort Monroe and a new training area for heavy field artillery and railway artillery established at Camp Eustis on Mulberry Island in upper Warwick County. Another innovation in the training at Fort Monroe came from the assignment of the antiaircraft artillery mission to the Coast Artillery Corps. Training during the winter of 1917 was handicapped by extremely cold weather as even Chesapeake Bay froze over. The establishment of Camp Eustis offered little relief to the overcrowded conditions on the Fort Monroe Reservation and in 1918 work began on a fill along the shores of Mill Creek north and northwest of the fort in the vicinity of the railroad crossing. In addition to training officer candidates, there was also a smaller expansion in the

training of noncommissioned officers and enlisted specialists at the school. From November 1918 to April 1920, the Soldiers Home was turned over to the War Department for use as an Army base hospital.

Work on the construction of Langley Field had barely begun before the declaration of war. The Fifth Aviation School Squadron was formed in June 1917 and in mid-October the United States Army School of Aerial Photography was established at Langley Field. This was followed in March 1918 with the formation of the School of Aerial Observers. The School of Aerial Photography was transferred in mid-1918, but the School of Aerial Photographic Reconnaissance remained, being redesignated the Air Service Flying School in August 1918. Major aircraft experimental activities had been shifted to McCook Field, Ohio, in mid-1917 because of delays in completing construction, but Langley Field retained responsibilities for experimentation in bombing, photography, radio and telegraphy, and testing of foreign aircraft. From late 1917 to early 1919, Langley was the center of aircraft experimentation and evaluation by both the Army and NACA. By 1918, there were ten aero squadrons, fifteen construction companies, and one balloon detachment at Langley Field.

Hampton's Battery D had hardly unpacked from its service on the Mexican Border when it was again mobilized. On April 2, 1917, the battery was sent to protect the harbor and shipyard at Newport News. They remained on guard in the Newport News area until August, when the battery was transferred to Camp McClellan, Alabama. On August 25, Battery D

The Red Barn at what is now Langley Air Force Base was the first barracks of the Army Air Corps School of Aerial Photography. From these beginnings in 1917, when aviation was in its infancy, aerial photography developed over a span of seventy years into the use of satellites which can photograph from orbit in space. Official U.S. Air Force photo

The majority of American pilots in the teens and twenties were trained on various models of the Curtiss JN-4 "Jenny." Official U.S. Air Force photo

This band is made up of members of a black construction battalion. The band played on post and also for military occasions throughout Hampton Roads until the end of 1918. Official U.S. Air Force photo

was assigned to the 111th Field Artillery Regiment of the Twenty-ninth Division. After ten months of training in Alabama, the division was shipped east to prepare for deployment to France. Battery D sailed from Philadelphia and after a miserable crossing reached Le Havre, France, on July 19, 1918. Training continued with road marches and gas mask practice. The 1918 epidemic of Spanish influenza struck the regiment heavily, but Battery D had only one fatality. On November 5, 1918, orders finally arrived to go to the front. The battery entrained for the Vosges sector and arrived on November 7. They were still awaiting orders to join the front-line units of the Twenty-ninth Division when the Armistice was declared on November 11. The troops returned to Newport News on May 25, 1919, and then marched in the Memorial Day parade in Richmond before being demobilized early in June. Seventy-one soldiers from Hampton and Elizabeth City County had been killed by hostile action during the course of the war.

Demobilization came quickly following the Armistice. The number of troops at both Fort Monroe and Langley Field decreased and reorganizations took place at both installations. The Coast Artillery Training Center was discontinued on May 15, 1923, and the headquarters of the Third Coast Artillery District activated the same day at Fort Monroe. The Coast Artillery School and harbor defenses of Chesapeake Bay continued at Old Point Comfort. At Langley Field, the Second Wing became the major tactical unit and the Air Service Field Officers School was established in 1920. This school became the Air Corps Tactical

School in 1926 when the air service was redesignated the Army Air Corps.

In the early 1920s, army aviator Brig. Gen. William Mitchell launched a controversial campaign for an independent air force. To prove the unique capabilities of the airplane in combat, Mitchell proposed using bombers to attack battleships. After studying various sites for the test, the Hampton Roads area was picked. Several German warships which had been captured at the end of World War I were anchored about seventy-five miles from the mouth of Chesapeake Bay, or about one hundred miles from Langley Field. On June 21, 1921, the First Provisional Air Brigade operating from Langley Field began the tests. Naval Air Service flying boats sank a submarine that day and two days later Army aircraft disposed of a destroyer. Further attacks in the following days caused heavy damage to a cruiser and the sinking of a battleship. That fall, the bombers from Langley Field sank three obsolete American battleships. Mitchell had proved that aircraft could sink battleships, but the dispute over the proper role and organization of the air arm continued for many years.

Langley Field also became the center of activity for lighter-than-air operations. Various types of balloons and airships were based at the field, including four foreign models. The Italian-built *Roma* was purchased in 1921 and brought to Langley Field for testing. The *Roma* was a large semi-rigid airship which received its buoyancy from highly inflammable hydrogen gas. Technical problems plagued its first three test flights. On February 21, 1922, the *Roma* left Langley on its fourth flight. The large airship flew over Hampton, Newport News, and Norfolk. While hovering over the Army Base at Norfolk the rudder failed. The nose of the ship dropped, the gas bag began to collapse, and the *Roma* slowly plunged to the ground. It hit power lines, igniting the hydrogen which in turn set the gasoline tanks of the engines on fire. The fiery crash killed thirty-four men; only eleven of the crew escaped. The *Roma* disaster ended the Army's interest in large lighter-than-air ships, although the Navy would continue their use for several years.

At Fort Monroe, the post and school celebrated their centennials in 1924 with elaborate ceremonies. The Twelfth Coast Artillery Regiment was formed at the post in that same year. The Twelfth was replaced

The dirigibles C-2, D-2, D-3, and what is probably the A-4 fly over Langley Field in the summer of 1921. Courtesy of the Casemate Museum

The dirigible Roma *was purchased in Italy, then assembled at Langley Field in autumn of 1921. Courtesy of the Planning Department, city of Hampton*

The Roma *prepares at Langley Field for its first American flight on November 15, 1921. Official U.S. Air Force photo*

the Second Coast Artillery Regiment in 1932. After the military deactivation of Fort Eustis, the railway artillery at that post was moved to Old Point Comfort. Instruction at the Coast Artillery School began to place more emphasis on antiaircraft artillery.

The Great Depression of 1929 had a profound impact on the military installations in Hampton. At Fort Monroe, the annual service practices with the large seacoast guns were cancelled to save money and the number of classes at the Coast Artillery School were reduced. Many of the officers of the garrison were detailed away from the posts on duty with the Civilian Conservation Corps. Both installations were devastated on August 23, 1933, when a major hurricane struck the Peninsula. Tides were more than six feet over mean high tide. At Langley Field, water was chest deep in many areas and the King Street Bridge was badly damaged. The 246th Coast Artillery of the

Virginia National Guard almost floated away at Fort Monroe when its barracks were torn from the foundations. Many buildings at both installations were also badly damaged, but there were no serious casualties. The destruction brought by the hurricane proved in the long run to be a blessing to the military installations of Hampton. Using the Work Projects Administration and other agencies established to counter the Great Depression, both Fort Monroe and Langley Field undertook extensive construction projects. At Fort Monroe, the Chesapeake Bay seawall was built to protect Old Point Comfort from future major storms. New quarters, administrative buildings, and hospitals also were built. The grass runways at Langley Field were also paved during this period.

In 1930, the Veterans Administration was created to consolidate into a single agency all federal activities dealing exclusively with veterans' affairs. The Soldiers

This is the flight line at Langley Field on May 23, 1921. The larger planes are NBS-1 bombers. Also on the line are DH-4 bombers and SE-5 advanced trainers. Official U.S. Air Force photo

This aerial view shows Langley Field on March 10, 1921. The large airship hangar is at the top, left. Official U.S. Air Force photo

Officers inspect aircraft at Langley Field, June 11, 1921. Courtesy of the Casemate Museum

Brig. Gen. William "Billy" Mitchell saw the potential of the airplane as an offensive and defensive weapon as early as 1916, when he learned to fly in Newport News. He directed bombing trials outside Hampton Roads using heavily-armored, captured German battleships. In proving that armored ships could be sunk from the air, he helped to change the character of modern warfare. Official U.S. Air Force photo

A phosphorous bomb nearly strikes the USS Alabama *on September 23, 1921, during the bombing tests conducted by Brig. Gen. Billy Mitchell outside Hampton Roads. Official U.S. Air force photo*

Home became the Hampton Veterans Administration Medical Center as a result of this consolidation. Extensive new construction expanded the old Soldiers Home to a modern 966-bed medical center. In addition there is a 120-bed nursing home care unit and a 475-bed rehabilitative domiciliary located at the Hampton facility.

In addition to the physical improvement, the last half of the 1930s marked significant changes for the military in the Hampton area. On March 1, 1935, General Headquarters Air Force came into existence at Langley Field. This new organization was the first step in the creation of an autonomous air arm within the United States Army and supervised all air tactical units. New equipment, such as the B-17 bomber, also arrived. The curriculum at the Coast Artillery School began to expand again and training slowly returned to normal. With the outbreak of war in Europe on September 1, 1939, some units from Fort Monroe deployed to protect Puerto Rico and new coast artillery units were formed at the post. The growing threat to the United States resulted in the mobilization of the National Guard. In September 1940, the 246th Coast Artillery Regiment from western Virginia reported to Fort Monroe to augment the regular Second Coast Artillery Regiment in the harbor defenses of Chesapeake Bay. New regular units were also activated at Langley Field.

The Japanese attack on Pearl Harbor on December 7, 1941, immediately galvanized the Hampton military installations. The coast defenses at Fort Monroe and the other forts under its command in the lower Chesapeake went on full alert. A garrison again occupied Fort Wool. The first radar-controlled seacoast battery went into operation at Fort Monroe. Brig. Gen. Rollin L. Tilton's Third Coast Artillery District at Fort Monroe became the Chesapeake Bay sector of the Eastern Defense Command with responsibility for defense of the coast from the Maryland-Virginia state line to below the Outer Banks of North Carolina. The Coast Artillery School continued operations, but the antiaircraft portion of the curriculum was transferred to a new school at Camp Davis, North Carolina. For a number of years there had been concern that there was no direct route from Fort Monroe to the James River Bridge to move troops and equipment in an emergency. With the outbreak of war, General Tilton and Col. E. A. Lohman, commander of Langley Field, received permission to build Military Road, which began with a new bridge out of Fort Monroe, crossed King Street coming out of Langley, and proceeded directly to the James River Bridge. Work began in 1942 on this road which eventually was renamed Mercury Boulevard. For the remainder of World War II, despite reorganizations and fluctuations in the number of troops available, Fort Monroe commanded the most important and strongest coast defense along the middle Atlantic shore.

Many units, including the Second Bombardment Wing, deployed from Langley Field to various operational theaters early in the war. From 1941 to 1943, units from Langley's Twenty-fifth Antisubmarine Wing conducted active operations, patrolling as far as six hundred miles from the coast. The First Sea Search Attack Group played a major role in developing new tactics, techniques, and equipment and in train-

A prototype Douglas World Cruiser flies over the Old North King Street bridge in 1924. Official U.S. Air Force photo

The King Street bridge leading to Langley Field was badly damaged by the August 23, 1933, hurricane. Courtesy of Charles H. Taylor Memorial Library

Brig. Gen. Frank Andrews and his staff take an aerial review at Langley Field on March 6, 1935, following the establishment of General Headquarters Air Force. Official U.S. Air Force photo

ing crews for antisubmarine operations. Following the phasedown of antisubmarine operations, Langley Field became a primary training center for airborne radar equipment. Langley, in contrast to Fort Monroe, had many black units assigned during the war, including truck companies and engineer battalions. By the end of the war, women soldiers were also assigned to both Fort Monroe and Langley Field.

Among the National Guard units mobilized prior to the outbreak of war was Hampton's Battery D,

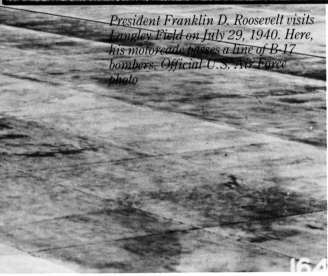

President Franklin D. Roosevelt visits Langley Field on July 29, 1940. Here, his motorcade passes a line of B-17 bombers. Official U.S. Air Force photo

111th Field Artillery Regiment, as part of the Twenty-ninth Infantry Division. E. Sclater Montague of Hampton had commanded Battery D since 1924 and rose to command of the regiment. The Twenty-ninth Infantry Division was called into active service in February 1941 and concentrated at Fort Meade, Maryland. That troop from Hampton participated in maneuvers in North Carolina and was still in the field when the war began in December. Returning to Fort Meade, the division reorganized and the 111th Field Artillery Regiment was broken up. The men from Hampton were scattered to other units of the division. The division sailed to England in late 1942 and spent the next year and a half in further intensive training. The waiting finally ended on June 6, 1944, when the Twenty-ninth Infantry Division led the American assault on Omaha Beach in Normandy. The division suffered twenty-four hundred casualties in the fierce fighting on Omaha Beach and then participated in the bitter fighting in the Normandy hedgerows and the assault on Brest. After a period of rest, the division again entered combat as the Allies penetrated into Germany, finishing the war on the banks of the Elbe River. Hampton counted 127 of her sons dead as a result of hostile actions since 1941.

Following the demobilization at the end of World War II, the military installations in Hampton again underwent major changes. The rapid growth of aviation during the war years and improvements in naval gunnery doomed traditional coast defenses such as Fort Monroe commanded. Early in 1946, Gen. Dwight D. Eisenhower, the Chief of Staff of the Army, directed that the Tactical Air Command (TAC) and Army Ground Forces (AGF) should be located in close proximity to each other and convenient to Washington. After studying various sites, the Army decided to locate TAC at Langley Field and AGF at Fort Monroe. On June 1, 1946, the Coast Artillery School transferred to Fort Winfield Scott in California and Fort Monroe ceased to be an artillery post. Shortly thereafter the two major commands moved their headquarters to Hampton.

Tactical Air Command headquarters has remained at Langley Air Force Base since 1946. Despite periodic minor changes in mission, TAC has been responsible for the organization, training, equipping, and maintenance of combat-ready forces capable of rapid deployment and employment and strategic air defense forces. The command at Fort Monroe, on the other hand, has undergone some significant changes in both name and mission since 1946. Army Ground Forces had responsibility for tactical units and the numbered continental armies as well as the training of the combat arms. In 1948, the command was reorganized as the Office of the Chief of Army Field Forces (OCAFF), with only responsibility for training. Another reorganization in 1955 redesignated OCAFF

as Headquarters, Continental Army Command (CONARC), which retained its primary mission of training and again assumed command of the continental armies. In 1962, the responsibility for combat developments was transferred to a new command, but CONARC received jurisdiction over the technical service schools and training. The latest reorganization took place in 1973. CONARC was broken up and its functions relating to the Strategic Army Forces, the Reserve Components, and unit training were transferred to the United States Army Forces Command. The United States Army Training and Doctrine Command (TRADOC) was established at Fort Monroe with the mission of individual training, doctrinal evolution, education, and combat developments. It commands the Army service school system and the Reserve Officers' Training Corps throughout the country.

The large seacoast guns were gone from Hampton, but in 1953 a battalion of antiaircraft guns headquartered at Fort Monroe took up positions to protect the lower Peninsula. These were soon replaced by NIKE missiles, which were stationed in Fox Hill and near Patrick Henry Airport until the 1960s.

Today the military is still a vital part of life in Hampton. TAC and TRADOC and its predecessors were responsible for the organization and training of the forces that fought in Korea and Vietnam. These major commands continue to form an important element of the defense of the United States. Hamptonians served proudly in Korea and Vietnam; twenty-four were killed serving their country during the Korean Conflict, and thirty-nine during Vietnam. Hampton continues its long tradition of citizen soldiers with its members of the 111th Field Artillery of the Virginia National Guard and the 302d Transportation Group of the United States Army Reserve. Although the military presence in Hampton has always primarily consisted of the Army and the Air Force, its citizens have also served in both the active and reserve components of the Navy, Marine Corps, and Coast Guard.

From 1941 until late 1943 Langley Field was a base for antisubmarine operations along the East Coast. This training exercise was conducted in April of 1942. Official U.S. Air Force photo

This aerial photograph shows Langley Air Force Base in September of 1983. Official U.S. Air Force photo

Fort Wool, opposite Fort Monroe, is shown about 1950. To the left are the casemates of the original stone fort. Seacoast batteries built in the early 1900s extend along the Hampton Roads face of the fort, and Battery Gates, built in World War II, is to the right. Courtesy of the Casemate Museum

This shows the main building of the Hampton Veterans Administration Medical Center which was built in 1937. Courtesy of the Veterans Administration Medical Center

This eight-inch railway gun was with Battery E, Fifty-second Coast Artillery at Fort Monroe in the late 1930s. Courtesy of the Casemate Museum

Company Twenty-two of the Virginia Protective Force, shown in May of 1942, was the first company of the Virginia home guard formed in World War II. Courtesy of the Syms-Eaton Museum

This view shows Fort Monroe from the air around the year 1950. To the right on Mill Creek shore can be seen the ferry dock which connected Hampton with Norfolk before the Hampton Roads Bridge-Tunnel was built. Courtesy of the Casemate Museum

ACKNOWLEDGMENTS

For assistance in preparing this chapter, I wish to thank the staff of the Casemate Museum, Fort Monroe, for furnishing pictures and the use of their excellent library; the members of the Tactical Air Command Historical Office, and Sgt. Chilton W. McPheeters, First Tactical Fighter Wing historian, Langley Air Force Base, for pictures of Langley and information about TAC; John Quarstein of the War Memorial Museum of Virginia; and Mike Cobb, curator of the Syms-Eaton Museum

CHEYNE,

St. John's Church has the oldest communion silver in continuous use in America, which was made in London in 1618. In the background is the Elizabeth City Parish Book of 1781. Courtesy of Syms-Eaton Museum

3

Chapter

Religion's Special Role

by the Reverend Chester Brown

For almost half of Hampton's 375 years there was only one church in the city; by 1985 there were more than 175. Seventeen of those churches lined one three-mile-long street, Todd's Lane. As Hampton grew and people came from all over the world, a great diversity of religions sprang up with a variety of traditions including Christian, Jewish and Moslem.

Religion has played a prominent role in the life of the people of Hampton since its earliest days. The Church and community were one in 1610 when the first settlers of the village of Kicotan (Hampton) brought the Anglican form of worship from their homeland. A strong belief in God was the basis of daily life in the seventeenth century. Frequent religious services strengthened the small community in its struggle for survival in the wilderness. Leaders of the church were often prominent in local government.

Hampton's oldest church, St. John's, built in 1728, located in the heart of the city, is the fourth church of Elizabeth City Parish. The parish is the oldest Episcopal parish in continuous service in the United States. Some two thousand tourists visit the church annually. It is a cruciform brick church built in the Georgian style. The interior, reflecting the ravages of war and the changing needs of an active congregation, is a mixture of styles with strong Victorian overtones.

The parish, begun with the settling of Hampton in 1610, was under the care of its first minister, the Rev. William Mease, for ten years. Although the site of the first church is unknown, the sites of the second church (1632-24) and the third church (1667) on opposite sides of the Hampton River are in the possession of the parish. Both churches were simple wooden structures. The parish still possesses the 1618 communion silver, the oldest in continuous use in the English-speaking United States, which came to it in 1627.

The present eighteenth century church was built in response to the demands of an expanded and more affluent population centered around the bustling port of Hampton. It suffered damage at the hands of the British in the Revolution and the War of 1812 and fell into ruin soon after as support by taxation for the Anglican (now Episcopal) church ceased with the formation of the new federal government. A dislike for all things identified with England, the rise of new religious denominations, and a crippled economy almost stamped out the Episcopal church in the United States.

In 1825, a revival swept through the Episcopal church and the old Elizabeth City Parish Church in Hampton was repaired and consecrated in 1830 with a

new name, St. John's. But thirty years later the Civil War visited the Peninsula and in 1861 Hampton and St. John's were burned by native sons to keep them out of Union hands. The sturdy Colonial brick walls remained and once again were repaired with funds sent from all over the nation, and in 1869 the tenacious congregation resumed services in the church entrusted to their care.

Over the years, Elizabeth City Parish has helped other Episcopal churches in the area to organize. The earliest, the Chapel of the Centurion at Fort Monroe consecrated in 1858, was served by the Rev. Mark L. Chevers in his dual capacity as rector of St. John's from 1827 to 1843 and chaplain of Fort Monroe from 1827 until his death in 1875.

The Episcopal Church of Phoebus became a mission in 1878 organized by the Reverend Mayo and the Rev. John J. Gravatt, rector of St. John's. Services were held in various locations until 1897 when Emmanuel Church of Phoebus was built. Interior woodwork and chancel furnishings were handmade at the woodwork shop of Hampton Institute. The membership grew steadily, and by 1958 Emmanuel's congregation had moved to their Parish Hall on what is now Mercury Boulevard until the church building was finished a year later. The Phoebus Church, a charming example of Victorian architecture made of wood, was sold to The Full Gospel Evangelical Christian Church, and was later demolished in the Phoebus redevelopment program.

The first black Episcopal congregation was formed in 1905 as the result of a meeting in Hampton between the Rev. Maximo F. Duty, rector of St. Phillips Episcopal Church, Richmond, and Mr. Richard Phillips. Their talks led them to the Rev. C. Braxton Bryan of St. John's. With the help of Mrs. Mary Cardwell, a group of ten interested persons were gathered and the small congregation began to meet at various places including, for a short time, the parish hall of St. John's. In 1907, the first St. Cyprian's Church was built on Lincoln Street. The Reverend Bryan and his successor, the Rev. Reverdy Estill continued to conduct services for St. Cyprian's on Sunday afternoons or Thursday evenings. In 1910, the Rev. Ebenezer H. Hamilton became the first permanent priest. From 1931 to 1960, St. Cyprian's and St. Augustine's in Newport News were served by the same priest. The congregation moved in 1963 to a new church built on the campus of Hampton Institute. In 1974 St. Cyprian's was admitted as a parish in the

This is how St. John's Church appeared shortly before it was burned during the Civil War. Courtesy of Casemate Museum

In 1892 St. John's Parish House was one of two parish houses in Virginia. Courtesy of Syms-Eaton Museum

This early twentieth century picture of St. John's Church offers a good view of the exceptional Flemish bond masonry. Courtesy of the Casemate Museum

Emmanuel Episcopal Church, organized in 1878, is located on what is now East Mercury Boulevard. Courtesy of C. Brown

This shows the First United Methodist Church as sketched in 1888. Courtesy of Syms-Eaton Museum

Saint Cyprian's Episcopal Church was built on West Queen Street in 1984. Courtesy of C. Brown

Council of the Diocese of Southern Virginia. By 1984 the membership had grown to 246 and the congregation moved to the new larger church built on west Queen Street.

In response to the development of the Northampton section of the city, St. John's decided to establish St. Mark's in 1963 as a parochial mission. Services were held in the clubhouse of the Northampton Woman's Club for about 122 members with the Rev. Winston Hope as vicar. The church building on Todds Lane was completed in 1964 on land donated for the purpose. St. Mark's was recognized as an independent parish of the diocese in 1966 and the Reverend Hope

was elected rector and served until his retirement in 1982. During the 1970s the congregation embarked on a program to enlarge and beautify the original building and by 1985 the membership had grown to 200.

Parallel to the Episcopalian revival, in the mid-eighteenth century a renewed interest in religion called "the Great Awakening" began in New England and spread rapidly throughout the Colonies. George Whitfield, a fiery, zealous English evangelist, preached up and down the Colonies, attracting many followers and laying a foundation for a broadly based religious revival. The most significant change in the religious scene during this period was the relative decline in

First United Methodist Church was located at the intersection of Bank and Queen streets when this picture was taken around the year 1936. Courtesy of Syms-Eaton Museum

Phoebus United Methodist Church was formerly the Mill Creek Methodist Church. This picture was taken around the year 1915. Courtesy of Syms-Eaton Museum

influence of the Puritans in the North and the Anglicans in the South, and a corresponding rise in influence of other Christians, namely, Lutherans, Roman Catholics, Methodists, Baptists, and Presbyterians. In the Colonies in 1660 there were forty-one Anglican Churches; by 1780 there were 906. While in 1660 there were only four Baptist churches, and five Presbyterian, in 1760 there were 457 Baptist and 495 Presbyterian churches in the Colonies.

The Methodists organized the first non-Anglican church in Hampton. It is reported that on August 26, 1772, one Joseph Philmore preached what is thought to be the first Methodist sermon in the city "in a large dining room," before "a fine congregation of the genteeler sort." It was not until 1789, however, that a Methodist "Society" was organized. This is considered to be the founding of the present First United Methodist Church, the oldest Methodist Church on the Peninsula, now a Virginia Historic Landmark.

The renowned itinerant Methodist evangelist, Francis Asbury, made two visits to Hampton. The first Methodist church was built in 1811 on land deeded by Mrs. Elizabeth Mallory for the sum of one dollar. The disruption caused by the War of 1812 greatly slowed the progress of the Methodists. It was at this time that the denomination experienced its first

Wallace Memorial United Methodist Church of Fox Hill was organized in 1895. Courtesy of C. Brown

Central United Methodist Church was built in 1904. Courtesy of Syms-Eaton Museum

schism. Later, as others would do when the Civil War came, Methodists divided North and South. Through the years Methodists have entered into numerous mergers so that by the twentieth century they have become one of the largest Christian groups in the world and the second largest Protestant congregation in the United States.

A Methodist church was organized in Phoebus in 1870. Beginning as a Sunday School, the church met on Curry Street under the leadership of Mr. and Mrs. O. P. Fernald. First called the Mill Creek Methodist Episcopal Church, in 1872 the name was changed to the Chesapeake City M. E. Church. When the town of Phoebus was founded the church changed its name a third time, incorporating the name of the new town, Phoebus Methodist Church.

In the early 1890s the need for a Methodist church in the western part of Hampton became evident, resulting in the establishment of Central United Methodist Church. In 1894 over sixty members of First United Methodist Church withdrew from the Queen Street church and formed the West End congregation which was described as "a veritable beehive of Methodist activity."

The Methodists bought the small frame structure from the Presbyterians for the sum of six hundred dollars. The lot had previously been given by John M. Willis for religious purposes. It was because of the location of this chapel that the street was named Chapel Street.

In 1904 the cornerstone for a new brick church was laid and the church was named Central Methodist Episcopal Church, South. In the almost one hundred years of its existence, the church continued to grow

Hampton Baptist Church is shown in approximately 1899. Courtesy of Hampton University Archives

Memorial Baptist Church on Lee Street was organized in 1903 in what was then Hampton's West End. Courtesy of Memorial Baptist Church

Central Baptist Church on West Mercury Boulevard was organized in 1950. Courtesy of C. Brown

and serve the community. In 1975 when Vietnamese refugees began to arrive in Hampton, Central, under the leadership of the Rev. Garry I. Shelton, led the resettlement of many families.

Baptists organized a church in 1791 with some ninety members, which became the Hampton Baptist Church downtown. Their work on the Peninsula began in the Grafton area and spread into Elizabeth City County around Bethel. A prominent Baptist in Hampton was Thomas Chisman, formerly a surgeon in the Continental Army. Baptist churches in Hampton in the years following represented several separate denominations, and a number of Baptist congregations remained unaffiliated, "Independent" Baptists, though in theory, every Baptist church is an independent organization, bound to others only on a voluntary and cooperative basis. The largest Independent Baptist church in the city, Central, boasted a membership of twenty-one hundred in the mid 1980s as it celebrated its thirty-fifth anniversary led by its only pastor, the Rev. G. Thornton Hall, the church's founder. In 1985, sixteen Baptist churches in Hampton were affiliated with the largest Baptist denomination, the Southern Baptist Convention with over fourteen million members. The largest Southern Baptist church in the community, Liberty on Todds Lane, had eighteen hundred members in the 1980s.

Before the Civil War the Hampton Baptist Church claimed at least six hundred black, and two hundred white members. During the war the blacks withdrew to form their own church, First Baptist. It was founded in 1863 in the Pee Dee section of Old Hampton with twenty-five members and the Rev. Zechariah Evans as its first pastor. First Baptist grew rapidly to a place of influence not only in the city, but throughout the state. Its second minister was undoubtedly the most prominent black man in Hampton. As a slave he was known as Billy, but as a sign of his newfound freedom, he chose a new name, William Taylor. Still, until his death he was Billy Colton to many Hamptonians. He was a homeowner and a carpenter. He was also a "fiery exhorter." In later years, The Rev. Dr. J. W. Patterson served the church for the first half of the twentieth century, enjoying one of the longest pastorates on record. Gen. Samuel Armstrong, founder of what is now Hampton University, laid the cornerstone of a new building on North King Street. By 1985 membership at First Baptist had grown to thirteen hundred.

One of the reasons for First Baptist's rapid growth was the presence of Union forces in Hampton during the Civil War which attracted many blacks. By the end of the war some twenty-five thousand refugees had flocked to the area. In response to this opportunity, many missionaries came down from the North, most of whom were Presbyterians and Episcopalians sponsored by the American Missionary Association, and by 1865 there were six mission schools serving the blacks of the Peninsula. The rigid Calvinistic views taught by many of them, especially predestination, did not appeal to the blacks, and most of them became Baptists or Methodists. In the same year that First Baptist was organized, the blacks of Phoebus established their own Baptist church, Zion. As with First Baptist, General Armstrong was instrumental, securing a property on County Street for the church. Its first minister, The Rev. William Thornton served the church until 1909. A well-known pastor of more recent years, The Rev. Dr. J. Dett Marshburn served from 1936 to 1972. Another black congregation was formed

This is how First Baptist Church appeared in 1929. Courtesy of Syms-Eaton Museum

Zion Baptist Church appeared this way in 1880. Courtesy of Syms-Eaton Museum

This photo of Queen Street Baptist Church was taken in 1935. Courtesy of Syms-Eaton Museum

in Hampton about this time as well, the Queen Street Church, first known as Second Baptist. In 1865 this church was founded by some of the refugees who had come down from Williamsburg. With a membership growing to six hundred, Queen Street Church became a familiar landmark at the corner of Queen and Armistead. In 1985 there were still some twenty-five Baptist churches in the city which had predominantly black congregations.

The African Methodist Episcopal Church is one of the largest Methodist groups in the country. Formed in 1787 over the issue of slavery, organized in 1787 by two free blacks, Richard Allen and Absalon Jones, the church spread throughout the country. The Bethel A.M.E. Church in Hampton was founded in 1864 and the first pastor was the Rev. Peter Sheppard. The sanctuary on Lincoln Street, built in 1972, served some four hundred members in its 121st Anniversary year.

The first Roman Catholic Church in Hampton, St. Mary Star of the Sea, was founded at Fort Monroe in 1860. At the time it was not unusual for a civilian church to be located on a military reservation, but over time it became one of the few in the country. There were three other parishes begun in the city: St. Rose of Lima in Wythe, founded in 1948; St. Joseph in Buckroe, founded in 1968; and Immaculate Conception, in Riverdale, in 1971.

Presbyterians trace their beginnings in Hampton to a meeting held at the home of Samuel Cumming on March 18, 1879. In less than a month First Presbyterian Church was organized with twelve charter members including Mr. Cumming as the first Elder. It was five years before the Rev. John Gray Anderson was called to serve as the church's first pastor. Mr.

Anderson was a busy man, for he divided his time among the Presbyterians in Hampton, Newport News, Williamsburg, and Smithfield. In the early 1890s, First Presbyterian sold its property on Chapel Street to the Methodists who organized Central United Methodist Church. The Presbyterians moved to the heart of the city on Queen Street. Then, in 1952 the Presbyterian church moved to the corner of Armistead and Victoria. An educational building served the church until 1963 when an impressive sanctuary was built, with a steeple and bell tower which could be seen from far out in the Chesapeake Bay. The LaCrosse Presbyterian Church in Phoebus, named for John LaCrosse, Phoebus resident and active Elder in the Hampton Church, grew out of a Sabbath school organized in 1895. Three other Affiliated Presbyterian churches arose in the city: Community on Fox Hill Road (1958), Wythe in Wythe (1940), and Northampton on Todds Lane (1961). There are also several independent Presbyterian churches in the city.

The Christian Churches appeared in Hampton in the late 1800s. These trace their origins to Alexander Campbell, who along with his father, Thomas, won many followers in the first half of the nineteenth century. The Campbells were greatly disturbed by the numerous divisions among Christians, but in their efforts to end denominationalism, they actually encouraged the forming of several new groups. A leader in the founding of Hampton Christian Church (Disciples) was William A. Tennis, a deacon in the Grafton Church. This church met for years on Chapel Street. In 1973 the property was sold to the Salvation Army and the church moved to the corner of Mercury and Andrews. First Christian, another Disciples church,

This photograph shows St. Mary Star of the Sea Church around the year 1870. The church is the low building on the right-hand side of the road. Courtesy of the Casemate Museum

The second St. Mary Star of the Sea Church was built in 1903 with stone brought from Europe as ship's ballast. Courtesy of the Casemate Museum

St. Joseph's Catholic Church of Buckroe was organized in 1968. Courtesy of C. Brown

This 1927 photo of First Presbyterian Church shows the facade which was remodeled in 1912-13. Courtesy of Syms-Eaton Museum

Northampton Presbyterian Church of Todds Lane was organized in 1961. Courtesy of C. Brown

Hampton Christian Church was organized in 1883 and moved to its new location on East Mercury Boulevard in 1973. Courtesy of C. Brown

Northampton Church of Christ on Todds Lane was organized in 1962. Courtesy of C. Brown

The United Church of Christ moved from downtown Newport News to Todds Lane in 1964. Courtesy of C. Brown

moved to Todds Lane from downtown Newport News in 1961. It was organized in 1888. The Hampton Church of Christ organized on Kecoughtan Road in 1945 with some seventy charter members. This group, though organizationally separate from the Christian Churches, also traces its beginning to the Campbells. The Northampton Church of Christ on Todds Lane was founded in 1962, and the Langley Church of Christ on Fox Hill Road was organized in 1980. A third group which grew from the work of the Campbells also called themselves Church of Christ but differed from the others by shunning the use of instrumental music in worship. One such church was built at the corner of Fox Hill Road and Fairfield Boulevard.

The United Church of Christ on Todds Lane moved to Hampton from downtown Newport News in 1964. This church is the result of a local merger of two Newport News congregations, one in the North End, the other in the East End; nationally, the church is the product of a merger of the Congregational and Evangelical Reformed Churches.

The sight of two neatly-dressed young men riding bicycles became a familiar one in twentieth-century Hampton. These easily-recognizable Mormon missionaries appeared on the scene shortly after the earliest meetings of the Church of Jesus Christ of Latter-Day Saints in the city were held in the home of Walter Stainback in Phoebus in 1937-38. The first Mormon chapel was built on Victoria Boulevard in 1950 with some eighty members in that congregation. In the same year a branch of the church was organized with Junny D. Smith, a high school principal, as president. In 1957, since membership had grown to 365, a ward (parish) was established and the Victoria Boulevard chapel was enlarged. The church moved to Todds Lane in 1964 and built a new and larger chapel. Two wards of about 450 members each shared the new chapel. In 1979 a stake (diocese) of the Church was organized for the Peninsula with 2,000 members and a $1.2 million building was constructed.

Lutheran worship services were held in Hampton as early as 1921 when the Reverend Louis J. Roehm, pastor of Norfolk's Trinity Lutheran Church (Lutheran Church-Missouri Synod), came over once a month. Meetings were held in the Wythe Community Center until about 1931. There was a disruption in

Emmanuel Lutheran Church on Kecoughtan Road was organized in 1944. Courtesy of C. Brown

these services, caused in part by the Great Depression, and Lutheran worship did not resume in the city until 1940 when another pastor from Trinity, the Rev. Paul Plawin, came over for monthly services. In the following year, the Rev. Byron P. Wallschlager of the Lutheran Service Center conducted weekly services at the Rouse Chapel on Twenty-fifth Street in Newport News. Within a month the group called its first pastor, the Rev. Phillip Priester, and selected Emmanuel as its name. In 1943 the congregation purchased the property at the corner of Kecoughtan and Shenandoah roads where the church was built and dedicated in 1944. Throughout the years Emmanuel Lutheran has been known for its day school which in 1985 had an enrollment of 116. The church also has operated a day-care center since 1980. Emmanuel is affiliated with the Lutheran church-Missouri Synod.

Three other Lutheran churches were organized in more recent years: St. Paul, at Mercury and Armistead avenues, was founded in 1953; Gloria Dei, on Fox Hill Road, began in 1965; and Hope, on Todds Lane, began its ministry in 1966. St. Paul and Gloria Dei are affiliated with the Lutheran Church in America, and Hope is affiliated with the American Lutheran Church. Gloria Dei operated a day school which in 1985 had an enrollment of 375.

The building of the Memorial Chapel signified the culmination of the development of the campus of Hampton Normal and Agricultural Institute for the years 1867-87. The church was funded as a gift from the estate of Frederick Marquand, a philanthropist who has resided in Southport, Connecticut. J. C. Cady, noted architect of New York, was engaged to draw the plans. When Memorial Chapel, located on the Hamp-

ton campus near the waterfront, was dedicated on May 20, 1886, Cady's personal criteria for the chapel, "permanence, dignity, simplicity, and welcome" were in evidence. Using the style of architecture known as Italian Romanesque, the chapel was built of brick and seated one thousand. The pews were built from yellow pine by Hampton students. In 1900 the chapel was described as being an undenominational church known as the Church of Christ. Until the mid-1960s all music for the services was without accompaniment.

The tower of Memorial Chapel was 150 feet in height and contained a four-faced illuminated clock which struck the hours and had a nine-bell chime. The largest of the nine bells weighed two thousand pounds and had the inscription "Praise God from whom all blessings flow." The bells were not electrified until 1951. Dominating the waterfront of Hampton University for almost a century, the tower of Memorial Chapel served as a point of reference for all who used the nearby waterways, particularly at night when the illuminated clock could be seen for many miles.

In 1985, a small wooden church which stood on the corner of Ivy Home and Kecoughtan Roads had a simple sign attached to the front of the building which read "Church of Jesus." Another small sign nearby signified that the building was designated as a state historic landmark. This simple church, known officially as Little England Chapel, was the only known black missionary chapel standing in the state of Virginia at the time it received its landmark designation around 1980.

Little England Chapel was thought to be representative of the many community institutions established in Hampton by blacks in the post-Civil War era.

This photo shows the Salvation Army building on Big Bethel Road. Courtesy of C. Brown

Memorial Chapel of Hampton University looked like this around the year 1890. Courtesy of Hampton University Archives

Little England Chapel was the site of regular church services in 1985. It was located at the corner of Kecoughtan and Ivy Home Roads. Courtesy of C. H. Hawkins

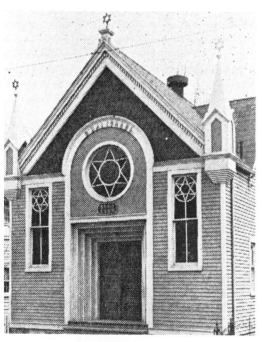

B'nai Israel Synagogue was located on Locust Street when this picture appeared in the 1915 pamphlet, Pen and Pencil Sketches. *Courtesy of the Hampton Heritage Foundation, Inc.*

This photo shows the Chapel of the Centurion around the year 1884. Courtesy of the Casemate Museum

Built by Hampton Normal and Agricultural Institute students between 1878 and 1880 as a Sunday School in the heavily populated black area then known as Cock's Newtown, the building was originally called "Sunday School" or "the Chapel." Daniel F. Cock, a white missionary from New York who instructed Indians in agriculture at the Normal School, gave permission for the chapel to be built on his land. The church also served as a kind of community center for the neighborhood. Captain Fred Cock gave the deed to the property to the Newtown Improvement Club and Civic Club in 1954 "to be used by the Congregation of the Newtown Improvement Club for non-denominational religious purposes."

In the spring of 1865, Bethesda Chapel was completed on property that later became a National Cemetery. It was founded by Chaplain E. P. Roe as a hospital chapel for sick and wounded Union soldiers at Camp Hamilton. Later that same year, the building was transferred by the War Department to the Presbyterian Committee of Home Missions of New York. As the number of patients dwindled, the chapel served the general community whose churches had been destroyed in the burning of Hampton in 1861. On November 7, 1869, Bethesda Chapel was reorganized under the American Missionary Association as an interdenominational church for Hampton Normal and Agricultural Institute (now Hampton University). The Rev. Richard Tolman was called as pastor in 1872 and immediately became active in religious affairs on the Peninsula. Students of the Institute were required to attend services until about 1936. The Indian students from the Western Plains, however, who had come to Hampton under the sponsorship of the Episcopal church were expected to attend services at St. John's Church.

The Victory Life Outreach, on West Queen Street, began its ministry in the Holiday Inn in October of 1981 with eight people. It served in two other locations before it moved into its present building in May 1984. In 1985 members numbered eight hundred. The Bible School graduated sixty-nine in 1985 with an expected two hundred students enrolled for the fall session.

Two synagogues served the Peninsula's Jewish population, B'nai Israel (Orthodox) on Kecoughtan Road and Rodef Sholom (Conservative) on Whealton Road. Rodef Sholom moved to Whealton in 1957 from Newport News and its congregation of some 250 families remained mostly oriented to that city. B'nai Israel was founded in 1904 by several Hampton and Phoebus businessmen who opened their homes for worship until a sanctuary could be built. Among the founding families are such well-known local names as Carmel, Cooper, Sears, Epstein, Fisher, Gold, Kirsner, Levy, and Goldstein. In 1908, having some twenty-two members, the first synagogue rose at the corner of Locust and Eaton streets. Here the first bar mitzvah in the city took place for Alfred Goldstein in 1914. It was

Liberty Baptist Church on Todds Lane was founded in 1900 and in 1985 was Hampton's largest church. Courtesy of Liberty Baptist Church

The Main Base Chapel, designated Chapel Number One at Langley Air Force Base, was photographed in 1985. Courtesy of U.S. Air Force, photo by Sergeant Ronald Golden

not until 1934 that a full-time rabbi, J. M. Freedman, was secured. It is noteworthy that a later rabbi, Allan Mirvis, served the synagogue for thirty-two years from 1942 until 1974. In 1957 the synagogue moved to its present Kecoughtan Road location serving some 90 families in the 1980s.

There are two military chapels in Hampton well worth a visit. One is at Fort Monroe and the other is at Langley Air Force Base. The Chapel of the Centurion at Fort Monroe (Episcopal/general Protestant), one of the most attractive examples of Victorian church architecture to be found anywhere, had an unusual beginning. On June 22, 1855, an explosion in the mixing room of the laboratory in the Fort Monroe arsenal killed two soldiers. Another, Lieutenant Julian McAllister, escaped. He was so moved by his miraculous escape that he headed an effort to raise funds for the building of a chapel. He was assisted by his commander, Capt. Alexander Dyer. Together they raised six thousand dollars, and the chapel was consecrated on May 3, 1858. It is named for Cornelius the Centurion, whose conversion is described by St. Paul in Ephesians 6. Organizations and individuals contributed battle flags which were hung along both walls near the beautiful stained-glass windows, products of such renowned studios as Tiffany, Lamb, Geissler, and Redding Baird. Religious services had been held at the fort since 1825, but the chapel offered an attractive place for worship. The Main Base Chapel

at Langley Air Force Base is located on Dodd Boulevard. It is a handsome, inviting Gothic brick structure, seating over four hundred people. It was built in 1935 to fit with the Tudor revival architecture of surrounding buildings. The pipe organ in the chapel was declared a historic property by the Air Force.

The only mosque at present in the state with authentic Islamic architecture was built in Hampton on Tide Mill Lane. The first services were held April 21, 1984. Serving some eight hundred members of the Tidewater Moslem community, the mosque and Islamic Center cost about $170,000. Both public officials and local Protestant and Catholic clergymen participated in the dedication of the center. A local Methodist minister remarked that "Moslems, Christians, and Jews are all working in the same direction for the glorification of God." Dr. Fahd Al-Nassar, director of the United Nations Office of the World Moslem League, speaking at the dedication, said that the center should be used as "a source of all good things, such as life, wisdom, love, brotherhood, unity and peace." Dr. Ahmed Noor, president of the Hampton Roads chapter of the Moslem Community Association, added that he hoped the center would be a "common ground for Christians, Jews, and Moslems to meet together and hold ecumenical discussions."

Hampton's churches have been an integral part of a growing city where diversity has proved both a blessing and a great resource. Through the years

Hampton's citizens have enjoyed a spirit of cooperation, and this spirit of community has also prevailed in matters of religion. In this respect as in many others, it is impossible to isolate Hampton from its Hampton Roads neighbors, especially those that share common borders. Many people who live in one city attend church in another. However, the nature of this history limits its consideration to churches geographically located in Hampton.

As neighboring citizens and communities have cooperated, so also have the downtown churches. Working together, the churches have begun such ministries as bringing Big Brothers to the Peninsula, and founding and partially funding a day-care center. A number of Hampton churches also joined in an effort to serve those who need shelter, food and clothing through an organization known as Hampton Ecumenical Lodgings and Provisions (H.E.L.P.). Each Easter and Thanksgiving many congregations hold joint services in various parts of the city. Throughout its first 375 years, religious life in Hampton prospered and contributed to the well-being of the community. Each of the congregations hope and pray to continue their service for many years into the future.

Churches in Hampton

The following list of churches reflects the names of those that have been organized, or have owned property at one time or another in Hampton. Where known, the date of organization is included. The list was drawn from the records of the Hampton city assessor.

Name of Church	Organized
A	
Abundant Life Tabernacle	1976
Aldersgate United Methodist	1937
Allegheny Wesleyan	
Antioch Baptist	1895
Apostolic Church of Christ	
B	
Beacon Baptist	1956
Berachak Baptist	
Bethany United Methodist	1853
Bethel A.M.E.	1864
Bethel Temple Assemblies of God	1955
Bethel Baptist	1968
Bethlehem Missionary Baptist	1979
Big Bethel Baptist	1942
(formerly Wythe Parkway Baptist)	
B'Nai Israel Synagogue	1904
Buckroe Baptist	1936
Buckroe Beach United Methodist	1951
Buckroe Church of God	
C	
Calvary Assembly of God	1939
Calvary Community Church	
Calvary Reformed Presbyterian	1955
Central Baptist	1950
Central United Methodist	1894
Chapel of the Centurian	1858
Church of Christ Holiness	

Church of God	
Church of God High Power	
Church of God in Christ Trust	
Church of God Redeemed	
Church of Jesus	
Church of Jesus Christ of Latter-Day Saints	1937
Church of the Lord Jesus Christ	
Church of True Apostolic Faith	
Clearview Baptist	
Coliseum Baptist Ministry	
Colonial Place Church of Christ	
Community Presbyterian	1958
E	
East Hampton Baptist	1956
East Hampton United Methodist	1902
Eastern Virginia Conference of Pentecostal Holiness	
Ebenezer Baptist	
Emmanuel Chapel Church of Christ	
Emmanuel Episcopal	1878
Emmanuel Evangelical Lutheran	1944
F	
Faith Church of God	
Faith Temple Church of God in Christ	
First Assembly of God	
First Baptist	1863
First Baptist of Lincoln	
First Christian of Newport News	1888
First Friends Church	1906

First Baptist Church, Lincoln Park on West Queen Street

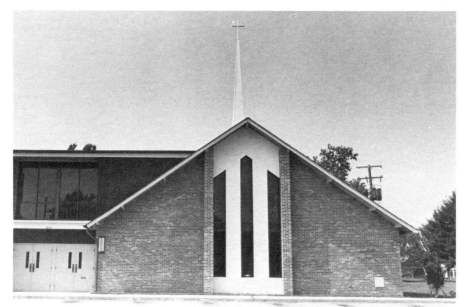

Sixth Mount Zion Baptist Temple on Kecoughtan Road

Phoebus Baptist Church on Fox Hill Road

Family Life Center of Liberty Baptist Church

Greenwood Pentecostal Holiness Church

Hampton Roads Seventh-Day Adventist Church on Kecoughtan Road

Central United Methodist Church of Fox Hill

All photos courtesy of C. Brown

Name of Church	Organized	Name of Church	Organized
First Hampton A.M.E. Zion		**M**	
First United Methodist of Fox Hill	1844	Memorial Baptist	1903
First Presbyterian	1878	Morning Start Baptist	c. 1865
First Riverview Baptist		Mosque	1976
First United Church of Christ	1900	Mount Olive Baptist	
First United Methodist	1789		
Fordham Baptist		**N**	
Fountain Baptist		New Covenant Church	1962
Fox Hill Central United Methodist	1899	Newmarket Baptist	1959
Fox Hill Road Baptist	1964	Newtown Improvement Club Church	
		Northampton Church of Christ	1962
G		Northampton Presbyterian	1961
Gloria Dei Lutheran	1965		
Good Samaritan		**O**	
Gospel Spreading		Old Fashioned Gospel Tabernacle	
Grace Baptist	1953		
Grace Fellowship	1974	**P**	
Gray's Mission and Baptist	1899	Park Place Baptist	
Greater Emmanuel Church of God in Christ		Parkview Church of God	1942
Greenwood Pentecostal Holiness	1931	Peninsula Missionary Baptist	
		Peninsula Rock	
H		Pentecostal Holiness	
Hampton Baptist Church	1791	Phoebus Baptist	1894
Hampton Church of Christ	1945	Phoebus Methodist Episcopal	1870
Hampton Christian	1883	Pine Chapel Baptist	1942
Hampton Evangelistic Center	1972	Progressive of Jesus	
Hampton Presbyterian		Providence Free Will Baptist	1983
Hampton Church of the Nazarene	1958		
Hampton Roads Baptist	1943	**Q**	
Holy Church of Deliverance		Queen Street Baptist	1865
Hope Lutheran	1966		
		R	
I		Redeemed Church of God	
Immaculate Conception Catholic	1971	Reformed Baptist	
Ivy Memorial Baptist	1913	Revival Temple	
		Revival Temple of Gospel Fellowship	
K		Riverdale Baptist	1967
Kingdom Hall of the Jehovah's Witnesses		Riverview Baptist	1902
		Rodef Sholom Temple	1957
L			
LaCrosse Memorial Presbyterian	1895	**S**	
Langley Air Force Base Chapel	1935	Saint Cyprian's Episcopal	1905
Langley Baptist	1949	Saint James United Methodist	1906
Langley Christian	1980	Saint John's Episcopal	1610
Liberty Baptist	1900	Saint Joseph's Catholic	1968
Lincoln Park Baptist	1912	Saint Mark's United Methodist	1960
Little Zion Baptist		Saint Mark's Protestant Episcopal	1963
Living Word Tabernacle	1978	Saint Mary Star of the Sea Catholic	1860

Name of Church	Organized
Saint Paul's A.M.E.	
Saint Paul's Evangelical Lutheran	1953
Saint Rose of Lima Catholic	1948
Salvation Army	
Seventh-Day Adventist	1899
Sixth Mount Zion Baptist	1900
Shell Road Church of God	

T

Third Baptist	
Trinity Baptist	1975
Trinity Tabernacle	1976
True Gospel Chapel	
True Mount Zion Holiness	
Tyler Memorial United Methodist	1943

U

Union Baptist	
Union Pentecostal Baptist of Hampton	
United Church of Christ	
United House of Prayer	
United Righteous of God	

V

Victory Baptist	
Victory Life World Outreach Center	1982

W

Wallace Memorial Methodist	1895
Way of the Cross Church of Christ	1970
Wesley United Methodist	1962
West End Baptist	
West Hampton Baptist	1943
Willow Oaks Church of God	
Wythe Presbyterian	1940

Z

Zion Baptist	1863

Acknowledgments

I wish to express my gratitude to the many people who have assisted me on this project. A special word of appreciation is due the following: the staff and congregation of the Hampton Baptist Church for allowing me the time to work on this history, for encouraging me in it, and for providing me the services of a secretary; Mrs. Barbara Ellington for her fine typing, editing and collecting information; Mrs. Carolyn Hawkins for her gracious advice and her assistance in gathering information, especially in the selection of appropriate pictures; the staff of Hampton University Library, especially in the archives; Dr. Finis E. Schneider, professor of mass media arts, Hampton University, for developing and printing some of the pictures used in this chapter; and the many people, often secretaries, sometimes pastors, of the various churches who graciously and willingly provided information.

*Whittier School, around the year
1895, was situated near what was to
become the famous Emancipation*
*Oak under which Lincoln's Emanci-
pation Proclamation was read. Courtesy of Hampton University Archives*

Chapter

Education: Important From the Onset

by Carolyn Haldeman Hawkins and Louise Watson Todd

Education in Kecoughtan began long before the British colonists arrived in 1607. Among the Indians, men of the tribe educated the boys in survival skills in nature's classroom, while the women taught the girls the arts of homemaking. Indian boys learned to hunt, fish, and fight. They learned how to make stone tools and weapons, and how to carve a log canoe. Among the fishing skills they learned were the making of weirs or fish traps, spear fishing, night fishing and the harvesting of shell fish. Indian girls learned to grind corn, nuts, and other foods in a mortar using a pestle. They also did much of the farming and gathering of walnuts, hickory nuts, and other natural foods. They learned pottery and basketmaking, produced clothing from deer hides and silkgrass, and practiced household tasks and cooking. Doubtless, the Indian natives shared their practical education with the newly arrived English settlers.

Early Education

It is noteworthy that within twenty-seven years of the landing of the colonists, a charity school was provided, indicating the settlers' early concern about having schools for their children. In 1634 Benjamin Syms, who was born in 1590 and lived in Isle of Wight County, willed two hundred acres of land, cows, a weeding hoe, and "other accommodations" with which to start a school near the Back River in Elizabeth City County. This was the first free school in America. Syms's will, dated February 10, 1634, was signed with an *X*, suggesting that he himself had received little formal education. The will makes the following statement:

Whereas there is due to me two hundred acres of Land Lying in the old Poquoson River and Eight Milch Cows...I bequeath it as followth Viz. The use of the said Land with the Milk and Increase Male of said Cattle to be for the Mantayance of an honest Learned Man to keep upon the said Ground a free school to Educate & teach the Children of the adjoining Parrishes of Elizb. City & Poquoson River. My Will and desire is that the Worshipful the Commander and the Rest of the Commissioners of this Liberty with the ministers and Church Wardens of the said Parrish where the said school is founded to see it from time to time justly and truly performed.

My Will and Desire is that when it please God there is sufficient Increase of the said Cattle that some part of them be sould for the Erecting of a very sufficient school house and the Rest of the Increase that are left to be disposed of before nominated and in Repairing the said School. My Will and Desire is that the Increase of the said Cattle after the said School Master is sufficiently stocked for his maintayance shall be spent according to the directions of the said Commander & Commitions with the rest of them to manteyne poor Children, or decayed or maimed persons of the said Parish.

Records show that Syms's bequest was accepted and sanctioned by the Virginia Assembly some ten years later. Although the exact date of its opening is unknown, it is certain that Syms School and others were operating by 1647. A document of that year entitled *A Perfect Description of Virginia* stated that the Syms Free School had "two hundred acres of Land, a fine House upon it, forty milch kine and other accommodations to it; the Benefactor deserves Perpetuall memory...." The same document pointed out that, "other petty (or minor) schools we have," indicating that Syms had provided a worthy example.

Twenty-five years after the gift from Benjamin Syms, Elizabeth City County received an additional bequest of five hundred acres. In 1659, Thomas Eaton, a physician who lived in Hampton, left a will which made the following statement:

—I have for the maintenance of an able school master (to) educate and teach the children borne within said County of Elizabeth City—

Given, granted, assigned, set over and confirmed and doo by these presents give, grant, assign, set over and confirm after the time of my decease for the use aforesaid, Five hundred acres of land whereon the (sd) Free school shall bee kept being a part of a dividend of six hundred and (f—) acres graunted unto me by pattent bearing the date the fifth day of June Anno 1638, Begining from the beaver damm...westerly towards the head of the Back River & Southerly...Woods, with all houses, edifices orchards and Rights to...belonging to it. Two negroes called by the names of...Twelve cows and two bulls, Twenty hogs, young and old, one bedstead, a table, a cheese press, twelve milch trays, an Iron kettle contayning about twelve gallons, pot rack and pot hooks, Milk Pailes, water tubs and powdering tubbs, to have and to hould the said land with all other the premises before mentioned for the use afores'd, with all ye male increase thereof, for ye

maintainance of the said schoolmaster...such a one as by the Commissioners, Mynister & Church Warden whom I doo nominate and appoint as trustees in trust for the ordering and settling thereof from time to time shall be thought fit, and I, the said Thomas Eaton do further order & appoint that no free education bee allowed but to such children as shal be borne within the said county.

There is little additional information available about Dr. Thomas Eaton. He may have been the brother of Nathaniel Eaton, the first head of Harvard, who later returned to England.

Syms Free School and Eaton Charity School operated in separate buildings, each on its own land, educating children in the "three Rs" until after the Revolutionary War. The two schools probably stood on adjoining sites, occupying land where Langley Field was later located. Eleven trustees administered both schools. The wills stipulated the surplus from property could be used to educate the poor only after provisions had been made for the schoolmaster and the upkeep of the buildings. Eaton's gift specified that only children born in Elizabeth City County should receive free education. Interpretations created problems because some children whose parents could afford to pay were attending school free. The officials were kept busy attempting to adjust the difficulties and keep the two schools in order.

During the Colonial period, parents who could afford it often hired tutors for their children, while some children were sent to England for their education. Because Hampton was an important seaport which would require a literate population to conduct business, it is most likely that a good number of the inhabitants could read and write and had an interest in assuring adequate education. Colonial Virginia laws required that orphans be educated. Consequently, the court and vestry of the church saw to it that all indigent children were bound in indenture to useful trades, because employers were required to teach their indentured to read and write. In his report to the Bishop of London in 1724, the Rev. James Falconer, rector of Elizabeth City Parish, wrote that there were two public schools in the parish and a good private school in which reading, arithmetic, Greek and Latin were taught. However, it appears that most of the early schools were strictly concerned with teaching the basics.

Among the most famous educators from the area was George Wythe, born in Elizabeth City County in 1726. Wythe later practiced law in the county and became the first professor of law in America's first law school at the College of William and Mary. Wythe was also a signer of the Declaration of Independence.

The Revolutionary War had a negative effect on education as with other aspects of Hampton's society. After the war, formal education reached a low ebb, despite the fact that ministers were teaching school during the week.

In 1803, local citizens sent a petition to the Virginia Assembly asking that Syms Free School and Eaton Charity School be consolidated and moved into the town of Hampton. On January 12, 1805, the consolidation was completed. The new school, built on Cary Street, was called Hampton Academy. The names of Syms and Eaton were dropped, but they would reappear a century later on a new school building on that very site.

From the beginning of the Syms and Eaton Schools the town residents complained about their locations. Because the schools were situated on their original property, they were not easily accessible to the poor children living in the town. After consolidation in 1805, the country folk began complaining about the inconvenience of the new school's location. A feud broke out between the town and country residents, causing tempers to run high. In the 1830s, during the period of great emotional stress over the problem of school location, Christopher Pryor, schoolmaster at Hampton Academy, horsewhipped a county school supporter. Mr. Pryor was dismissed and replaced by a Major Cooper, an elderly man who was considered to be just as competent as Pryor, though less severe. At the culmination of the feud, Major Cooper shot and killed a Pryor supporter, Thomas Allen, on July 4, 1837. The tragedy occurred on Queen Street where the First United Methodist Church was later built. Cooper was never prosecuted. He took a ship bound for New Orleans, and later his family joined him, after a large crowd of well-wishers saw them off. Evidently cooler heads prevailed because Pryor replaced Cooper at Hampton Academy that fall and received the usual three-year contract given at that time.

George Wythe in his later years, first professor of law at the College of William and Mary. Courtesy of Charles H. Taylor Memorial Library

In 1837, Hampton Academy was the public school in Elizabeth City County. The citizens of Elizabeth City County had for some time been arguing over locations and funds available for new schools. Fox Hill residents sent a petition to the General Assembly of Virginia requesting that a school be built in the Fox Hill-Harris Creek area. When the citizens' request was denied they founded the Fox Hill Academy, a private school.

An act of the assembly founded a public school system in Virginia in 1845. Elizabeth City County was among the first to adopt the new plan and appoint a board of commissioners to lay out the county in school districts. When the school districts were first established, land was taxed at approximately a half cent an acre, and the school tax amounted to four dollars. A petition of protest against the school tax made by local citizens prompted Col. John B. Cary, who had been master of Hampton Academy for several years, to rent the building and conduct a private school, using the name Hampton Academy.

The June 3, 1852, act of the assembly called for the transfer of the the Syms and Eaton school funds into the public school treasury. In September of that year the superintendent of the local school commissioners called on the treasurer of the academy board of trustees to deliver all money and property. When the transfer was made, the fund amounted to $10,706.55. This action marked the beginning of the public school system in Elizabeth City County and Hampton.

In 1854, a free school for all children was opened on Queen Street, conducted by William Robinson and his sister, Ellen. The following year, when Colonel Cary vacated the academy building, the school commissioners reclaimed it. They kept the name Hampton Academy and made the school the "District School" for the town of Hampton. That school building was supposedly wooden and described as having two sections end to end, one for boys and one for girls. Each room was forty feet by thirty-two feet wide. The boys and girls had separate entrances, and the boys played in the front yard while the girls played in the back. The school was surrounded by a fence enclosing a yard with three large shade trees on one side of the building.

In his memoirs, *When the Yankees Came*, edited by Parke Rouse, Jr., Benjamin West recalls:

In January 1845 I was sent to school to Colonel John B. Cary, who then taught in the old Court house....There were two rooms. The largest boys—young men really—were put in the smaller room and the little boys were also in this room, to be looked after by the older ones.

The next session Colonel Cary taught in the old academy on Pee Dee, where is now (1899) Hampton Academy....Father refused to send us to Cary because he thought the school should be kept as a free school only and no paid scholars should attend. He therefore sent me to Mr. William Hawkins, a Baptist preacher. I think he taught only one session, and then I went to another preacher, a northern man named Wheeler who at first taught in the basement of the Baptist church....For reasons I do not know, he moved his school to Old Point and taught in one of the casements of the fort (Monroe)....

From 1850 to 1855 I was sent to the free schools, and as the teachers were changed nearly every year and most of them were very poor teachers, my time was almost entirely thrown away.

Colonel Cary had built a private academy (on Pee Dee Point, facing Hampton Creek)...so father again sent me to him that fall of '55 and I remained with him till the fall of '59 when I entered the University of Virginia.

Cary made his a military school when he moved into his new academy; he had also a female department attached and employed a female teacher....Cary also built quite a large dwelling and kept boarders; the boys slept in the third story of the academy, the girls in his house, and all ate in his dwelling.

Col. John B. Cary had been principal of the private Hampton Academy for six years when he bought land adjacent to the older school to build Hampton Military Academy and his school for girls. In 1855, the two schools under his management stood next door to the Hampton Academy, which by then was administered by the public school system. The faculty of Hampton Military Academy held degrees from Princeton, Virginia Military Institute, the University of Virginia, and the Universities of Heidelburg and Leipzig. The cur-

This is an artist's conception of the successor to the Syms and Eaton schools, the Hampton Academy, as it is thought to have appeared from 1842 to 1861. Courtesy of the Syms-Eaton Museum

Hampton Military Academy was erected by Col. John B. Cary in 1855. Courtesy of Syms-Eaton Museum

Lith by G Hunckel & Son Bremen & Baltimore

HAMPTON ACADEMY

John B. Cary, Principal

Hampton Va.

95

riculum included Greek, Latin, mathematics and music. According to Lyon G. Tyler in his *History of Hampton and Elizabeth City County*, Colonel Cary was an enthusiastic teacher and a strong disciplinarian; in fact, the motto of his school was: "Order is Heaven's first law." The young men had a literary society called "The Old Boys" which would from time to time have outstanding speakers. Among them was former president John Tyler, who owned a summer home called Villa Margaret on a point of land on the east side of the Hampton River. After duty in the Confederate army, Cary became superintendent of Richmond schools and later served with the State Department of Education. He died in Richmond in 1898.

Another private school which functioned in Hampton was the Chesapeake Female College. As early as 1850, Hampton Baptists advocated the location of a Baptist school for females "in or near the town of Hampton." After no action was taken by the Baptist denomination, fifteen men organized a board and incorporated The Chesapeake Female College in 1854. A campus of forty acres overlooking the Hampton Roads was acquired and construction on an ornate five-story main building, designed to accommodate four hundred, was begun. Young ladies began attending the school in 1857, while construction continued. Norfolk and Portsmouth Baptists rescued the school from financial difficulties when they bought the school and property in 1859. The Chesapeake Female College was one of the principal seminaries for young women in Virginia before the Civil War. During the war, the federal government took possession of the school and converted it to the Chesapeake Military Hospital for officers of the Union army. In 1864, Gen. Benjamin Butler bought the building and property and then sold it to the federal government, which used it as a home for disabled veterans.

Although it had known its share of opposition, the school system in Elizabeth City was well established by the outbreak of the Civil War. Hampton Academy, as well as the Courthouse, Back River, Fox Hill, Hickman's Place, Sawyer's Swamp, Salters Creek and Little Bethel were all functioning as free schools when the war began.

During the turbulent days near the beginning of the War Between the States, the Hampton Academy and Cary's Academy were destroyed when Gen. John Bankhead Magruder, CSA, gave orders for his troops to burn Hampton rather than let it be of assistance to the Federal troops holding Fort Monroe. Capt. Jefferson Curle Phillips had the task of carrying out those orders. He had previously acted as treasurer of the school commissioners of Elizabeth City County, and through his efforts the mortgage bonds, representing the funds the Hampton Academy had inherited from the Syms and Eaton bequests, were taken to Richmond where they were kept safe until after the war. One legend explains that the bonds were taken to Richmond by Mrs. Phillips, who fastened them to the wire of her dress hoops. Another version states that Mrs. Phillips hid the bonds in the band of her apron. In any event, the bonds remained safe during the conflict and afterwards were returned and reinvested. Three and a half centuries after the original bequest, the money still paid interest which applied to the costs of educating the youth of Hampton.

Black Hamptonians were excluded from the school system prior to the Civil War. However, some blacks did receive informal instruction in reading and writing. One such individual was Cesar (Casar) Tarrant, a slave at the outbreak of the Revolutionary War. Owned by Hampton's Carter Tarrant, Cesar was a boat pilot so admired for his navigational skill and knowledge of local waterways that early in the war he was one of the seven pilots appointed by the Virginia Navy board to serve in the state's navy. For his "meritorious service" during the Revolutionary War, the Virginia Assembly passed an act on November 14, 1789, to purchase the freedom of Cesar from Carter Tarrant's widow, Mary. Cesar died in February, 1797, leaving a will, which from all indications, he had written and signed himself.

Unlike many localities in the South, Hampton had, for the most part, ignored laws prohibiting the teaching of reading and writing to slaves. Prior to the Civil War, a considerable number of local blacks, both slave and free, had taught each other to read. Among the most prominent teachers was Mrs. Mary Peake, a free-born black woman, who taught slaves in her home near Hampton Academy. Born in Norfolk in 1823, Mrs. Peake's maiden name was Mary Smith Kelsey. Her mother was a free mulatto and her father was an Englishman. As a child, she was described as being lovely in person and manners and "as she grew

The former Chesapeake Female College in the hands of the Union Army. Courtesy of Charles H. Taylor Library

This is an artist's view of the burning of Hampton in 1861. Courtesy of Charles H. Taylor Memorial Library

up, developed traits of character which made her a universal favorite." She became a gifted teacher in the 1850s and continued teaching through the early days of the war. Even after her home in Hampton burned, she moved to a cottage next to the then-deserted Chesapeake Female Academy and began teaching again. She was a tireless and dedicated worker until her untimely death from consumption in 1862 at the age of thirty-nine. A Hampton elementary school was named in her honor on the one hundredth anniversary of her death.

Another black, Peter Herbert, who had remained behind to care for John Tyler's Villa Margaret, opened a primary school in the cellar. Both the Brown and Herbert schools were functioning when the Rev. Lewis C. Lockwood, representing the American Missionary Association, arrived at Fort Monroe on September 3, 1861. Ever since May of that year blacks had been gathering in the area of Hampton and Fort Monroe in response to Gen. Benjamin Butler's declaration that runaway slaves were to be considered as contraband of war, and therefore would not be returned to their owners. The American Missionary Association, a New York-based philanthropic society, chose Hampton to be the site of its first missionary endeavors during the Civil War because of the large number of refugees in the area. One of Reverend

Lockwood's first actions was to intercede successfully with the military authorities on behalf of the two schools in order that they might operate openly and expand. This done, the missionary launched a public appeal in the North to furnish primers, additional missionary-teachers, and clothing.

The American Missionary Association incorporated the two schools it found here into its general program of establishing Sabbath and week-day schools, offering church services on Sundays, week-day classes for children, and evening classes for adults. Two additional schools opened by Christmas. A Mrs. Bishop, a free black woman, and two assistants taught at Fort Monroe, and a black man, Wilson Wallace, taught at a school near Mill Creek Bridge in Camp Hamilton (Phoebus). All of these schools had a similar structure in that one teacher taught all subjects, and the instruction was by rote, with class size ranging from sixty to one hundred in a single room.

After President Lincoln issued his preliminary Emancipation Proclamation on September 22, 1862, the number of fugitives arriving in the Hampton area grew considerably and more schools were necessary. Robert Engs, in *The Development of Black Culture and Community*, tells how missionaries and blacks created one of the largest local Sabbath and week-day schools by renovating the burned-out Courthouse in Hampton during 1862. C. P. Day took charge of its five hundred pupils, some of whom progressed so rapidly that he found it necessary to divide them into a "primary" department and a "higher" department, thus making it the first graded school for freedmen in the area. When General Butler arranged for government funds to be used to build another large school for black children in 1863, it temporarily relieved the pressure on the missionary schools. The school, known as the Butler School, was a large frame building in the shape of a Greek cross, which stood near the Emancipation Oak. At first six hundred students attended Butler, but another missionary school was established at Slabtown, a shanty community of freedmen on the road to Buckroe, and that helped relieve some of the overcrowding at Butler and at the other schools.

The government turned over the Butler School to the American Missionary Association in 1865, which supplied it with teachers until 1868. The approximately fifty to sixty missionary teachers who served

Butler School, built by the United States government for newly-freed slaves, was located near the Butler Oak, later named Emancipation Oak. Courtesy of Hampton University Archives

This is an artist's view of the Butler schoolhouse, founded in 1863 for freedmen. Courtesy of Syms-Eaton Museum

THE BUTLER SCHOOL-HOUSE.

This schoolhouse was located at Slabtown near Old Buckroe Road during the Civil War. The building was later used as a Sunday school taught by Hampton Institute students who are pictured here in 1892. Courtesy of Hampton University Archives

Lincoln School was located in downtown Hampton in 1900. Courtesy of Hampton University Archives

Samuel Chapman Armstrong was the founder of what is now Hampton University. Courtesy of Syms-Eaton Museum

in the Hampton area during the Civil War all contended with the problems of overcrowding, staff, and supplies. However, their students' enthusiasm for learning, as well as willingness to help construct or repair their own school buildings, overrode those problems and kept the morale of the teachers high. By war's end, six mission schools had been established in and around Hampton.

After the Civil War

When the Courthouse reverted to the Elizabeth City County authorities in 1866, the graded school for blacks which had been housed there was relocated nearby on Lincoln Street due to the efforts of Gen. Samuel Armstrong. As director of the Freedmen's Bureau, Armstrong had procured funds for the building of a new school using old hospital wards from Fort Hamilton. This school, called the Lincoln School, became part of the public school system in 1870 and served the black community until the turn of the century when it was replaced by Union Street School.

After the Civil War ended, the American Missionary Association felt that it could best continue its help to the freedmen by establishing a number of Normal Schools throughout the South to prepare blacks to teach. It was only natural that Hampton, as a major black population center, would be proposed as a site for one of these schools. The catalyst for this idea turned out to be the superintendent of the Freedmen's Bureau for the Hampton area, Gen. Samuel Chapman Armstrong. General Armstrong had always felt that the Freedmen's Bureau would only be able to provide temporary solutions for the thousands of former slaves who had gathered behind the Union lines on the Peninsula. As the son of missionaries who represented the American Missionary Association in Hawaii, a teacher in his father's manual training school, and the superintendent of black affairs at Fort Monroe during the Civil War, Armstrong became convinced that education was the best vehicle for black advancement. In July of 1867, he made formal petition to the American Missionary Society (formerly Association) to establish a school on the Wood farm, land along the Hampton Creek known as Little Scotland, anticipating that the Freedmen's Bureau might erect its buildings. The proposal became a reality when the American Missionary Society, along with the Freedmen's Bureau and several private donors, provided the nineteen thousand dollars necessary to purchase the farm and its buildings. Armstrong was asked to be principal.

General Armstrong's own purpose for the school differed from that of the American Missionary Society. He wanted to create not only a Normal School to train teachers, but also a school which taught agricultural and mechanical skills. In addition, he expected graduates to teach, not just in their own locality, but throughout the South. By the time the doors of the Hampton Normal and Agricultural Institute opened in April of 1868, three missionary teachers had already resigned in protest of Armstrong's "radical" plan. Two teachers and fifteen students, mostly from black families in the village of Hampton, attended the first session. To be admitted, one had to be of "good character," able to read and write at the fifth grade level, and be between the ages of fifteen and twenty-five. Students usually appeared at the school, were briefly interviewed by a teacher, and accepted on trial. A famous graduate of the school, Booker T. Washington, recalled in later years how he was asked to prove his worthiness for admission by sweeping a room.

For the first four years of the school's operation, Armstrong directed most of his efforts to giving it an independent base. The school's charter, granted by the Virginia legislature in 1870, provided for a nonsectarian board of trustees of seventeen members, not dependent on any association or government. Re-

ceiving one-third of Virginia's Morrill Act Land Grant in 1872 made the school virtually free of any connection with the American Missionary Society. The work of the Hampton school was brought to the attention of men and women of wealth in the North through newspapers, lectures, and word of mouth. Gifts to the school came year after year, enabling substantial progress in developing its physical plant.

In what turned out to be one of Armstrong's most successful ideas for raising money, he organized the Hampton Singers, who through concerts in northern cities raised subscriptions for the school. These student singers took their school books with them on their trips, studying and reciting as they traveled, and on their return, finished their school courses with credit. The group gave over five hundred concerts within a two and one-half year period. It is said that the Virginia Hall for girls, designed by the noted architect Richard Hunt of Biltmore fame, was "sung up" by the student singers.

The same philosophy of educating and giving practical training in the different trades to blacks was extended to Indians in 1878, when seventeen former captives of the 1873 Indian Wars arrived by steamer at the school wharf from Fort Marion at Saint Augustine, Florida. These Indians had been given the choice of being set free to return to their tribes in West or coming to Hampton for experimental training in the white man's ways. They had chosen the latter. It was soon apparent that the Indians were entirely unprepared for the standard Normal School program, and so could not receive the same education as the blacks at the school. Dietary differences between the two dictated separate dining facilities and dormitories. The school was able to make those accommodations. By the end of the first year it was evident that the

Indian program at Hampton Normal and Agricultural Institute had promise. This experiment at Hampton led to the policy of offering training and education to Indians on and off reservation schools in the country. An arrangement was made whereby the government would pay $167 yearly for each Indian enrolled. The Wigwam for boys and Winona Hall for girls were dormitories constructed and completed by 1882. A separate Indian School was established to teach the basic language skills. The program ran five years, at the end of which an Indian student would be ready to enter the Normal program. By 1900, over one hundred Indians had graduated from the Indian School. When the government withdrew its financial support in 1912, a number of Indians chose to work their way through. Forty-six were still enrolled as late as 1916, and Indians continued to attend Hampton until 1923.

Academic standards rose as Hampton Normal and Agricultural Institute students progressed. When Hollis Burke Frissell succeeded General Armstrong as principal in 1893, fifty buildings were serving 636 students, 188 Indians and 300 primary students. The 797 graduates sent out from 1870 to 1893 had taught 129,475 children in public schools throughout the South. The old Butler School, which had served as a practice school for student teachers since 1868, and which had been made a free school for black children in 1871, was replaced in 1887 through the generosity of a Brooklyn couple, Mr. and Mrs. D. W. McWilliams. The new school remained on the same site, but was renamed the Whittier Training School, in honor of John Greenleaf Whittier, who was a friend of Armstrong. The new school remained the property of the Normal School, serving for observation for student teachers, and Elizabeth City County continued to finance it as a public school for blacks in the neighbor-

This is the view looking toward the Hampton River from Hampton Normal and Agricultural Institute around the year 1876. On the left is Villa Margaret. Hampton Academy is across the river. To the right of it is Colonel Mallory's home, and the home of Thomas Tabb is to the right of the center barn. Courtesy of Hampton University Archives

This photograph shows the early faculty at Hampton Normal and Agricultural Institute, now Hampton University. At the top, far left, is Alice Mabel Bacon, founder of what is now Hampton General Hospital. Beside her is General Marshall. General Armstrong is sitting on the steps with his hands crossed, and Mr. Tolman is sitting directly behind him. Courtesy of Hampton University Archives

These black and Indian students were enrolled at Hampton Institute around the year 1880. Courtesy of the Casemate Museum

hood as had been done with Butler. Teacher training continued to be emphasized during the 1900s, and all seniors were required to practice teach at either Whittier or Lincoln School in town.

At the same time, an emphasis was placed on manual trades and agricultural knowledge. Shellbank Farm, consisting of six hundred acres located on what became Langley Air Force Base, had been purchased in 1879, and provided training for students in agricultural skills as well as supplying some food for the campus. Soon after the school was put on the list of accredited four year secondary schools for the state of Virginia, Hampton Normal and Agricultural Institute was called upon to train hundreds of soldiers in trades useful for World War I. The Hampton school supported a Student Army Training Corps during the war and also helped retrain disabled veterans. After the war,

Hampton Institute offered college courses, and on September 1, 1923, the school granted the bachelor of science degree in agricultural education for the first time. Formal accreditation as a standard technical and professional college followed in 1927. At the request of its trustees, the Hampton Normal and Agricultural Institute formally changed its name to Hampton Institute in 1930. During World War II Hampton Institute again established military training units. Following the war, Alonzo G. Moron, the first black president of Hampton Institute, arranged for year-round graduate study. Under Dr. William R. Harvey's leadership, Hampton Institute again changed its name on August 1, 1984 to become Hampton University, thereby reflecting high academic standards and the comprehensive activities of the school.

In 1890, what is now Hampton University sponsored an educational innovation which was to have far-reaching benefits for Hampton citizens. For several years previously Alice Mabel Bacon, a teacher at Hampton Normal and Agricultural Institute, had become increasingly concerned about the health of the ex-slaves she had been visiting in the neighborhoods around the school. At that time there was no formal training for black practical nurses in the South. As a solution, Miss Bacon formally proposed that a training school for black nurses be established in the Hampton area. The school would have its own hospital to provide experience for the nurses. Gen. Samuel Armstrong lent the support of Hampton Institute, and by February of 1891, the amount of $1,163 had been collected for the project. The Institute donated one of the buildings on its grounds, near the Emancipation Oak and Whittier School, and students converted it into a ten-bed, two-ward hospital. Miss Bacon christened the hospital "Dixie" after the horse she had ridden to visit the sick.

The school for nurses opened with one resident doctor and a superintendent of nurses. The first patient was admitted in May of 1891. Those who followed were both blacks and whites from the immediate neighborhood. On March 4, 1892, the Virginia General Assembly granted the nurses' school the formal title of Hampton Training School for Nurses and passed the following act of incorporation:

...to establish, maintain and conduct in the County of Elizabeth City, a training school for nurses (the object and purpose being to provide competent,

skilled and efficient nurses for the sick-room) and in connection therewith to establish, maintain, and conduct a hospital for the sick and afflicted.

This act established the Hampton Training School for Nurses as one of the earliest training schools for black nurses in this country.

During the summer of 1892, the new training school leased a nearby tract of land consisting of 3.4 acres from Hampton Normal and Agricultural Institute for two dollars a year. Hampton students picked up the hospital building and carried it across the fields to its new location near the Phoebus gate of the Soldiers Home where it was standing nearly a century later. After the building was enlarged, the training school and hospital operated on that site for twenty years. By 1897, there were thirty graduates of the nursing school, including one male who went into private-duty nursing. By July of 1906, patients were almost evenly divided between black and white; graduate nurses numbered seventy. The largest source of income for the hospital was donations. Nursing students who did private duty nursing returned their income to the school and hospital, providing the second largest source of income.

An exchange of land was arranged between the Hampton Training School for Nurses and the Hampton Normal and Agricultural Institute whereby the school of nurses received a deed of trust from the Institute for the former Villa Margaret property on East Queen Street. A new brick structure with sixty-five beds and nursing quarters located in a back wing opened in 1913 on that site.

This is a view of Hampton Normal and Agricultural Institute around the year 1898. The principal's home is at the left, Memorial Chapel is at the center, and Academic Hall is on the right. Courtesy of Syms-Eaton Museum

Memorial Chapel and Virginia Hall at Hampton Institute are shown as they appeared around the year 1895. Courtesy of the Casemate Museum

This international group of students posed at Hampton Institute around the year 1895. The seal of the emperor of Japan is on the sleeve of the young man on the far right. Courtesy of Syms-Eaton Museum

Over three hundred nurses had graduated from the training school when the trustees of the hospital changed the name of the Hampton Training School for Nurses to Dixie Hospital on July 31, 1933. Soon after that, the hospital needed the nurses' quarters for more patient beds, and Hampton Institute provided board, lodging and laundry for the nursing students until World War II, when the space was needed by the college. With federal aid, the hospital was able to build a brick nurses' home directly across the street.

The Hampton Training School for Nurses, as originally conceived, graduated its last class in 1956. By that time it had been in competition with Hampton Institute's own nursing program for twelve years. Dixie Hospital moved its location to Victoria Boulevard in 1959 and became known as Hampton General Hospital in 1973. However, the formal, corporate name of the hospital remained the "Hampton Training School for Nurses."

Another nursing school which had its beginnings in Elizabeth City County was the Elizabeth Buxton Training School. Soon after Dr. Joseph T. Buxton opened the Elizabeth Buxton Hospital on the Boulevard in 1906, he saw a need for nursing education. The

following year, he started the Elizabeth Buxton Training School at the hospital. Three years later, in 1910, four nurses received their diplomas at the first graduation exercises.

In the beginning, student nurses lived at the hospital, but a separate nurses' home was built in 1919 when the hospital needed more beds for patients. Although the average number of graduates was only two or three a year through 1926, the quality of education remained high throughout the existence of the nursing school. On January 1, 1927, the Elizabeth Buxton Hospital and its nurses' training program ceased to be a part of Elizabeth City County when the land on which they were located was annexed by the city of Newport News. Nevertheless, Hampton can rightfully claim to be the birthplace of two very fine institutions for educating nurses, The Hampton Training School for Nurses and the Elizabeth Buxton Training School.

The Virginia School for the Deaf and Blind had its genesis when William C. Ritter and his wife, Mary Alice, moved to Hampton in the 1890s after their graduation from the Virginia School for the Deaf and Blind in Staunton. Mr. Ritter, who was deaf, worked

Whittier School replaced Butler School in 1887. It was named after John Greenleaf Whittier, a friend of Gen. Samuel Chapman Armstrong. The school closed around the year 1930. Courtesy of Hampton University Archives

This advertisement for Hampton Training School for Nurses and Dixie Hospital appears in the 1896 Chataigne's Peninsula Directory. Courtesy of Charles H. Taylor Library

TWELFTH ANNUAL REPORT

OF THE

Hampton Training School

For Nurses

And Dixie Hospital

Hampton, Virginia

1902-1903

On March 4, 1892, Dixie Hospital was chartered as a non-profit corporation by the General Assembly of the Commonwealth of Virginia, becoming one of the few institutions left in the state with that distinction. This two-story building (which was still standing in 1985) was used as a hospital and training school for nurses for twenty years. Courtesy of the Hampton University Archives

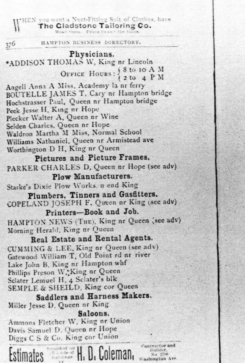

Buxton Hospital, pictured in 1915, was located in Elizabeth City County overlooking the Hampton Roads. Courtesy of Syms-Eaton Museum

107

THE BOARD OF VISITORS

as a printer for the *Hampton Monitor*. At that time, there was no school available in the state for blacks who were deaf or blind. Mr. Ritter became active in seeking to establish such a school.

When Harry R. Houston became proprietor of the *Hampton Monitor* in 1901, William Ritter continued to work there as foreman. By the time Houston was elected to the Virginia House of Delegates in 1905, he too, was convinced of the need for a school for deaf and blind blacks. He was successful in introducing a bill in the 1906 session whereby the General Assembly established the Virginia School for Colored Deaf and Blind Children. Mr. Ritter was appointed superintendent of the school, a post he held until 1937, and the Honorable Harry R. Houston served as the first president of the school's board of visitors. Mr. Houston is still remembered as the "patron saint" of the institution.

The Old Dominion Land Company sold the school

twenty-five acres fronting on Shell Road for a minimal amount and the school opened in the fall of 1909, with one building, twenty-four pupils, and three teachers. At first, only elementary education was offered the children, along with a few trades. Students assisted with new construction on the campus, as well as with growing of crops and dairying. By 1913, over a hundred students were attending the school. Blind boys were taught mattress making, chair caning, rattan work, and broom making, in addition to regular school work, while blind girls did needlework and cared for their rooms. Deaf boys attended classes in the morning and worked on the school farm in the afternoon. They also repaired shoes for the entire school population.

In 1980, the school was named the Virginia School for the Deaf and Blind at Hampton. The curriculum was gradually reoriented to follow closely that of regular public schools, with the addition of auditory training, speech, and speech reading for the deaf, and Braille and mobility training for the blind. The school also added a deaf-blind division, the only one of its kind in the state. Approximately two hundred students of both races attended the school in the mid-1980s.

When the Civil War ended, the Hampton families who had left began returning to rebuild their burned homes. When thought could again be given to educating the youth, a few schools were started in private homes to serve until the public school system could be reconstituted. During 1866 the public school commissioners of Elizabeth City County met and submitted their report for the year ending September 30, 1861. Dr. William F. Ruffner, state superintendent of education, received a county report in 1872. This indicates that education in Hampton had been resurrected by then.

The school mortgage bonds, in which the Syms-Eaton fund of ten thousand dollars had been invested, were returned to Hampton and recorded as "those bonds which are payable to the Trustees of Hampton Academy, and now, by operation of the Statutes, the property of the County School Board of Elizabeth City County." A new Hampton Academy, this time of brick, was built on the same site as the first wooden academy building. It served its neighborhood until it burned around 1900.

Charles F. Elliott in his book, *Fox Hill, Its People*

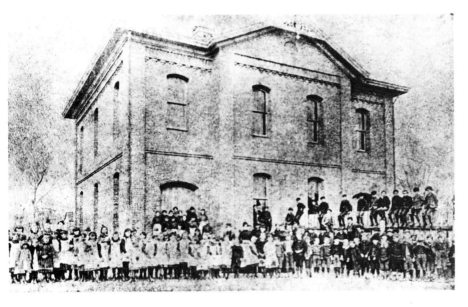

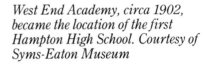

The brick-walled Hampton Academy was photographed around the year 1890. Courtesy of Charles H. Taylor Memorial Library

West End Academy, circa 1902, became the location of the first Hampton High School. Courtesy of Syms-Eaton Museum

and Places, describes a one-room school built in 1881 and located on the main road through Fox Hill:

> The late Harry Johnson of Fox Hill, who was 97 years old in 1972, said, that as a child, he went to this school. He said the desks were long wooden shelf-like affairs which were fastened to the walls of the room. The children stood to do their work but they had little stools to sit on while they listened to the teacher. The principal was Richard Watson of the community. It was said that Watson carried a shot gun to school each day because he loved to hunt and on his way to and from the school house he would bag a few rabbits and quail for the table.

By September 1888, education was being provided throughout Elizabeth City County and Hampton. A listing of public schools that fall included Hampton Academy, Lincoln, Fox Hill, New Market, Hickman (Harris Creek), Back River, Buckroe, Chesapeake (Phoebus), Bates, and Sawyer Swamp. By the turn of the century the following schools had been added to the system: West End, Riverview, Little Bethel, Big Bethel, Phillips, Bloxom, Davis, Semple Farm, and a second school on Back River.

Although high-school-level classes were introduced at Hampton Academy in 1887, not until 1899, when the West End Academy opened, did a real high school exist. Located where the Hampton Public Library would later stand on Victoria Boulevard, West End offered school work from the first grade through four years of high school. After Hampton Academy burned, students from both schools attended the new West End until 1902 when the downtown school reopened. The name Hampton Academy was dropped and the new school was called Syms-Eaton Academy in honor of the two benefactors of the public school system in Hampton. The opening of Syms-Eaton

109

proved to be quite a celebration which included a parade as well as a half-holiday by the local shop-keepers. Children attended Syms-Eaton through the seventh grade, with those promoted going on to high school at West End Academy.

The first high school class to graduate was that of 1904. A rear addition, built at the West End school in 1914, was specifically for use by the four high school grades. Gradually, this high school portion became known as Hampton High School. A successful bond issue enabled a building exclusively for high school students to open in 1922. When Hampton High School moved to its new building on the corner of Victoria Boulevard and Jackson Street, it signified the fulfillment of a long-held goal of a separate high school by many educators and parents in Hampton. The later building of Darling Memorial Stadium on adjacent land added a broad dimension to the importance of the school to the community.

The West End School was renamed in 1922 in honor of a then-recently retired superintendent of schools, John M. Willis. Later, in 1940, when the downtown Syms-Eaton Academy was closed as a public school, the name of John M. Willis School was changed to Willis-Syms-Eaton. Syms-Eaton Academy was used for various activities during the war years 1941-45. It housed the School Administration Offices for the city of Hampton for many years before being demolished in 1977.

Virginia passed a smallpox vaccination law in 1905, requiring all children of school age to be vaccinated. Ripraps, the school serving the Fox Hill area at that time, closed before the school year ended to protest the law, and the Ripraps principal, a Mr. Llewellyn, with some of his pupils, began the Fox Hill Anti-Vaccination School. Charles Elliott, in his history of Fox Hill, gives this account of the origin of the Anti-Vaccination School:

As a student of this time related, "One day Mr. J.M. Willis, the school superintendent, came to the school and announced that all children would have a medicine put in their arm with a needle." This was something that most of the people of Fox Hill had never heard of, so some of the children went running home in fear. This was the beginning of a new private school in the village. It was called the Fox Hill Anti-Vaccination School. The classes were made up of children from each grade, whose parents were against the vaccination law. The principal of the Fox Hill public school, Mr. Lewellen, was also against it. He left and became principal of this newly formed private school. The classes were held in the old Red Men's Hall located on Beach Road, near Johnson Road.

Graduation exercises were held at the new school. During the summer the principal entered the ministry, and the Anti-Vaccination School did not resume in the fall.

Consolidations closed several of the small schools throughout the county prior to World War I. For example, the Fox Hill School was built in 1917 at a cost of eighteen thousand dollars, and when this school was ready to receive students, three other small schools of the county were closed. These included the old Fox Hill School; Hickman's, located on Harris Creek Road; and the Bloxom's Corner School. River-view and Merrimac schools had already consolidated to become the George Wythe School in 1909. In 1917, a teacher was paid eight hundred dollars a year and a principal's salary was fifteen hundred dollars.

Approximately the same time the first Hampton High School was built, 1922, Union School on Union Street was developing into a high school for black students. Principal Y. H. Thomas expanded the curriculum at Union year by year until requirements for a high school were met. Six commencements had been held for Union High School students before the last class graduated in June 1931.

The following fall high school classes were held at Hampton Institute in anticipation of the opening of the George P. Phenix Training School the following year. Phenix, who was the first president of Hampton Institute, had convinced the General Education Board, an organization which assisted in the erection of demonstration practice schools at the secondary level, to contribute $150,000 towards building such a school at Hampton Institute. When the George P. Phenix Training School opened in September 1932, it housed both secondary and elementary students in a most modern twenty-five classroom building. The purpose of the school was twofold; first, it provided an opportunity for practice teaching at both elementary and

The opening of Syms-Eaton Academy on February 13, 1902, was cause for celebration. Courtesy of Syms-Eaton Museum

Students pose in front of Phoebus Grade School around the year 1904. This brick building replaced a wooden schoolhouse which had been open since the 1880s. Courtesy of Charles H. Taylor Memorial Library

A 1915 school bus loads students on the grounds of George Wythe School. Driver is Mr. Al Baines. Courtesy of Iva Maney Muth

This pamphlet lists the students enrolled in the Fox Hill Anti-Vaccination School, 1906-07. Courtesy of Rebecca Elliott

FOX HILL ANTI-VACCINATION SCHOOL
Ripraps, Va.
1906-1907

Irving L. Llewellyn
Miss Lettie Wallace
Assistant

PUPILS

EIGHTH GRADE
Vara Johnson — Pres.
Octavia Routten — Secy.
Hilda Holston — Treas.
Eunice Johnson — Poet
Effie Johnson — Prophet
Katie Johnson — Historian
Edith Johnson — Carlie Johnson
Stanley Johnson

SEVENTH GRADE
Elroy Llewellyn — Pres.
Nora Mason — Vice Pres.
Bennie Johnson — Secy.
Gracie Gordon — Kuney Johnson
Clarence Johnson — Norman Dixon

SIXTH GRADE
Goldie Johnson — Pres.
Beckie Barron — Vice Pres.
Raymond Johnson — Secy.
Rosa Wallace — Nora Elliott
Virgie Routten — Laura Copeland
Fannie Routten — Aloma Holston
Andrew Mason — Emmet Holston
Sydney Johnson

PRIMARY DEPT.
Mattie Oldfield — Mattie Barron
Dan Elliott — Jessie Lewis

Looking west from the Main Gate at Fort Monroe around the year 1870, the post school is visible as the small, one-story frame building on the left. Courtesy of the Casemate Museum

Class Colors .... Purple and Gold
Class Flower .... Red Rose

CLASS MOTTO.
"Launched, Not Anchored."

CLASS OFFICERS
*Arthur Holland .... President
Frank Wyche .... Acting President
Annie Mitchell .... Secretary
Rosa Prescott .... Treasurer

CLASS ROLL.
Ellen Burnett Hill
Rose Bernice Hill
Harris Hamilton Bright
Alpha Bannister Holland
Edward Norman Jones
Pauline Williams
Theresa Rudolph Thomas
Susie Beatrice Dabney
Minattie Adlener French
Eloise Christian
Albert Oscar Lewis
Jessie Edith Mitchell
John Taliaferro Lattimore
Delbert Hutchins Banks
Clemenza Arnelle Fields
Hazel Inez Truhart
Lillian Louise Banks
Thelma Ernestine Peeden
Henry R. Brooks, Jr.
Rosa Lurline Prescott
Lillian McGhee
Marie Matilda Boykin
Joseph Frank Wyche
Annie Mitchell
Elizabeth Glymph
Bruce Edwin Taylor
Grace Sample Wilkins
*Arthur Wilbur Holland

*Deceased

PROGRAM
SEVENTH ANNUAL COMMENCEMENT
UNION HIGH SCHOOL
June 3rd

Grace E. M...

Processional — "War Priest's March"—Mendlessohn
Treble Clef C...
Song — "Spring Greeting"—Strauss-Bliss
Rev. H. C. Wa...
Invocation — Clemenza F...
Salutatory — "No Temptation Without Determination."
Ellen B...

Valedictory — "Success Comes in Cans,"
Treble Clef C...
Song — "Mighty Lac' A Rose"—Ethelbert Nevin
Capt. G. A. Holl...
Presentation of the Speaker —
Rev. E. H. Hamilton, Rector Church of
Address — Resurrection, Corona, Long Island, N. Y.
Treble Clef C...
Song — "Roses of Picardy"—Weatherly Wood
F. M. Boggs, Chairman School Bo...
Address — R. M. Newton, Supt. of Sch...
Award of Prizes —
Presentation of Diplomas — Rev. H. C. Wa...
Benediction

The commencement program lists graduates of Union High School i 1931. Courtesy of C. H. Hawkins

secondary levels to education students at Hampton Institute, and second, it provided an elementary education for the children of Elizabeth City County who had previously attended Whittier and a secondary education for all the black high school students in Elizabeth City County and Hampton. Phenix was recognized as a public school and was under the supervision of the Virginia State Department of Education. Elizabeth City County at first paid tuition of $15 for each elementary pupil and $25 for each high school student, but in 1940, Hampton Institute made an agreement with Elizabeth City County whereby the school board would lease the Phenix School. The school board purchased all furniture, equipment, and supplies, and paid the operating costs for the 636 children enrolled. Teachers were selected by the school board, but with the approval of Hampton Institute. Phenix continued to serve as a demonstration school for practice teachers. This arrangement continued until 1962 when Phenix High School moved to a newly built high school facility on LaSalle Avenue. The name of the high school was changed to Pembroke High School in 1967, and the name Phenix was passed on to an elementary school which was torn down in 1984. Pembroke High School closed in 1980.

At the beginning of World War I there were two school districts: Wythe and Chesapeake. In 1922, the district school boards were abolished and the public school system of Hampton, Phoebus, and Elizabeth City became administered as one unit. The former county school, Woodrow Wilson, was transferred to Newport News on January 1, 1927, when the area it served was annexed by Newport News. At that time fifteen schools served all of Elizabeth City County.

World War II placed upon the public schools of the area the triple responsibility of carrying on the regular instructional program, rendering service in the various nationwide calls for assistance in the war effort and participating in community war projects. The children of the war workers who migrated into the area with their parents put tremendous strain on educational facilities and personnel. There was also a large turnover in students, as parents moved around the Peninsula in search of housing. Elizabeth City County had 6,542 students enrolled in its schools in 1940. By 1945, 8,500 students were enrolled. In an effort to help, the United States government built two schools in the

county specifically to serve the children of the war workers; one, Copeland Park, to serve a federal housing development of that name, and another, Langley View, to serve a housing development built for NACA workers. These two schools were turned over to the Elizabeth City County school system in 1950.

Until the 1960s Hampton public schools were segregated at all levels. The transition to a fully integrated school system began in 1960, thus anticipating the implementation of the Civil Rights Act of 1964. The school system was never under a court desegregation order, as it began desegregating its schools voluntarily. Several factors contributed to the successful manner in which integration in public schools took place. Among these was the foresight of C. Alton Lindsay, superintendent of schools. He worked effectively with the other administrators of the Hampton Public School System, the Hampton School Board, and the Hampton City Council, the NAACP, as well as with the Hampton PTA Council and the individual school PTAs throughout the city. Another factor contributing to the smoothness of the integration was the presence of Hampton University (then Institute), which has long had a positive influence on educational and economic affairs for the entire community. Also the high concentration of civil service and military families within the city was advantageous, since the federal government had desegregated a decade before.

After the Civil War many new private schools, small and large, helped to educate Hamptonians. The earliest known private school to operate in this area after the Civil War appears in an 1870 photograph of Fort Monroe. The Children's School, as it was designated on an 1880 map, was located where the YMCA was built at the turn of the century. In 1879, the Hampton Education Association was organized for the purpose of providing a private school. By February 1880, the Association had opened Banner School with thirty-six pupils taught by Miss Clara T. Price. Also called the Model School, it was located near Hampton Institute on East Queen Street and drew its support from such prestigious Hamptonians as Albert Howe, Samuel Armstrong, P. T. Woodfin, Thomas Tabb, and C. D. Cake. The school land was sold to settle debts in 1896. Nearby, the Misses Laura and Ruth Tileston opened their private school for girls in 1888. Miss

HEW PRAISES CITY SCHOOL SYSTEM, CITES COMPLIANCE ON CIVIL RIGHTS

Hampton Monitor highlights city school system's desegregation on February 23, 1973. Courtesy of Charles H. Taylor Memorial Library

C. Alton Lindsay was superintendent of schools from 1942 to 1968, during which time enrollment increased 400 percent. Courtesy of the Daily Press, Inc.

SUPT. GARLAND LIVELY
"We have complied!"

ROBERT J. DEWEY
City School Chairman

Public schools in Hampton are in compliance with, rather than in violation of the 1964 Civil Rights Act, according to latest reports from the Department of Health, Education and Welfare (HEW).

City school officials were shocked by published reports last week in which a federal judge said Hampton was among several school district still in violation of the act.

Judge John H. Pratt, a U. S. District Court judge, admitted however, that "some of the evidence and special information relating to compliance and non-compliance is nsomewhat out of date."

The action came in a suit brought by the NAACP and the ACLU because they thought HEW was delaying its enforcement of the Civil Rights Act.

School Supt. Garland R. Lively said he was surprised by the news story. "I'm very surprised that it would even be of concern. We feel we have done everything we could and we have the documentation."

Board Chairman Robert J. Dewey said, "It is clear and straight, city schools have complied" with the desegregation plans.

Dewey said Hampton fulfilled its desegregation play last fall at the start of the 1972-73 school year.

"In 1970-71, we felt we couldn't do everything at once and set up a two-stage plan," he said. "HEW wasn't really happy but they knew our circumstances and knew we were trying. As a result, in the fall of 1972, we received our compliance notice. Now, it is a dead issue to have done."

The Hampton chairman said confusion on the matter "stems from the age of the judge's information and from the construction of recent headlines, it puts the wrong information before the public when it essence, the information was two years old."

Superintendent Lively released a letter from Dr. Lloyd R. Henderson, director of the education division, office of Civil Rights, HEW, to the Hampton School Board Aug. 2:

"We have carefully reviewed the desegregation plan shown on the maps enclosed in your letter of June 15, 1972. In the agreements you reached with Miss Rosa Wiener in her discussions with you and your staff on July 14 and by telephone on July 26, and find that they meet the requirements of Title 6 of the Civil Rights Act of 1964."

The letter also said:
"In addition, you have made

Ruth had been teacher for the children of Samuel Armstrong, while Miss Laura taught at the Indian School at the Institute. Tileston Hall was so successful that the sisters moved to Brightview in Chesapeake City (Phoebus) and accommodated boarding students along with local girls. The school closed sometime around 1903 and the Tileston sisters left the area.

The cornerstone for the rather imposing Hampton Female College was laid on July 5, 1892, at East Hampton. This private boarding school, which a group of Hampton businessmen incorporated as the Hampton Female College Corporation, was erected under the management of Professor E. E. Parham. "Exceptionally fine educational advantages were offered at very moderate rates." Miss Bessie Fitchett was principal of the school when it burned to the ground in early September 1899. The school was able to relocate to North King Street. There it served a few boarding students along with local girls. Boys were allowed to attend the first three grades. Shortening its name to Hampton College, the school moved again, this time to College Place. In 1913, Miss Fitchett conveyed all the furnishings of the school to H. H. Savage, who continued to run the school at the same location after renaming it Pembroke Hall. Dr. George Vanderslice bought the school in 1919 and arranged for Miss Edith M. Collins to be principal, but the school closed permanently after a year or two. In the same neighborhood as Pembroke Hall, at 423 East Queen Street, Mrs. Kate Wise was principal of the Atlantic Coast School from 1917-19. The school advertised that it offered classes from kindergarten to college. Mrs. Wise moved the Atlantic Coast School to Newport News at the end of the 1919 session.

Prior to World War I private schools flourished in the black community in an effort to meet entrance requirements at Hampton Normal School. A. W. E. Bassett opened a school in a two-room building on Rip

Rap Road in 1895. Bassett later sold his school to Elizabeth City County to be used as a public school. Also around 1895, the Rev. Richard Spiller of First Baptist Church opened his school on nearby North King Street Extended. Nannie Gaddis and Julia White ran small schools in downtown Hampton. Around 1905 the Tidewater Collegiate Institute opened with the Rev. G. Edward Read as principal, and the Rev. Ebenezer Hamilton of St. Cyprian's Episcopal Church held classes in 1913 in a one-room schoolhouse located in the backyard of E. H. Spennie, next to Hampton Institute grounds.

A special institution which educated blacks was the Weaver Orphan Home. W. B. Weaver, Hampton Normal School class of 1875, was first instrumental in the building of the Gloucester Industrial School at Cappahosic, Virginia, which opened in 1888. When he relinquished his ties to that school, he brought his family to Hampton and purchased land on West Queen Street with the intention of opening an orphanage. The Weaver Orphan Home opened in 1904

Banner School, an early private school, had close ties with Hampton Institute. Courtesy of Syms-Eaton Museum

This 1892 view of the Hampton River shows Hampton Normal and Agricultural Institute in the foreground. Note that only a railroad bridge crosses the river at East Hampton. Banner School on the right is located on what would become East Queen Street. Villa Margaret and Colonel Mallory's home are at the center of the photo. Courtesy of Hampton University Archives

The 1896 Chataigne's Peninsula Directory *lists schools and academies in Hampton. Courtesy of Charles H. Taylor Memorial Library*

This 1985 photograph shows a former private school for blacks which was taught by the Rev. Ebenezer H. Hamilton, rector of St. Cyprian's Episcopal Church around the year 1912. It is located at 7 Gatewood Street. Courtesy of C. H. Hawkins

No. 2706   COTTRELL & COMPANY. Negotiate Loans on Real Estate.   Wash. Ave.

378   HAMPTON BUSINESS DIRECTORY.

*Downey Eli, Court nr King
Gibson John E, King nr Queen
*Lee William, King nr Mallory ave
Roche William W, Queen nr King
WOOD RANDOLPH R, King nr Queen (see adv)
Schools and Academies.
Armistead Julia Miss, Armistead ave nr Holt
Curtis Mary W Miss, Holt nr Armistead ave
Darden Anna B Mrs, Locust nr Academy
HAMPTON FEMALE COLLEGE, East Hampton
Edwin E Parham A M pres (see adv)
HAMPTON NORMAL AND AGRICULTURAL INSTITUTE (The), County rd nr bridge
HAMPTON TRAINING SCHOOL FOR NURSES, n e of Soldiers Home nr new cemetery Miss Alice M Bacon secy and treas Miss Susan B Swanton supt (see adv preceding page)
Ives Lillian A Miss, Melrose ave nr Armistead ave
*Spiller Academy, King extd Rev R Spiller pres
TILESTON HALL, Old Point rd nr Gatewoods cor

TILESTON HALL,
HAMPTON.
Select Boarding School for Girls.
Superior Advantages in
Art, Music and Modern Languages.
Special Training in Physical Culture and Athletics.
THE MISSES TILESTON.

Wilson Annie Miss, Hudgins la nr Queen
Winder Cornelia H Miss, King nr Hope
Ship Chandlers.
Armistead Bros & James, ft King
Shooting Galleries.
Leland Charles, Queen nr Hope

Jacob Heffelfinger, Foot of King St., Hampton.   **Coal.**   CLEAN. Good Quality, Full Weight.

Hampton Female College
HAMPTON, VA.

E. E. PARHAM, A. M., President.

Fall Session begins Second Wednesday in September. Spring Session, January 20. Commencement, first Wednesday in June.
This institution offers excellent accommodations for boarders. The building has electric lights, hot and cold water, Steam heat. Superior advantages in full English course. Mathematics, the Sciences, Latin, French, German, Instrumental and Vocal Music, Elocution, Art, &c.

Table First-Class.   All Delicacies of the Season.
RATES: $2 and $2.50 Per Day.   Special Rates by the Week or Month

Barnes Hotel,
KING STREET. HAMPTON, VA.
CLAUDIUS S. FOSTER,   -   Proprietor.
All the Advantages of Old Point Comfort at Cheaper Rates.
(379)

and furnished accommodations and schooling for about thirty-five children at the time. The schooling took place at the Home. Over eight-hundred orphan children lived in the home with the Weaver family during the orphanage's sixty-one year lifespan. The private orphanage received most of its financial support from local churches. After the death of Professor and Mrs. Weaver, their daughter, Anna Weaver Fagan, and her husband continued to run the orphanage for several years. The Weaver Orphan Home closed in 1965.

Besides Tileston Hall and Hampton Female College, several other schools were advertised in the Hampton business directories at the turn of the century. One, the Hampton Roads Military Academy for boys, briefly operated on a site on Chesapeake Avenue which later became part of Newport News.

Records kept by St. Mary Star of the Sea Catholic Church indicate that parochial education had begun at Old Point Comfort by 1889. A small school, located behind the rectory, served children of both civilian and military families at Old Point as well as the residents of Phoebus through the year 1903.

The Xaverian Brothers, represented by Brother Provincial Alexius, bought thirty-six acres of land near Buckroe on Mill Creek, with the plan of providing a home for aged and infirm brothers. However, the brothers began a school instead, the Old Point Comfort College, which was incorporated in 1898.

Brother Julian wrote in *Men and Deeds*:

Terry Allen, son of Lieutenant Allen of Fortress Monroe, was the first pupil, as a result of an urgent sermon on Catholic education by Father Mercer in church the preceding Sunday, when he spoke of the arrival of the Brothers and their readiness to conduct a school for the people of the neighborhood. The people were slow to respond. Catholics were few. . . . The place was thoroughly countrified and the largest town in the vicinity, Hampton, wholly non-Catholic. In consequence, day scholars were few. Five reported the first month, and only ten were enrolled by the end of the scholastic year. The only hope of a school lay in building for boarders.

A wooden structure with two stories and a basement was constructed to accommodate sixty boarders. This was soon enlarged with a structure three stories high. In 1905, the school developed into a regular military training school. Military discipline remained until 1916, when parents, objecting to the added expense of purchasing uniforms, brought pressure to discontinue the program. The *Bulletin* for 1907 describes Old Point Comfort College as having a college department with a bachelor of arts, a high school department, commercial business course, and a grammar department intended for younger students. By this time, a gymnasium with a pool, bowling alley, and separate chemistry building had been added. In 1921, it was decided to close Old Point to boarders and move novices there. However, the day school continued

This 1913 postcard shows the
Hampton Female Seminary. Courtesy
of Syms-Eaton Museum

This photo was taken from the 1909
Old Point Comfort College Bulletin.
Courtesy of Hampton University
Archives

until 1923. The Sacred Heart Noviate was located there until 1961, but the original buildings were not torn down until 1963.

A less successful Catholic boarding school for boys was the La Salle Institute. The *Daily Press* noted on September 15, 1898, that "the enrollment and examination of pupils in La Salle Institute, the new college of the Christian Brothers overlooking the Hampton Roads, began this week. The first name enrolled was James McMenamin, Jr., son of the owner of an extensive canning factory here." The three-story building located on ten acres which ran from La Salle Avenue to Church Creek served as a school from 1898 to 1904. Afterwards its building was converted to the Old Point View Hotel, then the Boulevard Inn rooming house. Following that it was converted into an apartment building which was in existence in 1985.

The same year Old Point Comfort College closed to day students, 1923, St. Mary Star of the Sea School opened in the Brightview Cottage in Phoebus, thanks to the efforts of Father Wilson from the Fort Monroe church of the same name. The school was run from its opening by the Dominican sisters and expanded its physical plant several times. In 1985, it was the oldest private school open in Hampton and had an enrollment of 310 pupils. During the 1950s, St. Rose of Lima's Catholic Church sponsored a school located in Wythe. Using buildings left from World War II, the parish opened its school in 1950. It eventually served grades kindergarten through eight, but closed around 1960.

In 1920, Hampton Institute sponsored the Winona School to serve children of faculty members. When the school closed in 1940, one of its teachers, Mrs. Mary McClean Sugden, continued to instruct some of her students in her home on Marrow Street. She named her school the Robert G. Sugden School, in honor of her late husband. In 1954 the school was sold to Mrs. Rose Cooper, who kept the name and moved the school to Ivy Home Road. From this site Sugden School served as a non-denominational elementary school for children from all parts of the Peninsula until it closed in 1980.

A friendly competitor of the Sugden School was Miss Porter's School. Edna Porter von Schilling began teaching in her home on Chesterfield Road during World War II. She expanded her school by moving to a larger home on Chesapeake Avenue and operating there until she closed the school in 1971.

In 1985 the three oldest private schools in Hampton were St. Mary Star of the Sea Parochial School, Emmanuel Lutheran School and Day Care Center, and Mary Atkins Elementary School. Emmanuel Lutheran School began in 1947 in a building of the church by the same name on Kecoughtan Road. In 1979 the school reorganized somewhat when it also began serving as a day care center. Mary E. Atkins opened her first formal kindergarten in 1955. She moved to rented rooms in a church and expanded her school through the fourth grade. When Mrs. Atkins retired, she sold her school to Mrs. Helen Simpson, who served as principal during the school's affiliation with Grace Covenant Church. Mary Atkins School later became part of the Hampton Christian Schools, Inc.

Finally, among private schools, Sarah Bonwell Hudgins Regional Center, located on forty acres just off Big Bethel Road, opened in 1965 as a training center for mentally retarded individuals in the community. Sarah Bonwell Hudgins offered programs which began from birth and extended throughout life for the mentally retarded and multi-handicapped.

The Hampton Public School System experienced a phenomenal growth during the 1960s and into the early 1970s. In 1960, there were seventeen schools. This number more than doubled from 1960 to 1972, reaching its peak in 1972 with a total of thirty-nine schools. The enrollment in 1972-73 was thirty-three thousand in contrast to seventeen thousand in 1960. The number declined to twenty thousand during the 1980s. The Hampton Public School System was two years ahead of the state in establishing a public kindergarten program. Classes for the five-year olds opened in August of 1968. The Center for Multi-handicapped Children opened in September of 1974. It was located in a separate building at the Robert E. Lee Elementary School to serve the entire Peninsula area.

Changes were made in the schools' curriculum in an attempt to meet the needs of the students. Among the innovations were the introduction of nine-week mini-courses, advanced placement courses, and "fundamental schools" which concentrated on teaching the basic subjects of reading, writing, and arithmetic in a structured environment.

Brightview Cottage, which served earlier as Tileston Hall, became the location of St. Mary Star of the Sea School in 1932. Courtesy of Syms-Eaton Museum

Armstrong Elementary School, which opened in 1921, was the oldest public school in operation in 1985. Courtesy of Armstrong Fundamental Elementary School

Numerous "alternative" programs were developed. In Vo Prep, and later, Alternatives, separate classrooms were set aside for those students having trouble adjusting to regular classes at the junior high level.

Vo Tech, for senior high school students, started in 1965 as the first jointly-operated vocational training center in the state, was located at the Mercedes Drive Campus in Copeland Industrial Park. The school board made plans to open New Horizons on Butler Farm Road in 1986-87 to serve the students of the community taking courses in health care, automobile trades, carpentry, and cosmetology. This new $6 million campus was also designed to house a special state magnet school for science and technology.

Located in the former Buckroe Junior High School building, the JTPA (Job Training Partnership Act) program, federally funded, taught economically disadvantaged adults on the Peninsula different skills,

including automobile service mechanics, air conditioning and heating, commercial cooking, clerk-typist stenography, building trades, machine technology, welding, and electrical wiring. The Buckroe school also housed some of the classes for the Hampton School System's Alternatives program.

Among the alternative programs, the Hampton School System developed ASPEN (Administers Secondary Program for Educational Needs). Located at Jefferson Davis Junior High School, the program began in 1980 to serve the trainable mentally handicapped. Students who were under fourteen years attended special classes in regular schools.

Another alternative program, PACES (Peninsula Area Cooperative Educational Services), opened in 1982 in the former Mary S. Peake Elementary School on Thomas Street. This program was developed for all the communities, to serve both the emotionally disturbed and the gifted and talented students. Hampton

119

Phoebus High School, which opened in 1976, had the newest public school building in use in 1985. Courtesy of the Daily Press, *Inc.*

had operated its own Gifted Program since 1971; with PACES it began a cooperative program.

In addition to developing its alternative programs, the Hampton Public School System revised and updated other programs in its curriculum. For example, the first language lab was put into operation in the 1960s; by the 1980s, many schools used modern language labs to increase the effectiveness of their language programs.

Beginning in 1961, Hampton and Norfolk began cooperative efforts to teach programs in math and elementary language using television. In the 1970s, the school system added computer science and computer math using terminals tied to the computer at the College of William and Mary. By 1973, the Hampton schools had their own computers. In 1983, each school began receiving their own micro-computers, purchased both by the school system and enterprising Parent-Teacher Associations, and in 1985 an elementary computer school was established.

Hampton's Junior High School changed, starting in the fall of 1985, when ninth-grade students were enrolled in the senior high schools. Junior Highs were scheduled to be phased out in the fall of 1987, with the move of sixth graders to the middle schools.

During the school year 1984-85, Hampton High School was selected as one of the best schools in the country. It received the National Award of Academic Excellence from the United States Department of Education, honoring 277 schools throughout the nation for their outstanding job in meeting the educa-

tional needs of students.

The 1960s brought a new and important element of education to Hampton and the rest of the Peninsula. Thomas Nelson Community College, a two-year institution of higher learning, was established in 1966 by the Virginia General Assembly as part of a statewide system of community colleges, and Hampton was designated as the site for this school. Land east of Big Bethel Road was purchased by the city of Hampton, and construction was begun on the initial phase of four buildings in August 1967. Dr. Thomas V. Jenkins, the first president of TNCC, and his staff operated from the William Claiborne Building in downtown Hampton until construction was completed. On September 20, 1968, classes began with 1,232 students enrolled.

Thomas Nelson Community College is named in honor of Thomas Nelson, Jr., a signer of the Declaration of Independence and an early colonial governor of Virginia, who was a merchant in Yorktown. He commanded several thousand Virginia militiamen at the seige of Yorktown during the Revolutionary War. Having spent his fortune for the cause of the Revolution, he died a pauper. Thomas Nelson Community College graduated its first class of students with associate degrees on June 13, 1970. The school serves not only Hampton residents, but also residents of neighboring communities. It is primarily financed by state funds, supplemented by contributions from the participating localities and the federal government. In 1985, the enrollment was 6,284.

Hampton Schools

The spectrum of Hampton's history is reflected in the names of its schools, beginning with the Kecoughtan Indians and going to the name of Christopher Kraft, former director of the Space Center in Houston. The following is a list of Hampton Schools as they existed in 1985, arranged alphabetically, with a historical vignette of each:

Aberdeen Elementary School, located on Aberdeen Road, opened its doors in 1938. It was built by the Works Progress Administration and deeded to the county school system in 1946.

Armstrong Elementary School, located on Matoaka Road, opened in 1921. The land on which the school stands was ceded to the Elizabeth City County School Board by the Armstrong Land and Improvement Company, from whence it gets it name.

Francis Asbury Elementary School, opened in 1916 on Beach Road in Fox Hill near the site of previous Fox Hill schools. It bears the name of the American preacher who was the first bishop of the Methodist Church.

Barron Elementary School, which opened in 1962 on Fox Hill Road, bears the name of an old Hampton family. Capt. Samuel Barron came to Virginia from Bristol, England, in the early seventeenth century. He later served as commander of Fort George. James Barron, the youngest son of Captain Barron, served as commander of the Virginia's Navy in 1779, having been appointed to this position by Virginia's governor. Both of Captain Barron's sons, Samuel and James, served in the Navy.

A.W.E. Bassette Elementary School, on Bell Street, which opened in 1971, was named in honor of an educator and lawyer, Andrew William Ernest Bassette, who was born in 1865 in Elizabeth City County. A graduate of Hampton Normal and Agricultural Institute, his teaching career spanned a period of thirty-nine years.

Bethel High School, on Big Bethel Road, opened its doors in 1969. The name Big Bethel refers to a Civil War battle fought in the vicinity, which in turn received its designation from its location on the grounds of the Bethel Baptist Church.

Booker Elementary School, located on Apollo Drive, opened in 1969, bearing the name of the distinguished Booker family of Hampton. George Booker, who was born in 1723, was prominent in the affairs of the county, serving as a trustee of the Syms-Eaton School. His great grandson, George Booker, born in 1805, became the first superintendent of public schools in Elizabeth City County. The Honorable Hunter Booker Andrews served as chairman of the School Board of the City of Hampton from 1959 to 1962. He was the first chairman of the Board of Trustees of the Hampton Roads Educational and Television Association.

Jane H. Bryan Elementary School, opened on North Mallory Street in 1955, was named in honor of an educator who taught three generations of citizens in Phoebus and the surrounding area. Miss

Jane Hamilton Bryan was born in Liverpool, England. She received her education in England and Germany, and migrated to Phoebus with her parents and two sisters. "Miss Janie," as she was affectionately known, and one of her sisters conducted a private school in Phoebus for many years. Her teaching career in the public schools began in 1902 and continued until her retirement in 1938.

Paul Burbank Elementary School, opened in 1967 on Tidemill Lane. It bears the name of Hampton native Paul Burbank, dentist, who served as chairman of the Hampton School Board.

John B. Cary Elementary School, on Andrews Boulevard, opened in 1958, bearing the name of the distinguished Hampton educator of a century ago. John Cary served as principal of both the public and private Hampton Academy before opening his own school, Hampton Military Academy. During the Civil War, Major Cary became commander of the Hampton Volunteers units.

William Mason Cooper Elementary School, which opened on Marcella Road in 1975, was named for the first black member of the Hampton City School Board. Dr. Cooper was born in 1892 and began teaching at Hampton Institute in 1929. He was director of the summer school in 1939 and in his latter days he served as consultant on education and interpersonal relations for the college, retiring from that position in 1958.

Jefferson Davis Junior High School, located on Todds Lane, opened in 1961. It was named in honor of Jefferson Davis who was president of the Confederate States of America from 1861 to 1865. Jefferson Davis was imprisoned at Fort Monroe when the Civil War ended.

Thomas Eaton Fundamental Junior High School was named to perpetuate the memory of Dr. Thomas Eaton who in 1659 willed 500 acres of land in Elizabeth City County to provide a school known as "Eaton Charity School." The City of Hampton School Board built the new junior high school in 1964 on Cunningham Drive.

Forrest Elementary School. When Bethel High School was built in 1969, Bethel Elementary School, which was opened in 1956 on Todds Lane changed its name. Forrest Elementary School honors the memory of Mr. Alfred S. Forrest who was principal of Wythe Elementary School from 1923. When a junior high school was built on grounds adjoining the elementary school in the early twenties, he served as principal for both. Mr. Forrest became principal of the new George Wythe Junior High School in 1950 where he served until his retirement in the early 1960s.

Hampton High School. On October 19, 1958, a new Hampton High School, nicknamed "The Little Pentagon," was dedicated on West Queen Street; however, Hampton High School had its real beginning in 1887, as part of Hampton Academy, located on the old Syms-Eaton grounds. The first graduating class of Hampton Academy, predecessor of Hampton High School, was in June 1896, consisting of two young ladies, Miss Blanche Bulifant and Miss Bessie Birdsall. The first independent Hampton High School was built in 1922 on Victoria Boulevard.

Kecoughtan High School opened on Woodland Road in 1963, having received its name from that of an Indian tribe which in 1607 was living in a village on the site of the present city of Hampton.

Christopher Kraft Elementary School on Concord Drive in Northampton, which opened in 1967, is named for Christopher Kraft, Jr., who was born in Phoebus in 1924. Mr. Kraft, noted for his contributions in the field of airplane-flight research, served as director of flight operations, NASA Manned Spacecraft Center, Houston, Texas and later, as director of the Lyndon B. Johnson Space Center, Houston, retiring from that position in 1982.

Samuel P. Langley School, located on Rockwell Road, opened its doors in 1942. It honors the memory of Samuel Pierpont Langley, aviator and physicist, who was a pioneer in the development of the airplane. The first United States aircraft carrier was named for him, and Langley Air Force Base also bears his name. The school was built by the federal government to serve NACA workers but it was deeded to Elizabeth City County School System in 1950.

Robert E. Lee Elementary School opened in 1966 on Briarfield Road, bearing the name of the commander of the Army of the Confederacy in the War Between the States. He spent three years before the war as superintendent at the United States Military Academy and afterwards during his last years he served as president of Washington College which, a year after his death in 1871, changed its name to Washington and Lee University.

C. Alton Lindsay Junior High School, on Briarfield Road, opened its doors to students in 1969. It bears the name of one of Hampton's most distinguished educators. Alton Lindsay served the community in public education over a period of forty-one years, beginning as principal of Armstrong Elementary School in 1927 and retiring as division superintendent of schools on June 30, 1968. Mr. Lindsay's tenure as superintendent was during the period of tremendous growth of the city. In 1942, when the school boards of the three political divisions of the community (Elizabeth City County, Hampton and the town of Phoebus) searched for a division superintendent, they found that Mr. Lindsay was the best qualified person. With the merging of Hampton, Elizabeth City and Phoebus in 1952, Mr. Lindsay served as the superintendent of the consolidated school system. While he was superintendent the city's population increased 400 percent.

The Luther W. Machen Elementary School opened its doors in 1970. Located on Sacramento Drive, it is named in memory of an educator and administrator whose career began in 1922 as a shop teacher in the old Hampton High School.

Mr. Machen developed the Teaching Materials Bureau, and was an active supporter from the inception of the educational and cultural television station WHRO-TV. In 1959, at the beginning of Hampton's boom in school construction, Mr. Machen became supervisor of construction, overseeing the building of more than ten structures, beginning with Hampton High School in 1958, and concluding with the Paul H. Burbank Elementary School in 1967.

Francis Mallory Elementary School opened in 1959 on Big Bethel Road. This school bears the name of one of Hampton's distinguished Colonial-era families. Francis Mallory was born in Hampton and educated at the College of William and Mary. He returned to Hampton to take up his career as a planter, attorney, and political leader. While serving in the Elizabeth City County Militia during the Revolutionary War, Mr. Mallory was killed in action in 1780 near Little Bethel in Elizabeth City County.

Merrimack Elementary School, opened in 1966 on Woodmansee Drive, was named for the ship which became the Confederate ironclad warship C.S.S. *Virginia*. On March 9, 1862, this ship engaged with the Union ironclad warship *Monitor* in an inconclusive battle.

Robert R. Moton Elementary School is another school named for a distinguished black educator, Robert Russo Moton. It was opened in 1948 on Old Buckroe Road. After graduating in 1890 from Hampton Institute, Robert Moton became the first black commandant of cadets at the school, which was equivalent to the position of a dean. He was the second principal of Tuskegee Normal and Industrial Institute, succeeding Booker T. Washington. Moton died in 1940.

Phillips Elementary School on Lemaster Avenue, which opened its doors in 1963, was named in memory of Benjamin Phillips, an early planter of Elizabeth City, and his many distinguished descendants who have contributed to public education and the community in general. Benjamin Phillips was born in 1760 in Accomac; however, he moved to Elizabeth City County in 1803 and settled in the Harris Creek area where he owned a prosperous farm.

Phoebus High School on Ireland Street was the last of the five high schools in Hampton to be built, opening its doors in 1976, and bearing the name of the geographic area in which it was built. The name honors the memory of Harrison Phoebus, a local entrepreneur who was born on a small farm in Maryland but settled in the Mill Creek community in 1864.

Captain John Smith Elementary School opened in 1968 on Woodland Road, receiving the name of the famous English adventurer who is remembered as the leader of the first English colonists in Virginia.

C. Vernon Spratley Junior High School opened on Woodland Road in 1970, bearing the name of a distinguished educator and jurist. Spratley was born in 1882 in Surry County and attended Hampton High School, the College of William and Mary, and the University of Virginia. He began his career in 1901 as a teacher of Latin and mathematics at Hampton High School, and was appointed principal of Stonewall Jackson Elementary School in Newport News in 1902. Mr. Spratley began the practice of law in 1906, serving as Phoebus and Hampton city attorney until 1923. He also served on the Hampton City Council as vice-mayor. In 1923, Mr. Spratley became judge of the Eleventh Judicial Circuit, receiving this appointment from Gov. E. Lee Trinkle. In 1936, Gov. George Perry appointed him to the Supreme Court of Appeals.

Benjamin Syms Jr. High School received its name to perpetuate the memory of Benjamin Syms, who in 1634 willed two hundred acres of land in Elizabeth City County to provide a charity school. The City of Hampton School Board built the new junior high school in 1963 on Fox Hill Road.

Cesar Tarrant Elementary School opened its doors on Wingfield Drive in 1970, and was named in honor of Cesar Tarrant, a black hero of the American Revolution. Cesar was a gallant navigator who early in the war was one of seven pilots appointed to serve in the Virginia Navy, a duty he performed for more than three years. For his meritorious service, the Virginia Assembly purchased Cesar's freedom from Carter Tarrant's widow. After he had become a free man, he worked toward getting freedom for his entire family and a few years later, Cesar's wife, Lucy, and their youngest child, Nancy, were freed. Cesar died in February 1797, still struggling to free the remainder of his family. His older daughter, Lydia, won her freedom, but apparently Cesar and Lucy's only son, Sampson, died a slave. The passionate desire of this Revolutionary War hero, Cesar Tarrant, was "to see justice done my children," a fitting ideal for the school system which honored him.

Tucker-Capps Elementary School on Wellington Drive, which opened its doors in 1963, bears the name of two outstanding leaders of the Colonial Period. Captain William Tucker and William Capps were two Englishmen who came to America in 1610 and settled in Kecoughtan. They represented Kecoughtan when the first General Assembly of the Colony of Virginia, America's first representative assembly, convened in the church at Jamestown.

John Tyler Elementary School on Salina Street opened in 1967, bearing the name of one of Hampton's most distinguished residents. John Tyler, president of the United States from 1841 to 1845, lived in Hampton during two summers preceding the Civil War. In 1858, he purchased Villa Margaret, located on the Hampton River across from where young cadets drilled at Hampton Military Academy, run by Tyler's friend, John Cary.

Wythe Elementary School, in the Wythe District of Hampton on Claremont Avenue, started as a four-room school building in 1909. In the early twenties, a junior high school was constructed on the adjoining grounds. When in 1950, a new and bigger junior high school was built a few blocks away, the elementary grades left the original building and moved to the vacated junior high school building next door. George Wythe, in whose honor the schools were named, was born in 1726 at "Chesterville" on Back River Road in Hampton. He was a teacher, a noted statesman, and a jurist. He was professor at the College of William and Mary, establishing there in 1779 the first professorship in law in the United States. Among the notables he taught were Thomas Jefferson, James Monroe, John Marshall, and James Madison. Wythe attended the Continental Congress in 1775, and signed the Declaration of Independence. In 1787, he helped to draft the Constitution of the United States. He died in 1806.

ACKNOWLEDGMENTS

We wish to thank the following people for their assistance: W. A. Ackerly; Kathleen Anderson; Mary Ellen Bowman; Casemate Museum Library; Joan Charles; Mary Todd Clark; Mike Cobb; Lillian Diamonstein; Harriet Donaldson; Gaynell Drummond; Edward Duckworth; Thornton Elliott; Thelma Todd Fox; Joe Frankoski; Jack Frost; Louise Masters Gayle; Eleanor Gustafson; Hampton City School Administrative Offices staff; Blanche Cutchins Haldeman; Edward Haldeman; S. Frear Hawkins, II; Rhomie L. Heck; Jesse H. Hogg, Jr.; James, Richardson, and Quinn, P.C.; Francis W. Jones; Gerry L. Lassiter; C. Alton Lindsay; Dr. Joseph Lyles; Dr. Robert H. Lynn; Fritz J. Malval; Elizabeth Messick; Newport News West Avenue Branch Public Library; Cynthia Poston; R. Cody Phillips; Cora M. Reid; Theresa F. Sanchez; Martha Shields; Helen Simpson; Peggy Stead; Dr. Betty M. Swiggett; Charles H. Taylor Library staff; Virginia School for the Deaf and Blind at Hampton staff; Joan Fuller Traynham; Phyllis Wharton; Donzella Willford; and Barbara Wood.

*Henry Wriothesley, third earl of
Southampton, was treasurer of the
London Company and later its presi-
dent from 1620 to 1625. The city of*
*Hampton, Hampton Roads and the
Hampton River were named in his
honor. Courtesy of the Mariners
Museum*

5

Chapter

Seafood, Steamers, and Streetcars

by William Hudgins

To appreciate the role that business and industry had in the colonizing of Virginia and thus Hampton, it is helpful to consider the history of England in the latter part of the sixteenth century. Years of war with its European neighbors had produced a financial drain in England and her natural resources were being depleted. Many goods had to be imported, causing an imbalance in trade payments. In Elizabeth I's court, a soldier, explorer and businessman, Sir Walter Raleigh, became deeply interested in exploration and sent several expeditions to American to establish a colony there. His ventures centered on the Pamlico Sound region of what is now North Carolina. Raleigh named this area Virginia in honor of "The Virgin Queen," Elizabeth. At first, Raleigh financed the expeditions from his own personal funds, but as time went on and costs increased, he brought other individuals into the project. These individuals were later to play a prominent part in the formation of the Virginia Colony. In 1603 Queen Elizabeth died and James I ascended to the throne of England. James feared and distrusted Raleigh and charged him with treason, whereupon Raleigh was imprisoned in the Tower of London. Because of his imprisonment, Raleigh's rights in the Colony of Virginia reverted back to the Crown.

In 1606, the King chartered the Virginia Company in London for the purpose of colonizing Virginia. James was very desirous of a permanent colony in the new world because of the prestige and revenue that would be derived, but he did not want the expedition financed by either himself or his government. Thus a royal grant was extended. The charter, dated April 10, 1606, listed among its founders the following persons: Sir Thomas Gates (commander of one of Sir Francis Drake's vessels on an expedition to Virginia around 1586); Sir Thomas Smith, first treasurer (i.e. chief executive officer); Rev. Richard Hakluyt; Robert Gilbert (a nephew of Raleigh); Sir George Somers; Edward Maria Wingfield (to become first president of the council); Captain Gabriel Archer; and the Rev. Robert Hunt (to be chaplain of the expedition to Virginia). Most of these individuals had been associated with Raleigh in his previous attempts to colonize Virginia.

For every twelve pounds, ten shillings (approximately sixty dollars) paid into the treasury, the company guaranteed to give the payee a "hundred" (of land). Also, there was a promise of another hundred when the first area had been cultivated. It is not certain how much land a hundred amounted to. Some authorities believe the term referred to its physical size of 100 acres or 100 hides (of 120 acres each). However, there was no regularity in size, for some of the Virginia

Two F-15 fighter jets returning to Langley Air Force Base fly over a waterman's craft. Courtesy of the Daily Press, Inc.

hundreds contained as many as 80,000 acres.

Under the command of Capt. Christopher Newport, who had acquired a maritime reputation by former expeditions against the Spanish, the Virginia Company fitted out three vessels, the *Susan Constant* (or *Sarah Constant*), the *Godspeed* (*Goodspeed*) and the *Discovery*. On December 19, 1606, the three vessels set said from Blackwall, London with the *Susan Constant* under the command of Captain Newport, the *Godspeed* under the command of Capt. Bartholomew Gosnold and the *Discovery* under the command of Capt. John Ratcliff. Captain Newport was also commander of the squadron. Clearly, all of the early activities set on colonizing Virginia were organized and carried out using "a business" as the reason. The first chapter of this history tells how the settlement progressed.

Seafood

Seafood was the predominant natural resource of the area. The colonists were astounded by the abundance of seafood and the ease with which it was obtained. Capt. John Smith listed the following fish observed by the colonists: sturgeon, porpoise, stingray, mullet, white salmon, eel, catfish, perch, toadfish, herring, shad, rock, trout, flounder, bass and sheepshead. Later, in the seventeeenth century, there was mention of drum, croaker, and bluefish (taylors), and in the eighteenth century spot is mentioned as inhabiting the waters of the lower Chesapeake Bay. Smith also recorded the presence of oysters, crabs, and whales.

The great variety of seafood that Hampton has been blessed with is due in large part to its geographical location. Its numerous inlets and creeks with deep and shallow water and easy access to the open sea make the area a natural hatchery for fish and crabs. Also, there are excellent seedbeds and rocks for growing oysters and clams.

Nevertheless, seafood was slow to develop as a commercial industry. Not until the middle of the eighteenth century did the seafood industry begin to grow; and really not until after the Civil War did it make its appearance in Hampton. At the conclusion of the Civil War Northerners came south and brought Yankee ingenuity, enterprise, and capital. Nowhere in Hampton was this more evident than in the oyster and crab business.

Oysters were the first seafood the colonists encountered. On Monday, April 27, 1607, one day after landing in the new world, an exploring party discovered oysters roasting over a deserted fire. A few days later, when they arrived at Kecoughtan, the colonists ate oysters served by their Indian hosts. The newcomers could not believe the abundance, size and accessibility of the oysters. At low tide, huge clusters of them formed reefs and could be harvested by hand. In 1610, astounded colonists reported oysters thirteen inches long, and a century later they were described as being four times as large as the English variety. Even in the nineteenth century, the oysters were described as being as long as seven inches. Warm and nutritious

S. S. Coston

J. S. Darling

J. E. Robinson

James McMenamin

local waters accounted for the abundance and size of the oysters. In addition to providing food for the colonists, oysters supplied them with shells that were used as flux for iron smelting and for making roads, garden paths and mortar for bricks.

Oysters were plentiful in area waters in the early seventeenth century. Even so, an Eastern Shore resident in 1753 suggested that oysters be cultivated. However, it was not until the nineteenth century that the oyster industry, as it is today, began. In September 1821, eight schooner owners were given permission to "transfer oysters from Elizabeth City County" and the state for harvesting the following year. Later, during the mid-1800s, fishermen came from outside the area

to work the local beds and local harvesters began to think of conservation as over-harvesting of these beds threatened to exhaust the resource.

The oyster industry for all intents and purposes started in Hampton in 1881 with the formation of J. S. Darling and Son. Darling was born in 1832 in New York City and migrated with his family to Hampton in 1865. When he came to Hampton, Darling also brought with him a vessel load of lumber to build houses. Among other businesses, some of which are discussed below, Darling and his son Frank in 1884 formed an oystering firm, J. S. Darling and Sons, that remained in business until 1979.

In fact, the post-Civil War fledgling oyster business

was dominated by northern natives, including James McMenamin and Charles E. Hewins of Massachusetts, Michael H. Haas of Pennsylvania, Harry Libby of New Hampshire, and William N. Armstrong, a native of Hawaii and a brother of the founder of what is now Hampton University. Hewins and a native Virginian named Dexter went into business together buying and planting oysters. In 1881, Hewins and Darling became involved in a court suit having to do with the staking and planting of oysters on Hampton Bar. Before the case could be legally settled, the Readjuster Legislature of 1881 convened and passed a bill that permitted Darling and Hewins to rent grounds on the Hampton Bar for twenty-five cents per acre per year. The records show that in 1884 Darling paid rent on 350 acres and in 1885 Hewins rented 80 acres. The ruling which opened the Hampton Bar in 1882 provided the major push for expansion of the oyster industry of Hampton.

Although there were a number of oyster packers and planters in the city during the latter part of the 1800s and early 1900s, J. S. Darling and Son became the largest such firm in the world and made the Hampton Bar oyster world famous. During the oyster season, the firm characteristically employed approximately 160 shuckers and another hundred for operating two steam dredges and a fleet of twenty-five to thirty canoes. The plant could process approximately two hundred thousand bushels of oysters annually. Once the oyster was removed from its shell it was packed in quart or gallon metal containers, which in turn were placed in iced tubs for shipment. Oysters were shipped the same day they were opened and this insured their arrival in a fresh state. The empty shells were carried out of the plant on chain conveyors and dumped on piles that reached as much as fifty feet in height. The enormous piles of oyster shells in the rear of the Darling plant were a landmark for many years. Many of the empty shells were placed in Back River for new oysters to anchor upon.

In 1900, J. S. Darling died and the business was carried on by his son, Capt. Frank Darling. Upon Captain Darling's death in 1941, his son J. S. Darling, II, became president of the firm until his death in 1951. At this time George C. Bentley assumed the management of the business until it closed in 1979. Darling and Sons was the only seafood firm that dealt exclusively with oysters.

Other mollusks played a lesser role in Hampton's seafood industry. Clams, plentiful in the waters surrounding Hampton, particularly on Hampton Bar, began to be processed by some of the seafood plants at about the same time as the oyster. Clams are usually dredged from the bottom, rather than tonged as are oysters. However, the processing of clams for shipment is similar to that of the oyster. In recent years, the clam like other local seafood has been adversely affected by pollution, and it has never achieved the fame of the oyster or Chesapeake Bay blue crab. During the 1960s and 1970s Hampton saw a rise of a new seafood—the scallop. Although the scallop is not a native of the Hampton waters, many of the boats in the scallop business brought their catches into Hampton to be sold and processed. The scallop business has declined greatly in the last few years resulting from the depletion of the scallop beds, another example of the effects on a natural seafood resource of the lack of proper conservation management.

As with mollusks, the evolution of the crab industry in Hampton was slow in coming. In the early sixteenth century crabs were abundant and remarkably large. One account relates a variety of crab twelve inches long, six inches wide which provided a meal for four men. Despite this abundance, crab meat did not become a popular food staple until the late 1800s. This was due in part to the conservative eating habits of the English in the early days of the colony and, later, to the lack of refrigeration and mechanical ice making. For those who tasted the crabmeat from the Chesapeake Bay blue crab, it became a favorite seafood, but it had to be eaten at or near its native habitat.

In 1878, James McMenamin developed a process which assured the success of the crab industry. McMenamin was born in Ireland but came to Boston in the 1840s because of the potato famine. After the Civil War, McMenamin moved to Norfolk and became a court clerk. While in Norfolk, McMenamin became fascinated by the Chesapeake Bay blue crab and set about developing a process by which its crabmeat could be preserved. From 1871 to 1878 McMenamin spent all of his spare time and money experimenting with canning crabmeat using a teakettle and a few crabs. By 1879 McMenamin had perfected his method for canning crabmeat which in essence involved adding the right amount of salt and water and allowing a proper amount of time before sealing the

Oyster tongers filled the Hampton River in the early 1900s. Courtesy of Charles H. Taylor Memorial Library

Log canoes for oyster tonging are seen from the King Street steamboat wharf looking east toward the Queen Street Bridge around the year 1916. Courtesy of the Syms-Eaton Museum

Piles of oyster shells were a common sight at the packing plant of J. S. Darling and Son. Courtesy of the Syms-Eaton Museum

The oyster shell pile at Robinson Oyster Plant on Chesapeake Avenue is adjacent to Robinson Creek in this 1927 photo. Courtesy of the Syms-Eaton Museum

steamed meat in an airtight metal container. Also in that year McMenamin established a crab plant on Hampton River to process and can crabmeat.

In June 1882, this plant burned and McMenamin built a new plant across the river especially designed for canning crabmeat. The new plant was completed in September 1882, and encompassed a large iron warehouse, packing rooms and other buildings having a total floor space in excess of twenty-thousand square feet. In 1880 McMenamin & Company was one of the largest firms in Hampton, employing 350 people in the busy season (the three summer months) with a third of the force employed for five months. In addition to crabmeat McMenamin also canned fruits and vegetables. In 1880, McMenamin estimated the value of his products at twenty-five thousand dollars. At the height of the business, sales reached five million dollars.

During the busy season, a fleet of fifty or sixty small boats would go out in Hampton Roads and the Bay and set trot lines. A trot line was a heavy line, as much as fifteen-hundred feet in length, with chunks of bait tied at intervals. At each end of the trot line was an anchor and a float. The "crabber" would spend the day pulling his boat from one end of the trot line to the other picking the crabs off. At the end of the day, motorized boats or tugs would come around and pick up fifteen or twenty of the small boats and tow them back to the crab plant. When the crabs reached the plant they were placed in large baskets that in turn were placed in large cookers and steamed. After steaming the meat was picked from the shell and

canned. McMenamin insisted on a high level of sanitation. All bowls and pans were sterilized, all the pickers were required to have clean hands and they dressed in immaculate white hats and sleeves. Steam fans kept the air of the picking and packing rooms free of insects and the rooms were washed down every day to prevent any accumulation of scrap.

Canned crabmeat from McMenamin & Company was shipped and carried all over the world. In 1909 when Robert Peary reached the North Pole, McMenamin's crabmeat accompanied him. The product also received many awards. In 1880, just two years after he started in business, McMenamin won a first place medal in the Berlin Exposition and after that awards flowed in: 1881, at the Richmond fair; 1883, the grand award of the London exposition; 1889, the blue ribbon award at the Paris World's Fair. On April 20, 1901, James McMenamin died, having, it has been said, "put the crab in 'Crabtown'." The plant continued to operate until it was sold and demolished to make way for Bluewater Yacht Yard.

Crab, like oysters, could be shipped fresh after the development of mechanical refrigeration and ice making. The first shipment of fresh crabmeat from Hampton was made by the Coston Company, founded by Samuel S. Coston. After the crabmeat was picked, it was put in one-pound metal cans which had small holes in the bottom. These cans were packed in ice and shipped. The process resulted from a conversation Coston had had with his friend, Charles Rector, founder of famous New York and Chicago restaurants, in 1902.

An oyster lugger with a load of oysters on deck enters the Hampton River. In the background is the snow-capped roof of Cedar Hall, home of Capt. Frank Darling. Courtesy of the Mariners Museum

Instead of trot lines modern crabbers use crab pots which are wire mesh cages with bait inside. Once a crab gets in the cage, it is virtually impossible for him to find his way out. A line and marker secured to the pots ensure that they can be found, pulled up, and emptied. In the spring and summer, hundreds of these markers dot Hampton Roads and the Bay. Modern methods have also extended the season. In the winter, when crabs burrow, well-equipped crab boats dredge for them.

Early explorers to Virginia found an abundance of fish but despite this, early colonists came to the new world with no nets or fishing gear to take advantage of this food source. The colonists traded trinkets to the Indians for seafood and in the summer of 1607 were able to catch sturgeon, shad, and herring in shallow water with a minimum amount of equipment and effort. In the hard winter of 1607-08 the colonists ate fish that they found frozen in icy rivers.

The Indians used a variety of means to catch fish including spears, bow-and-arrow, and fish hooks made of bone. The colonists soon realized, however, that unskilled labor and Indian fishing methods would not provide a steady supply of fish. As a result the colonists requested that fishermen and netmakers be sent over.

When the colonists arrived in 1607, they found an abundance of sturgeon in the lower Chesapeake Bay and its tributaries. The sturgeon was the largest fish to enter American fresh waters to lay its eggs. The eggs, or caviar, were already a delicacy to the English who imported their caviar from the Baltic countries.

Modern methods of harvesting oysters include mechanical tonging, although hand tonging is still widely used. Courtesy of Syms-Eaton Museum

McMenamin's Crab Meat—Packed in three sizes: 4, 8 and 16 oz. cans.

4-ounce can will make Three Deviled Crabs.
8-ounce can will make Six Deviled Crabs.
16-ounce can will make Twelve Deviled Crabs.

McMenamin's canned crabmeat was widely advertised. Courtesy of Marguerite S. McMenamin

In 1907 these crab pickers worked at the S.S. Coston Plant. Courtesy of Syms-Eaton Museum

McMenamin's Crab Shells which we furnish with our Crab Meat. The shells are used in preparing Deviled Crabs, and other attractive dishes, as shown on the following pages. They can be procured from your grocer.

One carton, containing 3 Shells, accompanies our 4-ounce can.
One carton, containing 6 Shells, accompanies our 8-ounce can.

With such an abundance of sturgeon the colonists felt they stumbled upon a profitable industry.

Capt. Christopher Newport returned to England from Jamestown in the summer of 1607 carrying a small amount of picked sturgeon with him. Although this shipment was ill-cured and found little favor, the commercial potentialities of the situation were obvious. The fact that the English gentry held sturgeon products in such high esteem and the natural desire of merchants to be free from Baltic domination of the sturgeon-products market encouraged the Virginia Company to dispatch Capt. Samuel Argall to Virginia in 1609 with instructions for the colonists to fish for sturgeon.

In the summer of 1609 the colonists sent a cargo of pickled sturgeon and caviar. Later the same year and the next, additional cargoes of sturgeon and caviar were shipped in the *Blessing* and the *Hercules*. However, poor packing and curing caused the shipments to arrive in poor condition. Additional instructions were sent to Virginia for the preparation of sturgeon products, but it was not until 1620 that there is a record of more shipments of sturgeon, which apparently arrived in good condition. The early Virginia colonists lacked knowledge of curing and pickling the fish, the weather was hot and they had improper salt

Crabbers of McMenamin and Company tend trot lines around the year 1900. Courtesy of Marguerite S. McMenamin

Note the bowsprit and decorative carving beneath it on this fishing boat underway in the Hampton River. Courtesy of Syms-Eaton Museum

for the curing process. Tobacco growing also soon occupied the full attention of most Virginians and the ill-fated commercial fisheries, including that of sturgeon, were virtually forgotten until the middle of the eighteenth century.

The colonists realized that they urgently needed a dependable supply of food fish, not as seasonal or erratic as the river fisheries that were producing herring and shad. This realization led them to attempt to establish a cod-fishing fleet to fish during the seasons when codfish were found off the coast of Virginia. However, the lack of seaworthy fishing vessels and skilled fishermen doomed this effort to failure and colonists began to import salt codfish as a main food staple.

With improved fishing methods and increased interest in seafood, fishing became a commercial enterprise. By the end of the eighteenth century, salt herring was being exported abroad. Large cargoes of Virginia salt herring were shipped from Hampton to the West Indies, especially Jamaica.

In the 1750s shipments of sturgeon to England began again and continued in volume until the Revolutionary War. As late as the early 1900s four or five large sturgeons (five hundred pounds or larger) were caught in the Chesapeake Bay off of Buckroe-Grandview-Back River. But overfishing took its toll. The last large sturgeon was caught in the Bay off Hampton in the mid 1960s. The story of the sturgeon in the Chesapeake Bay and its tributaries pointedly shows

the need for appropriate conservation of our natural resources.

As with other facets of the seafood industry, really large-scale growth of fishing and related activity is tied to post-Civil War recovery. In 1879, J. S. Darling and a partner, William H. Smithers, erected a menhaden fish oil factory at Factory Point, the northeastern most tip of the city at the mouth of Back River. They had established a similar plant earlier on the Eastern Shore of Virginia, but had lost it (and a good deal of money) to a storm in October 1878. The new plant consisted of a factory building and several long, frame buildings for drying, covering approximately six acres. Sailing schooners were used to catch the menhaden (also called "bunker fish") and bring them into the factory for processing, which consisted of cooking the fish in large kettles and extracting the oil. After cooking, the remaining matter was dried on wooden racks. Oil that drained from the drying fish was collected in troughs built around the perimeter of the drying racks. The oil collected was packaged in barrels and sold to paint and medicinal compound manufacturers. The factory could produce between nine hundred and sixteen hundred barrels of oil per season. The refuse was bagged and shipped by schooner up the bay to be sold to farmers as fertilizer. The factory began operations in late spring and ceased operating at the end of summer. It employed approximately two hundred people, with seventy actually operating the plant and the remaining personnel

*This is a view of a typical fish pound.
Courtesy of Syms-Eaton Museum*

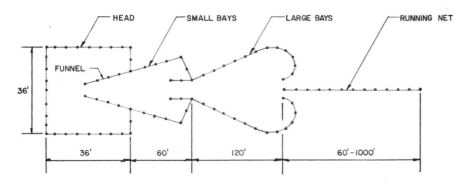

*Arrows show the direction fish swim
in a pound net. Drawing by Charles F.
Elliott*

*This fish camp of the early 1900s is
located along the shore of Hampton
Roads at what is now Merrimac
Shores. Note the pound boats on the
beach. Larger camps were located at
Buckroe Beach and Grand View.
Courtesy of The Mariners Museum*

*This photo shows a pound boat off
Buckroe Beach. Courtesy of Charles F.
Elliott*

137

operating the boats. When the plant was closed, the employees worked at oystering. The factory remained in operation until it was washed away in the devastating 1933 hurricane.

Pound net fishing as practiced in the area evolved from a combination of the weirs used by the Indians, and the seines, casting nets, and setting nets used by the early colonists. The pound net is a large, heavy net held in place by long wooden poles driven into the sea bottom which functions as a stationary fish trap or "pound." The technique was used extensively in Hampton Roads and the Chesapeake Bay from the 1800s up until the 1950s. In 1940, there were ap-

proximately 130 pound nets in the bay between Old Point and Back River, with an average cost per pound of five hundred dollars. Today, the same area of the bay has only 3 pound nets, since fish are not now as abundant as they once were and the fact that a pound net today may run as much as five thousand dollars to install. A pound net commonly known as the "Lane," installed at the end of Beach Road, had been in place for over 130 years by the mid 1980s. Its name originated from the fact that the fishermen used the road or "lane" as a guide to drive the poles each year.

Many of the fishermen that fished pound nets lived in fish camps along the shore. The fish camps

were nothing more than small tin-roof shanties where the fishermen lived, ate and stored equipment. On the weekends, the fishermen would go home. At one time there were almost one hundred fish camps between Buckroe and Back River.

To fish the pound nets from the shores of the Chesapeake Bay required a unique craft, the pound boat. It was "designed" by local watermen for use in local waters and built by local boatbuilders. The pound boat was a scow-type fishing boat designed to be launched and retrieved through the surf. The first pound boats were approximately twenty feet long, but they eventually grew to an average length of thirty-four feet with a six-foot beam and a three-foot depth. Most of the boats were built of yellow pine planking with oak frames, and were extremely seaworthy. They were constructed of heavy timbers which allowed them to be pulled up through the surf with five to seven tons of fish in them.

Shipbuilding and Boatbuilding

The first shipbuilding in the new world by the English took place as soon as the colonists landed at Cape Henry in 1607. More precisely, the newcomers assembled the sections of a shallop that had been brought over from England to explore shallower waters. The shallop was a small (thirty feet or less) heavily constructed, and undecked boat carrying a main and staysails, usually singlemasted.

Obviously, though, the first marine craft constructed in what became Hampton was Indian. As the colonists sailed from Cape Henry to Kecoughtan, they saw a dugout canoe of approximately forty-five feet in length. Capt. John Smith described the larger canoes as being forty-five inches deep, forty to fifty feet in length, and capable of carrying forty men. However, most of the dugout canoes were smaller, carrying ten, twenty, or thirty men. All of the canoes were propelled by paddles in lieu of oars. Dugout canoes were one of the foremost means of transportation during the early days of the colony as well, primarily because they drew very little water and thus could traverse the shallow waters. From the dugout canoe the colonists evolved such various craft as the piragua, Rose's tobacco boat and the Chesapeake Bay canoe and bugeye.

In 1612, Samuel Argalls came to Virginia and established a shipyard at Point Comfort to repair ships and boats that had fallen into disrepair. In 1613, he built a frigate at the yard. In 1702, large ships were careened at Old Point Comfort as they came to the colony to burn and bream the bottom for the teredo (shipworms) or to apply caulking or coating.

A major advantage the Chesapeake Bay offered was ready access to fresh water anchorage to protect ocean-going ships from barnacles and the teredo worms that eat unprotected bottom planks. The worms were a problem only from June until the first great rains after the middle of July, when they disappeared until the next summer. Four methods protected vessels from the worms. The simplest procedure was to move the vessel to fresh water for the period the worms were active. Another method was to coat the bottom of the vessel with pitch, tar, lime, or tallow. A third method was to anchor the vessel where the tidal current was strong and would not allow the worms to fasten onto the planking. The fourth method was heaving down or careening the vessel as soon as the "worm season" was over and burning and breaming the bottom of the vessel before the worms had a chance to bury themselves into the planking.

A shipbuilding industry was inevitable in Hampton. In this coastal city, water was the best means of transportation. Rivers and creeks and the Chesapeake Bay itself to be crossed. Large ships anchored in the rivers had to be lightened, and fishing and crabbing and oystering were waiting to be done. Obviously, a large and varied number of vessels was needed.

Colonial shipyards were simple in nature, requiring only a plot of ground on the bank of a river, creek or stream, a pier with sufficient water to float the vessel, a small building or shed in which to store tools and materials and a suitable supply of timber. There was an excellent supply of timber available in the Hampton Roads area, consisting of heart pine, cypress, white oak and live oak.

By the mid 1700s Hampton had become a commercial center. The maritime trade stimulated shipbuilding, which in turn fostered ancillary industries such as lumber, hemp, iron, cordage, sailcloth and naval stores. In April, 1767, John Hatley Norton came to the Virginia colony as his father's agent and resided in Yorktown. He wrote home that his cousins, the Walker Brothers, had a shipyard located at Hampton and were building ships of white oak for the West Indies trade.

Another pre-Revolutionary War shipyard in Hampton was located where Settlers Landing Road met the Booker T. Washington Bridge two hundred years later. Just prior to the Revolution it was owned by William Williams who sold it and moved to Harris Creek. Later the shipyard was owned by James and Samuel Barron and became known as "the shipyard on the South Quay." This yard produced the *Gloucester*, later converted to a prison ship, and the *Liberty* which was involved in more than twenty battles and was the largest ship built, mounting thirty-two guns. This shipyard also became headquarters for the Virginia Navy, controlled by a board of naval commissioners of whom Col. Thomas Whiting of Hampton was president. After the Revolutionary War, George Hope who had worked at the shipyard bought it from the Barron brothers. In colonial times, a cove extended from the Hampton River almost to Queen Street and sheltered two small boat yards: one nearest Queen Street owned by Jimmy Betts and the other purchased by Hope and added to his larger shipyard. Sometime prior to the Civil War, a shipyard and marine railway stood on the east bank of the Hampton River near where the former Dixie Hospital

Frigates were careened for cleaning during the Colonial Period. Courtesy of the Mariners Museum

This is the scene at a Colonial shipyard. Courtesy of the Syms-Eaton Museum

A new vessel is about to be launched at Darling Marine Railway. The vessel on the railway to the left is ready for repairs and painting. Courtesy of the Syms-Eaton Museum

was built.

Some time in the mid to latter 1800s a boat yard was established on Hampton River just to the west of the future Booker T. Washington Bridge. In 1872 it was taken over by William Hall from J. H. Gosline. Hall was born in 1832 in New York City and became a ship's carpenter and spent many years at sea in the clipper ships. Upon taking over the yard, he made many improvements among which was the addition in 1904 of an electrically operated railway. An existing railway of smaller capacity was also electrified. The yard offered general shipwrighting, caulking and sparmaking and supplied all types of marine paints, cordage hardware, and general ship chandlery.

In 1914, the boat yard and marine railway was taken over by Darling and Sons to build and service craft used in their oyster business and became known as the Darling Marine Railway. As the seafood industry developed in Hampton, the actual construction of new vessels virtually stopped and the yards and marine railways were increasingly used for repair and maintenance of the boats used in the seafood trade. From 1952 to 1980, the railway was managed by George C. Bentley and provided service to workboats, barges, tugs, yachts, and various military craft. In 1980, the railway was purchased by the city of Hampton and leased to Fass Brothers Seafood to service their vessels. Later, it became Hampton Marine Railway and worked on larger vessels. How-

ever, the size of vessels was restricted by the twelve-foot channel and in March of 1985, the railway was closed and the city of Hampton made plans to use the site for a proposed downtown hotel. With its closing, the last marine railway on the Hampton River disappeared.

In addition to the shipyards and marine railways on the Hampton River, there were small shipyards located on Harris Creek, Back River, and Wallace Creek. These yards built primarily schooners used in the local seafood industry and in the coastal trade. The vessels varied in size from 40 to 125 feet in length, had one to three masts and had a capacity of 40 to 497 tons.

The largest shipyard ever to operate in Hampton was the Newcomb Lifeboat Company which came into existence during World War I and was located on the south side of Sunset Creek where Hastings-Radist (Teledyne Corporation) later located. The company started under the auspices of the United States Shipping Board Emergency Fleet Corporation to provide submarine chasers and merchant vessels for the Navy. The firm had contracts for ten wooden sub-chasers, 65 feet in length. Also, the firm received a contract to build four wooden-hull 350-foot ships without engines. Later, two of the hulls were cancelled. The two hulls that were built and launched, the *Kahoka* and the *Luray*, were never completed or documented.

Two ships are being built at Sunset Creek by the Newcomb Lifeboat Company. At left on the stocks is the Luray and on the right is the Kahoka. Behind and to the left of Luray is Cedar Hall, home of the Darling family. Behind the Kahoka is the clock tower at Hampton University. Courtesy of the Mariners Museum

In this aerial view, the Newcomb Lifeboat Company is shown around the year 1918. In the background on the north side of Sunset Creek is Park Place. Courtesy of the Mariners Museum

The Kahoka is launched at the Newcomb Lifeboat Company. In the background to the right of the ship is a dredge that was used to deepen Sunset Creek at the launch site to a depth of 18 feet. Courtesy of the Mariners Museum

This aerial view of the Newcomb Lifeboat Company shows the Kahoka after launching, with the Luray still in the stocks. In the left foreground are two homes at Park Place and in the background is Ivy Home Road. Courtesy of the Mariners Museum

The Port of Hampton

As noted in the introduction, a major reason for establishing a colony in Virginia was to secure a source of supplies and resources that could be shipped back to England. In the early days of the Virginia colony, Hampton was the port through which the goods and supplies were shipped back to England as well as the port receiving goods and supplies sent to the new colony. In 1633, a public warehouse and inspection point for tobacco was established on Hampton River. In April, 1691, Hampton was established as an official port and as the customs port of the lower James River District. The public wharf was probably located where the King Street wharf was later erected. Near the wharf were public and private warehouses for storage of tobacco and other goods and products destined for overseas, as well as storage for goods and supplies coming into the colony. Ships entering the harbor from abroad and headed up the James River dropped off cargo at Hampton destined for James River plantations.

Tobacco was by far the largest export of Hampton, followed by grain (corn and wheat). Other commodities included were hemp, flax, cotton, foodstuffs (pork, ham, beef, beans, peas and, later, fish), furs and skins, lumber, and naval stores. Imports consisted of tools, hardware, building materials, cloth, fabrics, clothes, furniture, linen, china, silver, and pewter from England. From the northern colonies imports consisted of codfish, mackerel, cheese, malt, furniture, and rum. Imported from the West Indies were rum sugar, salt, molasses, ginger, cocoa, citrus fruit, and wine.

By the beginning of the eighteenth century, Hampton had become a busy seaport and by mid-century, it had become a commercial center. King Street had an international air about it with sailors from many parts of the world visiting the wharf. Ships anchored in the Hampton River came from other colonial ports such as Boston, New York, Philadelphia and Norfolk; from the British ports of Bristol, Liverpool, London and Glasgow; from the British island colonies of Bermuda, Barbados, Jamaica, Antigua, and St. Kitts; and the Madeiras. By the mid-1700s the total tonnage of vessels arriving in the port of Hampton was only slightly less than that in New York. Although 279 ships called in New York in 1754, compared to 169 in Hampton in 1752, the Hampton tonnage was 10,557 compared to 11,525 for New York. However, this is

somewhat misleading since the port of Hampton was not precisely the same as the town of Hampton. The port of Hampton then included the south side of Hampton Roads as well. In 1680 a new commercial center for trade had begun to develop on the north bank of the Elizabeth River, known as Norfolk. By 1738 Norfolk had grown large enough to petition council the appointment of a deputy collector of customs to reside in the town, thus saving the Norfolk people from having to make frequent trips across Hampton Roads to Hampton for the necessary trade documents. Norfolk soon had the largest share of the trade in the lower bay, but it had not yet become an independent port and was still considered part of the port of Hampton.

After the Revolutionary War, Hampton declined as a commercial center. There were several reasons for this. First, the custom house was removed from Hampton and located in Norfolk; second, trade with the West Indies declined; and, third, large ships were unable to enter the Hampton River because of shallow water. Contributing to the latter, the river was silting which inhibited further port development. From 1800 on, Norfolk became the commercial center of the lower bay.

The King Street Wharf is shown around the year 1853. Courtesy of Charles H. Taylor Memorial Library

King Street Wharf was a busy place in the mid 1900s. In the background is the Blackiston House, where the Georgetown Condominiums were located in 1985. Courtesy of the Mariners Museum

The Old Dominion Line's side-paddle passenger steamer Luray *is docked at the Old Dominion pier in Hampton River. Courtesy of the Mariners Museum*

Salt

When the English arrived in Virginia in April of 1607, they found food supplies to be bountiful. However, they could catch or trap only that which could be eaten in a given day due to the lack of salt available for preserving. The Indians had no salt or seasoning except the salt ash from hickory and some other woods. As time went on the colonists became more established, saltmakers were sent over from England to build saltworks.

Mr. William Capps, one of the first two burgesses to represent Kecoughtan when the General Assembly of the Colony of Virginia convened in the church of Jamestown on July 30, 1619, was given the privilege of erecting a saltworks in 1627. Early saltworks were located near the ocean or the bay. Salt was obtained by two methods. The simplest was solar-evaporative process. A faster method for producing salt involved placing the seawater or brine in sixteen-foot square shallow copper or iron containers called salt pans, with fire for heat.

In 1776 the Virginia General Assembly appointed John Cary to build and operate a saltworks in Elizabeth City County. He located his saltworks between Fox Hill and Buckroe in an area known today as the Salt Ponds. The area is very marshy and has a canal running through it. This saltworks was of such importance during the Revolutionary War that it was placed under guard by the local militia. Mr. Cary, as manager of the salt works, received two shillings a bushel for all the salt produced. The salt was sold at a rate of fifty shillings per fifty pounds, and each family member was rationed one peck of salt.

It is interesting to note the effects politics had upon local salt production and hence the development of the local fish industry. Although salt was locally produced, the efforts were not wholly satisfactory due to the low salinity of the local waters. The salt that was produced was therefore not suitable for curing many foodstuffs, notably fish. Liverpool salt was considered too weak for curing fish and locally produced salt was deemed of "too corroding a nature." Lisbon salt was considered the ideal salt for curing fish. As a result, the Virginia colonists imported salt directly from England, the West Indies (Turks Island and Tortuga—known as the Sallitudes), or indirectly from southern Europe (Spain, Portugal and Isle of May in the Cape Verdes Islands) by way of England or the northern colonies at double the transportation cost.

This was done intentionally. Under a provision of the navigation laws, New England and the middle colonies were allowed to import salt directly from southern Europe, but the southern colonies were forbidden to do so. This seeming inequity resulted from the Crown's grand plan to encourage fishing in the northern colonies, Newfoundland, Nova Scotia, and Quebec, and to discourage it in the southern colonies where tobacco, rice and sugar were marketable staples. The plan was not wholly successful in this region, as this chapter has already noted.

Agriculture

The first explorers to the Virginia coast realized that the land offered a number of natural resources. As early as 1529 it was noted that the natives lived on maize, fish, game, various fruits, melons, nuts, berries and peas. However, the two plans that had the most impact on the early colonists were tobacco and maize or Indian corn.

When the colonists landed in Kecoughtan in 1607 they found that the Indians used tobacco for ceremonial occasions rather than to satisfy a habit or for personal gratification. The Indians burned tobacco as an incense and used it as a sacrifice to the sun to pray for fair weather on a journey, or threw it into a stream or river which they were going to cross to beseech the spirit dwelling therein to grant them a safe passage. The peace pipe, filled with tobacco, was of great importance in their councils during all negotiations. At first tobacco was not well received by the Englishmen as it was considered a stinking, nauseous unpalatable weed harmful to health. However, it shortly became the principal exported crop of the Virginia colony and, in fact, was the currency or medium of exchange during the infancy of the Colony.

The individual associated with the success of tobacco as an exportable crop was John Rolfe, a confirmed smoker. In 1612 Rolfe found that tobacco would grow well in Virginia and could be sold in England at a good profit. In fact tobacco became extremely popular in England and an insatiable demand for it sprang up overnight. By 1619, tobacco was virtually the only crop exported and was the main crop of the Virginia colony during the seventeenth century. Many fertile acres of Elizabeth City County were devoted to tobacco planting.

Rolfe's early experiments with tobacco resulted in the abandonment of the native tobacco plant and the importation of South American seed. From this importation of seed, two distinct varieties of tobacco emanated: oronoco, strong in flavor, with a coarser, bulkier, and sharper leaf, grown around the Bay and the back country on all the rivers; and sweetscented tobacco with finer fibres, a rounder leaf, and, as the name suggests, a mild taste. It was predominantly grown on the banks of the Hampton, James, York, Rappahannock and Potomac rivers. Elizabeth City County was known as one of Virginia's "sweetscented" counties. The sweetscented tobacco, particularly that grown in Elizabeth City County and on the peninsula between the James and York Rivers, was considered the best tobacco available anywhere by the English but the stronger oronoco tobacco was in great demand on the Continent, particularly by smokers in nothern and eastern Europe. Thus, although the English considered the oronoco tobacco inferior, it had a wider market and thus more profitable to the planters than the sweetscented tobacco.

From 1622 until the Revolutionary War, tobacco dominated the Virginia economy as well as that of Maryland. In 1622 England imported sixty thousand pounds of tobacco, in 1628, five hundred thousand pounds and 1.5 million pounds by the end of 1639. By the end of the seventeenth century, tobacco production exceeded 20 million pounds in Virginia and Maryland and in 1775 it exceeded 100 million.

The reasons tobacco became the dominant crop of colonial Virginia are many. First, and foremost, was the fact that the Chesapeake Bay and its tributaries allowed ocean-going ships ready access to the plantations. Some of the tributaries were navigable for approximately a hundred miles. In turn, the tributaries had branches that were navigable for as much as fifty miles. Thus, this natural waterway system allowed the rapid and continued expansion of tobacco production. One may fully appreciate the waterway system when one realizes that the tobacco, prior to shipping, was packed into casks and that a cask of sweetscented tobacco weighed between 950 and 1,400 pounds while a cask of oronoco tobacco weighed between 750 and 1,150 pounds. For the weight considered, water transportation was easier, cheaper, and less damaging to the tobacco than overland transportation. Tobacco required less acreage than grain to grow, and thus less clearing of forest. Tobacco had a relatively small bulk-to-weight and price-to-weight ratio than grain.

From the time tobacco was first grown as a crop until approximately 1624, planters received "luxury prices" for their production and profits that would never be achieved again. From 1624 on, the price of tobacco fluctuated violently, but the dominant trend was down. But because of cheaper credit, lower freight rates, falling prices of manufactured goods, and a sharp increase in the rate of production, the cost of growing tobacco declined significantly. This permitted the planters and merchants to sell the tobacco at lower prices which in turn expanded the market for the staple. This was an extremely important step, because if the costs of producing and marketing the tobacco had not declined, Virginia tobacco would have remained a high-priced luxury item with a limited market. Without a growing market for the staple, the rapid growth of population and hence settlement that occurred in Virginia between the 1620s and the 1660s would not have taken place. Also, the port of Hampton would not have reached the importance that it achieved.

When the colonists first arrived at Kecoughtan

they found that maize or Indian corn was the chief staple of the Indians' diet. The importance of corn in the lives of the Indians can be seen by the fact they reckoned time by dividing the year into five seasons: the budding of corn, the earing of corn, the highest sun, the corn-gathering, and the call of the goose.

Corn also became very important to the colonists in the early days as they learned to mill it to make a bread of corn meal, called pone. Milling was one of the first, if not the first, industry of Elizabeth City County. In 1635 William Claiborne erected a windmill on his land on the west side of Hampton River on what today is known as Blackbeard Point. In the same year, another windmill was constructed on the east side of the river at the mouth of Mill Creek (then called Point Comfort). At that time, the maximum fee that could be charged for the milling operations was one-sixth of the grain. By 1637, scales were required to weigh the grain.

In the late 1600s a grist and saw mill was built at the head of Back River. This mill was distinguished from the other mills of Elizabeth City County by the fact that it was water-powered. A Frenchman, Bertand Servant, who may have been a Huguenot refugee and who came to Virginia in the early 1660s, sponsored this ambitious enterprise. In 1689, Servant brought Isaac Molyn, who may have been French also, a Negro woman named Toma, and three workmen to Elizabeth City County from New England to build the mill and dam. It appears that the mill's design was a success, for by 1692 Molyn and Toma were the only ones required for operating it. With the success of this mill, other water-powered mills soon followed in the Back River area.

Grain continued to be a locally grown commodity up to the turn of the century. Prior to the Revolutionary War considerable quantities of wheat, corn, and flour were exported, particularly to the West Indies. After the Civil War, grain was still a major crop as evidenced by the fact that there were five grist mills in Hampton in 1860. Of these mills three were steam, one was tidal, and one was a windmill. In the latter part of the 1860s, J. S. Darling bought or erected a steam driven grist mill on South King Street and by 1870 was grinding almost as much grain as all of the other mills combined. In 1880, another mill was established in Hampton with new equipment but it did not match the production of Darling's mill. Grain not

ground locally was usually shipped in pungies to Richmond and Baltimore.

Grain and tobacco were not the only cash crops. Ever since 1607, the colonists realized that many crops would grow well in Elizabeth City County, and in fact the county was a major truck farming area of the state up until World War II. This success was due largely to the light loam soil of the area, mild climate and ready access to northern markets. The big money crop at that time was sweet potatoes which, when harvested, were usually sold to captains or owners of schooners and other vessels who transported them in bulk, anywhere from six hundred to fifteen hundred bushels. Towards the end of the nineteenth century and the early twentieth century Elizabeth City County reached its zenith as a truck farming area. The principal crops were corn, various garden vegetables, melons, strawberries and various nuts. Peas, Irish potatoes, and strawberries were taken to Old Point Comfort and shipped by boat to Baltimore. The growing of fruits in the area also became popular and there were large orchards of peaches, plums, pears and apples. Peach growing, in particular, became very profitable. Although some peaches were shipped to northern markets, the majority of the fruit was consumed locally.

With the advent of World War II and the great influx of people into the area, much of the land that had been used for agricultural purposes was turned into residential areas. At the conclusion of the war, new industry and the military presence in the area continued to draw people. Finally Elizabeth City County and the city of Hampton consolidated in 1952 resulting in higher property taxes. These factors made it economically unfeasible to use land for agriculture and as a result agriculture dwindled to almost nothing.

Other agricultural enterprises had less impact on the area but are interesting, nonetheless. In 1620 a settlement was established in Elizabeth City County at Buckroe for the purpose of growing mulberry trees and hence to raise silkworms. This endeavor was under the direction of an Englishman, John Bonnell, who remained in England. However, a group of Frenchmen from the Langued'oc region of France came to Buckroe with Bonnell's instructions for establishing a silk industry in Virginia. In 1623 the settlement at Buckroe numbered thirty persons among whom were Anthony Bonnell, James Bonnell, Peter

Arundel, David Poole and Elias LaGuard. However, the envisioned silk industry did not thrive and was abandoned.

Wine production was also short lived. When the colonists arrived at Kecoughtan in 1607, they noted the abundance of grapevines in the area. Because of the number of vines, the colonists hoped to establish a wine industry in Elizabeth City County, but, like the silk industry, it was unsuccessful.

Another kind of harvest also provided an industry for the settlers. When the colonists landed at Kecoughtan, they found an abundance of game including squirrel, deer, fox, rabbit, racoon, beaver, otter, muskrat, mink, ducks, geese, swans, bear, pheasant, partridge, turkey, opossum, pigeons, and larks. With such a quantity of game readily available, it was only a matter of time before a fur industry was established. William Claiborne of Elizabeth City County realized this, and during the 1630s and 1640s had a virtual monopoly on the fur trade of the Chesapeake Bay. His trappers ventured up the bay as far north as Kent Island which is opposite the town of Annapolis today and established a trading post in 1631. Claiborne refused to accept the authority of Leonard Calvert, the governor of Maryland, and there were constant conflicts and in 1644 war broke out. It was from Elizabeth City County that Claiborne's forces embarked for Maryland. The overall result of the dispute was that Claiborne, with help from some of the Puritan settlers in Maryland, drove Calvert out and seized control of the colony. However, in 1657, Oliver Cromwell ordered the restoration of the Calvert government and Virginia lost authority over Kent Island and some other territory.

Public Transportation

Ease of transporting goods into and out of Hampton played a large role in the city's development, but transporting people over land and water became increasingly important, too, and an industry in itself. In 1888, James S. Darling, Sr., envisioned an electric railway or trolley car line from Hampton to Old Point. On February 24, 1888, he organized the Hampton and Old Point Railway Company with himself as president and major stockholder. The Schmelz brothers, prominent local bankers, also participated in the organiza-tion. In 1889 the trolley line began operation, with four and a half miles of track which included a branch line leading into the Soldiers Home.

The trolley line was an immediate success, and in 1890 it was extended to Newport News where Collis P. Huntington had opened his shipyard the year before. Houses, lots, and rents had become very expensive in Newport News and people found that they could live more cheaply in Hampton, even after paying the trolley car fare. Thus, an overnight demand for housing in Hampton materialized and the West End of Hampton began to develop around the trolley line.

On February 28, 1890, the Newport News Street Railway Company was incorporated with Col. C. M. Braxton as president. At first this line had horse-drawn cars, but in 1892 Braxton electrified his line. On December 24, 1892, the company extended its service to Hampton. The main trolley line that connected the cities of Hampton and Newport News was flanked by a road that was appropriately named Electric Avenue. Many years later when trolley car service was discontinued and the tracks taken up, a multi-lane concrete highway was built in their place and on October 21, 1953, the name of the road became Victoria Boulevard.

In 1894 the Buckroe, Phoebus, and Hampton Railway Company was formed and trolley cars were available to take people from Hampton to the newly organized beach resort. In 1896 the Hampton and Old Point Railway Company and the Newport News Street Railway Company merged to form the Newport News, Hampton and Old Point Railway Company with Capt. Frank W. Darling, son of J. S. Darling, Sr., as president. Soon after the merger, the company acquired the Buckroe, Phoebus, and Hampton Railway Company and replaced its tracks with sixty-five pound steel rails. This allowed excursion trains operated by the Chesapeake and Ohio Railroad and pulled by steam locomotives to run from Richmond to Buckroe during the summer months. The merger of the three formerly independent companies allowed the addition of more modern equipment and freight service. The freight service especially was of inestimable value as it allowed the goods and produce of Hampton and the surrounding Elizabeth City County to be transported to the wharf at Old Point for shipment up the bay or to northern ports.

In March 1898, the Newport News, Hampton and Old Point Railway Company was redesignated the

Newport News and Old Point Railway and Electric Company. By 1902 it had some forty miles of track and sixty street cars. About this time, a rival company, the Peninsula Railway Company was formed. In May 1900, these two firms merged with the Chesapeake and Hampton Roads Railway and the Peninsula Light and Power Company to form the Citizens Railway, Light and Power Company.

At the turn of the century, still another trolley car company emerged. This was the Newport News-Hampton Roads Railway and Electric Company under the presidency of W. J. Nelms. In 1905 this firm was known as the Hampton Roads Traction Company. Its line ran through the East End of Newport News and crossed Salter's Creek, from whence it ran the full length of Chesapeake Avenue (the Boulevard) and turned north at LaSalle Avenue and so into Hampton.

As each trolley company emerged, it had to have its own source of power or generating facility. All operated steam power plants to run turbine-generators to produce electricity for the trolley lines. Three powerhouses were in Hampton; one was located on the north side of Sunset Creek where Hunt Oil Company later located; another on the south side of Sunset Creek near where Hastings Instrument Company Division of Teledyne Corporation built and the third was located near the C & O Railway station at the end of Washington Street. All the powerhouses used coal brought in on barges. The facility located on the north side of Sunset Creek was the largest and provided the electrical power for the Newport News and Old Point Railway.

A great rivalry existed between the Newport News and Old Point Railway and Electric Company, (Citizens Railway, Light and Power Co.) and the Hampton Roads Traction Company and the rivalry, it is said, extended through the personnel of each company to the point where car tenders and conductors hardly spoke to each other. Finally, rate wars and cut-throat competition had resulted in poor service to the public and the threat of revocation of the two companies' franchises. As a result, the Newport News and Hampton Railway Gas and Electric Company was formed from the merger of the two rivals on January 13, 1914. The new trolley car company obtained modern equipment. The new cars had double trucks and four-motor driven air-brakes, manufactured by the pioneer firm of J. B. Brill Company of Philadelphia. Other cars were ordered from Perley and Thomas of High Point, North Carolina. The cars could achieve a speed of thirty-eight miles per hour on the open main line right-of-way.

The president of the consolidated new company, John N. Shanahan, had his own private streetcar furnished with plush carpets, overstuffed wicker chairs, and brass spitoons, and the windows were

This streetcar is parked at the car barn.
Courtesy of the Charles H. Taylor
Memorial Library

Officers of the Newport News and Hampton Railway, Gas and Electric Company in 1916 are, standing, left to right, A. E. Steirly, superintendent of the power plant; Frank Lawton, superintendent of the gas works; Richard Booker, treasurer; Thornton Jones, mayor of Hampton, in charge of freight; W. F. Crosten, superintendent of the gas department; William Stewart, secretary to the president; Fred Sanford, superintendent of ice, coal, and wood; George Caskey, auditor; and Chester D. Porter, general manager. Seated, from left to right are: B. J. Meggison, superintendent of transportation; John Shanahan, president; and E. F. Peck, executive vice president. Courtesy of Charles H. Taylor Memorial Library

embellished with shades and curtains. This car was kept highly polished at all times, and was available for hire to meet local or visiting luminaries either at the steamboat dock at Old Point or at the Chesapeake and Ohio Railway Station. The new company also used open cars and trailers. These were popular in the summer and in the event of rain, canvas sides were rolled down. These cars were closed in and rebuilt into all-season, center-door cars in about 1920. The last new streetcars that operated on the Peninsula were purchased just after World War I. At the height of operations, there were approximately sixty streetcars in service.

With the introduction of the gasoline engine the heyday of the streetcar was passing. On May 2, 1923, the Citizens Rapid Transit Corporation formed to provide bus service within Newport News. The initial equipment consisted of three buses. Soon buses became a popular means of transportation. On November 10, 1924, Virginia Public Service Company purchased the Citizens Rapid Transit Corporation and on December 1, 1926, the Virginia Public Service Company and the Newport News and Hampton Railway, Gas and Electric Company merged.

The worst blow to the streetcar came from the hurricane of August 23, 1933 which washed out and completely destroyed all the tracks along Chesapeake Avenue (the Boulevard). The line was never rebuilt

and buses were substituted for the streetcars. This trend continued with buses replacing streetcars in both cities. In Hampton, along with the Boulevard route, buses took over the Phoebus to Old Point run, and by the late 1930s, buses had so replaced the streetcars, that only the "mainline" from Phoebus to Newport News remained. The life of the streetcar on the Peninsula, however, was extended with the outbreak of World War II. The need for transportation of any kind during the war allowed the trolleys to keep running and the forced retirement was thus delayed until the end of the war.

In May 1944, the Virginia Public Service Company was merged with the Virginia Electric and Power Company (VEPCO) and under the terms of the merger VEPCO was required to divest itself of all its transportation facilities. A local corporation formed, Citizens Rapid Transit Company, and on April 1, 1945, acquired VEPCO's street railway franchise and facilities on the Peninsula, and also those of its bus-operating subsidiary, the C.R.T. Corporation. Soon afterwards, the C.R.T. Company obtained formal approval from the local cities and the State Corporation Commission to abandon streetcar service on the lower Peninsula. The final blow came on January 13, 1946, when a streetcar derailed in front of the Dixie Hospital on East Queen Street because of a soft spot in the roadbed. The next day, the C.R.T. board of

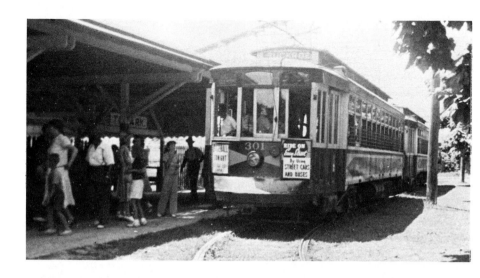

A streetcar stops at Buckroe Beach Amusement Park. Courtesy of Charles H. Taylor Memorial Library

directors held an emergency meeting and decided to cease streetcar operations immediately. At the end of operations there were approximately two dozen trolleys and upon termination of operations, the cars were dismantled in the company's shops and the wheels and electric motors were disconnected from the cars and sold separately. Some were even sold to companies in South America. The cars were sold separately and used for diners, residences, shops and chicken coops. By 1950, all of the track had been taken up.

Although Hampton and Elizabeth City County were blessed with good water transportation facilities, local citizens also desired long-distance rail facilities. In 1871, a team of investigators came to the Peninsula to look at Newport News as a possible site for the eastern terminus of the Chesapeake and Ohio Railroad. Their report was favorable, but because of the depression of 1873, the railroad delayed construction. Later, when it looked as though the line would be built, the railroad seemed to favor a site at Yorktown which would mean building a shorter line than the one to Newport News. However, land speculators who bought the Yorktown acreage drove up the price, and the line to Yorktown was discarded.

In February 1880, a group of Peninsula citizens met at the Barnes Hotel in Hampton and formed the Newport News Land Company for the purpose of securing the terminus of the Chesapeake and Ohio Railroad at Newport News. A committee from the land company commenced negotiations with the president of the railroad, Collis P. Huntington, and its directors. In March 1880 the Virginia Legislature approved a plan allowing the Chesapeake and Ohio Railroad to construct a line from Richmond to the Newport News waterfront, and shortly thereafter, the board of directors of the railroad authorized construction. Work began immediately and on May 1, 1882, the line was completed. A branch line from Newport News to Hampton was completed by the end of the year. The

line ended at Phoebus, a station named in honor of Harrison Phoebus who, among his many activities, had played a major role in negotiating for the location of the railroad on the Peninsula. By 1885, the Chesapeake and Ohio Railroad extended from Newport News, Virginia, to Big Sandy River, West Virginia, a distance of approximately 512 miles. At the West Virginia terminus, the line connected with lines extending south to New Orleans and west to San Francisco. This gave the farmers and seafood dealers of Elizabeth City and Hampton a means to transport their products to western markets.

Earliest provisions for public transportation were, not surprisingly, on the water. In 1866, George Schermerhorn, a New York steamboat captain, came to Hampton with his steamer *Mystic* and provided service between Hampton and Norfolk. Captain Schermerhorn built up a brisk service in both freight and passengers, and later sold his small shipping line to the Old Dominion Steamship Company, which hired him to command the ship that operated between Hampton and Norfolk. This connector line provided the residents of Hampton and the surrounding county a means of shipping their seafood, vegetables, fruits, lumber, and other products to Norfolk and hence on to New York via Old Dominion ocean-going vessels, which left Norfolk each day except Sunday and arrived in New York approximately one day later thus assuring that the seafood and crop product would arrive in a fresh condition. Special ships were run in the late spring and early summer to transport nothing but strawberries, grown on the Peninsula, to northern markets. During the late spring and summer, farmers lined up for blocks to unload their produce for shipment. During the week ending June, 1886, between fifteen hundred and two thousand barrels of "truck" farming produce were shipped daily over the wharf at Old Point Comfort. The Old Dominion Steamship Company had been formed in June 1867 by N. L.

A Chesapeake and Ohio Railroad excursion train stops at Buckroe Beach Amusement Park in July of 1939. Courtesy of the Casemate Museum

The Old Bay Line steamer City of Norfolk *ties up at the Government Dock at Old Point Comfort around the year 1958. Courtesy of the Casemate Museum*

McCready to provide steamship service between New York and Old Point Comfort, Norfolk, Newport News, and Richmond. The company was formed by a merger of the New York and Virginia Steamship Company that had in 1851 started permanent steamship service between New York, Norfolk, and Richmond. The Old Dominion Steamship Company also operated numerous feeder lines that went up most of the rivers.

In December 1839, the Baltimore Steam Packet Company was organized and on March 10, 1840, began making a daily trip between Baltimore and Norfolk with a stop at Old Point Comfort. During the Civil War, the company continued its daily service, carrying large amounts of freight and a few passengers. In 1865, the Company became known as the "Old Bay Line" and this name remained synonymous with the firm until it ceased operations in the early 1960s.

A new competitor to the Old Bay Line emerged in 1876 with the beginning of service between Baltimore, Old Point Comfort, and Norfolk by the People's Line, a subsidiary of the Chesapeake Steamship Company. The rivalry between the People's Line and the Old Bay Line was short lived for in 1877 a compromise agreement was signed by the presidents of the two lines which, among other things, discontinued operations of the People's Line to Old Point. While the competition between the two shipping lines resulted in reduced freight rates, the settlement also benefitted the customers as the Old Bay Line reorganized its fleet of ships for more efficient service.

In March 1891, the Norfolk and Washington Steamboat Company was formed and provided service between Washington, Old Point Comfort, and Norfolk. As time passed, smaller lines went out of existence until Old Point Comfort was served by only the Old Bay Line and the Norfolk and Washington Steamboat Company. On February 8, 1949, the Old Bay Line took over the Norfolk and Washington line. The wharf at

Old Point Comfort was also government-owned and maintained. With a decrease in use and thus less revenue from rents and faced with a major rehabilitation of the wharf the Army decided to abandon the wharf and have it razed. The Old Bay Line made the last northbound steamship stop at the wharf on the evening of December 30, 1959. By the Spring of 1961 the pier had been completely torn down and all pilings pulled up.

ACKNOWLEDGMENTS

I would like to thank the following individuals for their assistance with the portion of this book on Businesss and Industry: Mr. W. A. Ackerly, Mr. Charles R. Amory, Mr. Charles F. Elliott, and Miss Marguerite S. McMenamin.

153

An artist depicts Capt. John Smith and his party visiting with the Indians at Kecoughtan. Courtesy of Syms-Eaton Museum

6

Chapter

Hospitable Hampton

by Carolyn Haldeman Hawkins

It can be said that hospitality to tourists in Hampton began in 1607 when the English travelers anchored their ships near the Indian village of Kecoughtan and received a most cordial welcome from the natives. It is recorded that the visitors were escorted to the shore, given a feast and provided with entertainment. The following year John Smith and a sizable party from Jamestown were forced by extreme winter weather to spend an entire week at Kecoughtan. We are told that Smith and his men "made merry and feasted on oysters, fish, flesh, and wild fowl…and were quite comfortable in the dry, warm native huts."

Within a few years, Hampton had become a port as well as home to many seafaring men. Again, a cordial welcome was extended to all. Inns and ordinaries were scattered throughout the community where sailors could stay while their vessels were anchored in the harbor. In 1638 an act of the assembly provided that all inn-holders and ordinary-keepers should be rated at six pounds of tobacco or eighteen pence in money for a meal or gallon of ale, to be paid at the discretion of the guests. In 1639 the royal governor issued commissions to several persons in Elizabeth City County that gave permission to keep a common ale house and a "victuating" house.

It is interesting to note that in 1689 court was

being held in the ordinary kept by Worlich Westwood; no doubt the justices enjoyed the convenience. In 1697 licenses for keeping ordinaries were granted to the following persons: Anne Anderson, William Smelt, Sarah Middleton, and Mary Downes. "Too many ordinaries for a town so small," said the governor to the justices in 1699. He commanded the local lawmen to enforce the law permitting only two ordinaries to a town. The justices revoked the licenses of everyone except William Hudson and William Smelt, and ordered several women to shut up their "tippling houses." Interestingly, in 1699 Elizabeth City County was credited with being the first county seat in the New World to provide a building for courts of justice. It is unknown how long the reform concerning the limitation of ordinaries lasted, but probably not long. Pre-revolutionary Hampton was always known to have at least a half dozen open at any one time. The royal customs house located in Hampton accounted for dozens of grogshops and bawdyhouses along the wharves.

During the early 1700s a ferryman could have a free license to keep an ordinary at his landing. Rachael Skinner kept the ferry which crossed between the town of Hampton and Brooks Point on the east side of Hampton River, and the ordinary which went with it, from 1736 to 1738. Ms. Skinner was apparently more interested in her tavern than in her ferryboats because complaints concerning scheduling were made against her, and she was replaced by a man.

Coleman Brough had set up an inn on South King Street near the wharf in the 1680s. In 1766 his descendents were running the leading tavern in Hampton, The Kings Arms, also located near the wharf. The Kings Arms provided accommodations for most of the prominent visitors, including George Washington. Two other well known taverns at the time of the Revolution were Francis Riddlehurst's The Bunch of Grapes and John Jones's Lower Brick Tavern. Prior to the Revolutionary War, innkeepers were kept busy in the fifty-acre port town. As Virginia's major port as well as home to the state's navy, Hampton had no problem keeping its inns and taverns full during most of the 1700s.

With the removal of the royal customs house after independence, Hampton declined to the point that grass grew in the streets. Nevertheless, taverns, inns, and ordinaries continued to exist throughout the community. In all of Elizabeth City County, but particularly Hampton, taverns continued to be regulated as to the prices they might charge. In 1786, Justice Wilson Miles Cary signed a court order establishing the rates of one shilling, one sixpence each for supper or breakfast. In the closing years of the eighteenth century, the general customs house was removed, causing a real decline in business in Hampton.

For those whose occupations involved providing lodging or entertainment for the traveler, the coming of the first steamboat which ran between Norfolk and Hampton was cause for real celebration. In January of 1819 an article in the *Norfolk and Portsmouth Herald* suggested that an excursion to Hampton on the steamboat *Sea Horse* would "afford a tenfold more pleasing recreation, upon cheaper terms, instead of a ride into the country through dusty roads on a dry summer day." The steamboat would prove to be a tremendous boon to recreational travel. Additional accommodations were prepared for the anticipated influx of visitors. The following advertisement was placed in the *American Beacon* newspaper by John B. Cooper in February 1819:

THE HOUSE OF ENTERTAINMENT IN HAMPTON

The Subscriber has taken, and put in complete and handsome order, that very spacious, airy and commodious BRICK BUILDING in Hampton, on the right side of Main Street, leading from the Wharf, and only the third house therefrom, which he has opened for the accommodation of the public, under the appellation of the "STEAM-BOAT HOTEL."....Gentlemen and Ladies from Norfolk and other places, desirous of visiting Hampton, either for recreation or health, can be accommodated, at all times, with private rooms and will be boarded on reasonable terms for any period they please. The Steam-Boat holds out a strong inducement to parties of pleasure from Norfolk, who may be disposed to make a trip to Hampton, as they can return the same day.

The building of Fort Monroe at Old Point Comfort began in 1819. In order to provide accommodations for construction workers, permission was obtained to erect a modest hostelry. The Hygeia Hotel was built next to the moat, facing west, in 1822. Henry Clay was an early visitor to the first Hygeia. He spent the night there in February of 1822 when the steamboat on which he had passage made harbor close by due to inclement weather. A few months later on May 29, a small article in the *Norfolk and Portsmouth Herald* mentioned that a Public House at Old Point Comfort had opened for the reception of visitors. The following year the owner of the hotel reported that he was contemplating the building of a large addition, which when completed would increase the number of rooms to twenty. In addition, bath houses were to be erected immediately for the "accommodation of the Ladies."

Year by year Old Point Comfort increased in popularity as a summer resort for well-to-do Southerners. The Hygeia Hotel expanded several times until it was described in 1841 as being "large and commodious." Having as its name, Hygeia, who was the Greek goddess of health, helped to spread its fame as a health resort.

At the beginning of the Civil War the Hygeia

Hotel was partially converted into a hospital ward while the rest of the building continued to function as a hotel. Curiosity seekers who were finding lodging at the Hygeia became annoying to the federal authorities, and also the hotel building itself interfered with the training of the Fort Monroe guns just behind it. Consequently, the hotel was ordered torn down.

In 1863, one of the proprietors of the original Hygeia was given permission to erect a small one-story restaurant close to the beach near the Baltimore Wharf. Its name was the Hygeia Dining Saloon. Throughout the next decade, this small eating establishment grew in size and reputation, eventually accepting overnight guests. A new and larger building, the second Hygeia Hotel, was constructed in 1872. The new hotel was a three-story building, designed in the style of the Second Empire and surrounded by open verandas on all levels.

In 1873 the Hygeia owners got into financial difficulties and filed for bankruptcy. Thomas Tabb, Harrison Phoebus, and G. S. Griffith, Jr., were assigned as trustees for the creditors. They put the property up for auction and advertised the sale in the *Southern Workman* as follows:

First Class Hotel Property for sale. The Hygeia Hotel, Fortress Monroe, Virginia, will be sold on Thursday, the 9th day of April at 11 o'clock A.M. on the premises. This is one of the most superior summer resorts of the country, located immediately at the confluence of Hampton Roads with Chesapeake Bay. The bathing is not surpassed along the Atlantic Coast and the scenery is magnificent.

The Hotel Buildings are constructed in the best manner, and are capable of accommodating two hundred guests. All the appointments of this establishment are of the first class. It is furnished throughout in the most elegant manner....

Samuel Shoemaker, an official of the Adams Express Company near the Old Point Dock and a friend of Harrison Phoebus, bought the hotel at the auction and put Phoebus in charge. Harrison Phoebus had no previous experience in the hotel business, but he was anxious to learn everything he could about hotel management. He visited other hotels and studied their organization, all the while looking for innovations and improvements for the Hygeia. By 1881 Phoebus had greatly enlarged the hotel so that it had become an enormously long, four-story structure with accommodations for one thousand guests. Under his management the second Hygeia Hotel became one of the best known hotels in the United States and was visited by almost every noted Southerner and by many of the foremost Northern figures in finance or industry. It was open year round, being a favorite with its Southern trade in the summer and with its Northern clientele in the winter. *The Home Bulletin* of the Old Soldiers' Home reported in its December 13, 1884 issue that the Hygeia:

...is substantially built, luxuriously furnished with many of the rooms *en suite* and fitted with all modern improvements; has...Otis' hydraulic passenger elevators, gas and electric bells or Creighton's oral annunciators in every room; closets, and bathrooms, including hot sea baths on every floor, and the most perfect system of drainage to be found in any hotel or public building in the country. The wide verandas afford spacious and convenient

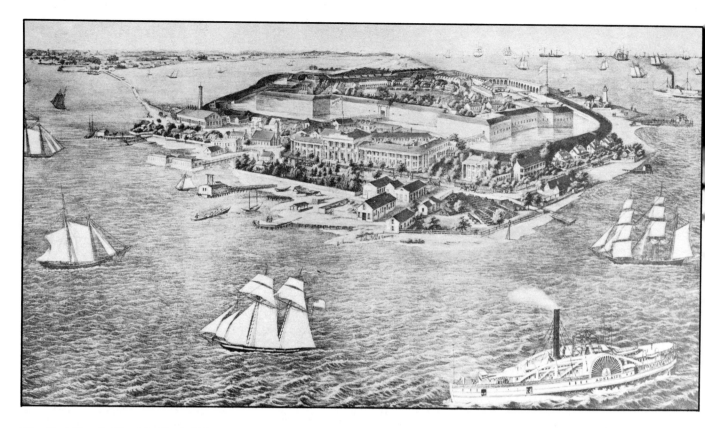

The first Hygeia Hotel built at Old Point Comfort was located along what later became Ingalls Road between Cannon Park and the moat footbridge. It overlooked Hampton Roads and Newport News Point. Courtesy of Charles H. Taylor Memorial Library

The second Hygeia Hotel is shown in 1873. It was located next to Old Point Wharf. Courtesy of the Casemate Museum

Harrison Phoebus was the successful manager of the second Hygeia Hotel. Courtesy of the Casemate Museum

The Hygeia Dining Saloon was located next to the Baltimore Wharf in this 1870s photo. Courtesy of the Casemate Museum

Looking north from the dock, the Hygeia Hotel is shown in 1881 with its addition complete. In 1985 the seawall at Fort Monroe was located approximately where the men are standing. Courtesy of Syms-Eaton Museum

The Hygeia Hotel is in the foreground as it appeared in the 1880s. Courtesy of the Casemate Museum

In the 1880s ox carts were used by visitor and vendor alike. Pictured is "Aunt Charlotte," known as the "Pie Woman," in her vendor's cart. Courtesy of the Casemate Museum

promenades, and during the cold weather over 15,000 square feet of them are encased in glass, enabling the most delicate invalid to enjoy the sunshine and fine water view without the slightest exposure. A spacious pavillion with a floor of 7,000 square feet, is set apart for dancing, and choice music is furnished by the United States Artillery School Band through the year. The dining room is a large apartment of 60 by 150 feet, with a lofty groined roof, and is thoroughly heated and commands a water view that is unrivaled on this continent. The table is unsurpassed....

Within a short time a complete set of baths, including the Turkish, Russian, Thermo, Electro, Magnetic, Mercurial, Sulphur and Vapor baths have been introduced which combined with celebrated Hot Sea Baths, adds another and more wonderful agent to the therapeutic advantages of the Hygeia, as beneficial as it is unique.

After the Civil War four of Hampton's leading tourist attractions were located near the Hygeia Hotel. They were Fort Monroe, situated one hundred yards in back of the hotel; the Home for Disabled Soldiers, located two miles from the hotel at the entrance of the Hampton River; the National Cemetery, located between the Soldiers' Home and the fourth attraction, the Hampton Normal and Agricultural Institute. Some visitors came just for the day on boat or rail excursions. Land transportation in the area was practically primitive due to the poor conditions of the area roads. Hampton's most common conveyance, a two-wheeled cart, was pulled by a horse, a mule or oxen and was used by both visitor and native. The Hampton and Old Point Chariot Line, run by Leonard Sheetz, made connections with all boats. The fare was fifteen cents for one trip between Hampton and Old Point.

As early as 1877, Norfolk Sunday schools were having picnics on the park-like grounds of the Soldiers' Home. Military authorities at Fort Monroe made sightseers feel welcome to attend the meeting of the guard in the mornings as well as the dress parades in the late afternoons. Open-air concerts open to the public were performed by the coast artillery school band during the summer weeks, and a military band usually played at the Hygeia Hotel while the guests were dining and again for after-dinner dancing. On a more serious note, many visitors to Hampton were relatives and friends of soldiers of the Union Army who were buried in the National Cemetery.

Naturally, not all visitors were able to stay at the elaborate Hygeia Hotel. Many took advantage of the more economical hotels and boarding houses located in and around Hampton. One family who benefitted from the presence of the predominance of young ladies from the North on the faculty of the Hampton Normal School was the Daniel Cock family who lived in a large brick home on the west bank of the Hampton River across from the school grounds. The families and friends who came to visit the teachers would often board with Daniel Cock and then arrange to be rowed back and forth across the creek. Cock's business was so good that he found it necessary to build an additional house in his yard to accommodate the visitors. Cock's Ivy Home was advertised regularly in the *Home Bulletin* during the 1880s.

Serving the Old Point area about this same time was a small hotel, the Sherwood Inn, originally built as a private residence in 1843 by Dr. Robert Archer. The cottage changed hands several times until Mrs. S. F. Eaton bought the property in 1867. She expanded the building and began operating it as a boarding house. Mrs. Eaton sold the house to George Booker in 1887. He enlarged it and named it for his family's

The park-like grounds of the National Soldiers Home are pictured around the year 1895. Courtesy of the Casemate Museum

The cornerstone of the Soliders Monument at Hampton was laid on October 3, 1867, as shown in this Harper's Weekly *sketch. Courtesy of the Casemate Museum*

plantation, Sherwood, located at what became Langley Field. The New Sherwood, as it was called, had a capacity of 175 guests by 1889.

John Chamberlin, whose backround was in gambling clubs, race tracks, luxury hotels and fine restaurants, formed a company in 1887 which raised capital and secured congressional authorization to construct another hotel at Fort Monroe. Construction was progressing in 1890 but came to a halt due to insufficient funds. The Hampton Roads Hotel Company completed the construction and the Chamberlin Hotel, as it was called, opened to the public on April 4, 1896. The hotel was 754 feet long and was said to be the first resort hotel entirely illuminated by electric lights. The structure cost an estimated $5 million and had six stories, 554 rooms and 1,000 beds, "200 of the rooms having private baths of handsome design into which may be turned hot or cold, fresh or salt water." The Hygeia and the Chamberlin, each stretching out along the beach with the Old Point Wharf between them, must have presented an impressive scene to the visitor arriving by water.

An added enticement to visit Hampton might have been the opening of the Hampton Roads Golf Club in 1893. It was one of the earliest golf courses in the United States and reputedly the first in Virginia.

At Daniel Cock's "Ivy Home," guests were rowed across the Hampton River. In 1985 the house on the right was known as the Paschow Herbert House and was one of the oldest structures standing in Hampton. Courtesy of Hampton University Archives

The course had nine holes which were laid out between the present-day Hampton Roads Avenue and La Salle Avenue. The Chamberlin Hotel helped with the maintenance of the course until it built its own links nearer the hotel on part of the old glebe land between Hampton and Phoebus.

After the death of Harrison Phoebus in 1888, the Hygeia Hotel seemed to go into a slow decline from which it never recovered. In 1902 the secretary of war ordered the second Hygeia to be torn down. The land upon which it stood became the Continental Park. The Chamberlin remained, its own reputation as a luxury hotel well established.

Tourists and visitors were being welcomed in other parts of Elizabeth City County and Hampton at the same time Old Point Comfort was gaining its reputation as a fun spot for pleasure-seekers. In the actual town of Hampton the Barnes Hotel, founded in the 1870s on South King Street near Queen, was the most popular. It was frequently used as a meeting place when important issues needed to be discussed. For example, George Benjamin West recorded in his diary that a meeting of all the owners of the waterfront near the West farm at Newport News Point (then in Elizabeth City County) took place at the Barnes in late 1879 or early 1880. Its purpose was to come up with an offer to Collis P. Huntington that would induce him to bring his railroad to the Point. By the 1880s J. J. Barnes's hotel could accommodate one hundred guests. Although advertised as a "popular Summer Resort open all the year," the hotel found its steadiest customers to be the salesmen of the day. The Barnes

Hotel was also the town's favorite banquet hall, serving such groups as the Knights of the Pythias elaborate foods in great quantity. In 1889 the hotel was renamed Hotel Hampton, but when Capt. George Schermerhorn bought the property in 1890, he returned the original name. The Barnes Hotel occupied a high place in the community and was famous throughout Virginia for its food and drink. Its proprietor advertised that the hotel had "all the Advantages of Old Point Comfort at Cheaper Rates." Captain Schermerhorn had the hotel torn down in 1902 and replaced it with the Kecoughtan Building, home for several businesses. An annex to the Barnes Hotel continued to run under the name "Barnes Hotel" until it was razed several years later.

Several other hotels were located within walking distance of the cross streets, King and Queen, in downtown Hampton. The Augusta Hotel on East Queen Street was one of these. It began serving the public around 1895 after W. A. Plecker bought the property from George A. Schmelz. After the Barnes was razed, the Augusta became the prominent hotel of Hampton. Several boarding houses were also being advertised at the turn of the century, one being William Rudd's, located near the Hampton wharf.

Mary Ann Dobbins Herbert obtained part of an old estate known as the Buckroe Plantation after the Civil War. She opened a boarding house for summer guests near her beach on the Chesapeake Bay in 1833 and soon afterwards had a bathhouse constructed for her guests, along with a pavillion for dancing. Edward B. Chiles, a Hampton businessman, built the first

John Chamberlin is pictured in a sketch attributed to the New York Herald in 1890. Courtesy of the Casemate Museum

"Young lady with two officers" was the first advertisement for the hotel, which appeared in 1896. Courtesy of the Casemate Museum

The first Chamberlin Hotel is seen as it appeared from the Old Point wharf in 1901. Courtesy of the Casemate Museum

public bathhouse at Buckroe a year later. Mr. Chiles transported his patrons from town to the beach in horse drawn beach-wagons.

A railway company under James S. Darling of Hampton acquired land at Buckroe Beach for the construction of a hotel which operated June 21, 1897. It was christened the Buckroe Beach Hotel and featured a large pavillion for dancing. Mrs. Herbert's much smaller boarding house became known as the "old Buckroe Hotel." It was destroyed by fire in 1912.

With the completion of Darling's new building, Buckroe Beach began to be known as somewhat of a resort. The large pavillion for dancing, an added amusement park, along with the two-mile stretch of sand were the featured attractions. However, "There was no mixed bathing in 1900," remembered a Hampton resident, "males and females were required to bathe separately in roped-off areas....All ladies were

In this 1916 photograph of the Hampton Roads Golf Club, the tennis court is on the right. The clubhouse faced the Hampton Roads. Courtesy of Syms-Eaton Museum

This photo shows the first Chamberlin Hotel facing east, the Adams Express Building and Mrs. Kimberly's Store around the year 1905. Courtesy of the Casemate Museum

Barnes Hotel was located on the east side of South King Street near Queen and is seen in this picture around the year 1890. Courtesy of Syms-Eaton Museum

The Augusta Hotel on the north side of East Queen Street is shown as it appeared in 1915. Courtesy of Syms-Eaton Museum

Located on the corner of East Queen and South King streets, The Fair served as a gathering place for townspeople. The United Virginia Bank occupied this site in 1985. Courtesy of the Plannng Department, city of Hampton

In 1900 Buckroe Beach attractions included, from left to right, a bath house, the Buckroe Hotel, an amusement park and a dance pavillion. Courtesy of Charles H. Taylor Memorial Library

required to wear black stockings." Despite these restrictions, the Buckroe Beach Hotel under the management of Charles H. Hewins, enjoyed great popularity as a family hotel offering excellent cuisine as well as a dignified atmosphere. The hotel was particularly popular among residents of Richmond, and for many years special excursion trains ran from Richmond to Buckroe Beach, bringing bathers to the resort.

A few miles from Buckroe, in 1890 a Mr. Laser built a hotel fronting the Chesapeake Bay, east of the community called Fox Hill. He named it The Grandview and used an attractive horse-drawn wagon to pick up hotel guests who arrived at the Hampton and Phoebus train stations and the Old Point wharf. Like Darling, Mr. Laser built a dance pavillion near his hotel.

Some black citizens of Hampton, recognizing a need for a place on the water for bathing and recreation, formed a company known as the Bay Shore Hotel Company and purchased waterfront property on Buckroe Beach in the fall of 1897. The first directors were J. H. Evans, J. I. Fountain, Thomas Harmond, D. R. Lewis, F. D. Banks, R. R. Moton, Alexander Gardiner, J. M. Phillips, and R. R. Palmer. The hotel opened in the summer of 1898, and from then until 1933, Bay Shore is believed to have been the only resort in this section of the country open to blacks.

In 1895 Chesapeake City, later named Phoebus, had at least four hotels; the Chesapeake Hotel, Clark's Palace, the Atlantic Garden Hotel, and the Phoebus Club Hotel. Two additional early hotels in the town were the Hotel Richelieu and the Hotel Klondyke. For more sedate lodgings, one might have stayed at Brightview Cottage overlooking Mill Creek and Fort Monroe. Brightview was a pre-Civil War home which had been used as a convalescent hospital during the war and then converted to a hotel around 1895. It served mostly military families and military guests.

There was no problem getting a drink in Phoebus at the turn of the century. Fifty-two saloons were listed as being in Phoebus in the 1900 *Hill's Directory*. The town of Hampton had twenty-three saloons listed as being within its borders that year.

In April of 1902 regional directors were appointed to promote the selection of Norfolk, Virginia, as the site for the 1907 Jamestown Exposition. Those representing Hampton and Elizabeth City County were Frank Darling, John Rowe, H. L. Schmelz, E. C. Kaiser and S. Gordon Cumming. William Baulch represented Old Point. One of the biggest arguments used for locating the Exposition in Norfolk was the attractiveness of not just Norfolk, but the entire Hampton Roads area to tourists. Each locality was encouraged to promote its recreational and historical attributes. After it was determined that Norfolk would be the site for the Jamestown Exposition, plans were made for a great naval and marine exhibition in the waters of the Hampton Roads.

Local hotels reacted immediately to the news that an exposition would be located "just across the Roads" in 1907. New construction and intensive "sprucing up" became top priorities. A special publication, *The Industrial Edition of the Hampton Monitor*, was compiled especially to praise the virtues of Hampton and the surrounding area, with special attention given to the hotels of Phoebus and Hampton. Albert E. Walker, editor and compiler, pointed out that "no locality in America offers more points of historic interest than immediately surrounding Hampton. No tourist, or student of American history, can visit this locality without being impressed with its great historical importance and interest." Following these remarks W. A. Flecker, M.D., was called upon to describe the Tidewater, Virginia, climate. This he did by calling it as "nearly perfect as any climate could be in the entire Western Hemisphere; the reason for this being the prevailing winds which were 'abundantly laden with ozone, of which ocean breezes always contain a superabundance'... To the fantastic climate of the area which Tourists and Health seekers would be happy to find, one could add the 'almost entire freedom from malaria and other zymotic diseases'."

Among the new business additions to Phoebus after 1900 was a leading hostelry, Fuller's Hotel. Mr. Phillip A. Fuller, proprietor and manager, was described as an up-to-date hotel man who had not done anything by halves to prepare accommodations for the rush of the exposition. The then-newly completed annex for 475 guests could also feed more than 500. The hotel was touted as having a reputation of supplying the best meals on the Peninsula. Atlantic Garden Hotel was supposedly known to nearly every soldier and sailor who had visited this section of the United States since its opening. Its stock of wet goods was said to be "large, varied, and selected with sound

This picture of the Bay Shore Hotel was taken in 1919. Courtesy of Syms-Eaton Museum

In 1900 the Chesapeake Hotel flew its flags to celebrate the incorporation of Phoebus. Courtesy of the Syms-Eaton Museum

This is how South Mallory Street in Phoebus looked around the year 1900. The Hotel Phoebus is located on the far right. Courtesy of Syms-Eaton Museum

The American Hotel on East Mellen Street, pictured in approximately 1930, was replaced by the Phoebus Post Office in 1938. Courtesy of Syms-Eaton Museum

Fuller's Hotel, located on the corner of County and Mallory Streets, is pictured in approximately 1903. Courtesy of Syms-Eaton Museum

judgement." Atlantic Garden advertised "rooms with all the very latest improvements at rock bottom prices." Clark's Palace, already one of the most ornate buildings in Phoebus, and Porter's Corner, were both recognized for their extensive renovations for the Jamestown Exposition.

The leading hotel in downtown Hampton at the time of the Jamestown Exposition was the Augusta Hotel owned by Joseph F. Rowe and his wife, Sarah. An advertisement at the time read that the Augusta stood "on the shore with open doors, prepared to shelter and feed the wayfarer and stranger." Rates were $2.50 American plan, $1.50 for lodging and breakfast. Other hotels operating downtown at that time were the Barnes Annex on Queen Street, the Hoffman House and the Hub Hotel, both on West Queen Street. Out of town, the Old Point View Hotel, located at the corner of La Salle Avenue and the Boulevard, and a nearby boarding house, Bay Bank,

offered additional accommodations.

The United States Atlantic Fleet arrived in Hampton Roads April 15, 1907, and took their stations at the Man-of-War Anchorage, which was west of the Old Point Comfort Light and northwest of the Hampton Bar and Hampton flats. During the remainder of the month foreign naval detachments arrived and took berths assigned to them near the United States vessels. Approximately seventy-five ships anchored in the Man-of-War Anchorage by the opening of the Jamestown Exposition on April 26, 1907. Many visitors to this side of Hampton Roads, as well as natives, took in the exposition. A small ferry ran from Hampton and two ferries ran from Old Point to carry sightseers through the anchored fleet and on to the exhibits located on the Norfolk shoreline.

Buckroe Beach continued to be a successful venture. Mr. Chilies built a new bathhouse with showers in 1909. Sclater Montague reported that in

Clark's Hotel on Mallory Street was one of the most ornate buildings in Phoebus at the time of the 1907 Jamestown Exposition. Courtesy of Syms-Eaton Museum

Hoffman House, 120 West Queen Street, was a boarding house from the early 1880s until the early 1900s. During that time the building had a third floor and porches on both the second and third floors. Boarders stayed on the second and third floors, and the ground floor was usually occupied by a retail business. The above photo was taken in 1981. Courtesy of the Planning Department, city of Hampton

Looking east on Queen Street around 1910, the Hub Hotel and Restaurant can be seen on the left. Courtesy of Syms-Eaton Museum

Copyright, 1907
W. N. Jennings

1913 Buckroe Beach was the center of amusement attractions on the Lower Peninsula. During the 1914 and 1915 seasons, bathers paid twenty-five cents for a suit and towel. Ladies had the additional costs of ten cents for a bathing cap and another ten cents for black cotton stockings, still a requirement to swim at Buckroe. In 1918 Claude Wagoner constructed the thirty-five room Wagoner Hotel which stood overlooking the water until it was razed in 1958.

Grandview became more appealing to the general public when Mr. Frank Cummings of Hampton built a bathhouse near the Grandview Hotel. An amusement area and dance pavillion were constructed in the same general area in 1925. One of the predominant features of the pavillion was a revolving crystal ball suspended from the center of the room. An unusual display of light was created by flashing colored lamps onto the ball. This crystal ball was thought to be the only one of its kind used on the East Coast.

In 1915 the Sherwood Inn was owned by J. B. Kimberly, who had a newsstand next to the Chamberlin Hotel. At that time the Chamberlin was the favorite gathering place for Fort Monroe officers. Naval officers were known to frequent the premises also. Guests were given the opportunity to ride in an open bus-like touring car which visited Phoebus. Soldiers' Home,

the National Cemetery, Hampton Institute, Town of Hampton and Old St. John's Church. The round trip was fifty cents.

Hotel business in the area picked up at the time of World War I when soldiers and sailors from the military bases poured into town. When the war came, the Chamberlin was taken over by the military for quarters for officers of the Army and the Navy. In 1918 the United States Army bought the Sherwood Inn to use as temporary officers' quarters.

The Chamberlin had hardly been back in civilian hands when a devastating fire broke out on its third floor March 7, 1920. Within a few hours the beautiful hotel had burned to the ground. Fortunately, no lives were lost. Old Point Comfort was left without a luxury hotel for the first time since the Civil War. Despite the protests of the Fort Monroe post commander at the time, in 1926 the War Department gave the Old Point Hotel Corporation permission to build a new hotel where the first Chamberlin had stood. It opened in 1928 as the Chamberlin-Vanderbilt, a massive eight-story brick and concrete structure adorned with two tall domes. An elaborate interior included special baths and an indoor pool supplied with sea water.

Also in 1928 Phoebus was still considered by some to be a tourists' haven although the number of hotels

As part of the 1907 Jamestown Exposition, a naval review of battleships was conducted offshore at Old Point Comfort. Pictured at left is the Maine, with the Indiana in the center and the Rhode Island at the right. Courtesy of the Casemate Museum

The Sherwood Inn at Fort Monroe is pictured as it looked in approximately 1915. Courtesy of the Casemate Museum

Only charred remains of the first Chamberlin Hotel remained after a devastating fire on March 7, 1920. Courtesy of Syms-Eaton Museum

The Hygeia Hotel at 6 South Mallory Street in Phoebus was operated by William M. Davis in the years 1915 to 1919. Courtesy of Syms-Eaton Museum

In this photo of the Chamberlin Hotel as it appeared during the 1930s, note the cuppolas which were removed for security reasons and never replaced. Courtesy of Syms-Eaton Museum

An excursion train brought passengers to Buckroe Beach in 1931. Courtesy of Charles H. Taylor Memorial Library

In this 1931 view of Buckroe Beach, the Buckroe Hotel can be seen on the left and the dance pavillion on the right. Courtesy of Syms-Eaton Museum

A 1920-vintage carousel with hand-carved horses was a special attraction at Buckroe Beach Amusement Park, shown here in 1931. Courtesy of Syms-Eaton Museum

Waves break at Buckroe Beach during a storm. Courtesy of the Planning Department, city of Hampton

had dwindled to four: The American, Fuller's, The Liberty and The Palace. In Hampton, the largest hotel, Hotel Langley, formerly the old Augusta, changed owners. Rutherford B. Thompson and his wife Elizabeth purchased the hotel in 1928. At that time, the guest rooms were upstairs, and downstairs shops were located on both sides of the main lobby. The Thompsons ran the hotel until 1949 when they sold it to a local organization, The Hampton Hotels, Inc.

Severe storms in the twenties and thirties took their toll on the area beaches. The August 1933 storm tore down almost all of the buildings at Grandview. The beach there remained desolate, except for a few fish shanties, until the 1940s. Buckroe suffered similar devastation, but immediately began a massive clean-up and rebuilding campaign with the help of the WPA. At Bay Shore, the hotel and all the park facilities which had been developed since its opening were almost completely destroyed by the hurricane. The financial difficulties arising from the storm damage caused the resort to eventually be put up for sale by the federal government, which held an unpaid loan. Mr. Joseph E. Healy, president of a Hampton bank at the time, was instrumental in aiding black investors headed by Charles H. Williams to recover Bay Shore in the early 1940s. The New Bay Shore Corporation, as the new organization was called, expanded and developed the site once again.

Prior to the 1933 storm, the Sherwood Inn had followed the fate of the Hygeia Hotel. After having served as an officers' mess, as well as having provided temporary quarters for military families since World War I, The Sherwood Inn was razed in 1932. The land which it had occupied so many years became Sherwood Park.

During the mid-1930s the Chamberlin Hotel continued to draw visitors to the area with its luxurious accommodations and magnificent view of the Hampton Roads and Chesapeake Bay. However, tourists may not have cared for a local ordinance passed in 1936 which forbade dancing and music, live or by juke box, in local taverns. This action was taken "in an effort to discourage the lawless element." Also in 1936 topless bathing suits for men appeared at Buckroe Beach. Then Judge C. Vernon Spratley responded by calling for a jury to decide "if the sight of a topless swim suit was offensive to the casual eye."

When World War II began the Chamberlin was used as temporary housing for the military once more. The high domes of the hotel were removed as a precautionary measure and were never again replaced. Fortunately, military housing was more readily available during the second war than it had been during the first. The only two hotels advertising during the war years were a reduced Fuller's in Phoebus and the fifty-room Hotel Langley in Hampton. Restaurants were the booming business which served the large transient population of that time. Bay Shore and Buckroe Beach amusement parks were able to continue their operations during the war, thus providing pleasant diversions for both civilians and military personnel.

As life returned to normal after World War II, thought was given to preserving the past. In 1951 the Fort Monroe Casemate Museum had its beginnings. It took its name from its location within the casemates, (chambers) in the wall of a fort where guns are positioned. The Casemate Museum at first emphasized the casemate in which Jefferson Davis, president of the Confederacy, was confined and the Battle of the *Merrimack* and the *Monitor*. In 1952 Miss Margaret Sinclair was instrumental in opening the Syms-Eaton

173

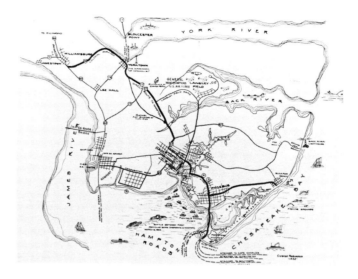

This 1935 tourist map shows attractions of Hampton and the vicinity. Courtesy of Charles H. Taylor Memorial Library

Take a family voyage on the Kicotan Clipper along the paths of mighty warships and atomic submarines, where the Monitor met the Merrimac and pirate ships once roved. You'll see yesterday, today and a little of tomorrow in the 12 outstanding attractions on the Hampton Tour.

HAMPTON TOUR **VIRGINIA**

For more facts, contact Mr. A. S. Greenwell

The Casemate Museum lies within the walls of historic Fort Monroe. This photo was taken in approximately 1972. Courtesy of the Casemate Museum

The Hampton Tour was advertised in 1971. Courtesy of the Hampton Coliseum, city of Hampton

The Aerospace Park and Information Center was photographed in 1985. Courtesy of the city of Hampton Department of Parks

The Syms-Eaton Museum exists to collect, preserve, and present the history of Hampton. Temporary exhibits are based on historical dates and events. In addition, the staff gives programs for groups of all ages. Courtesy of Syms-Eaton Museum

An elevated crosswalk across Mercury Boulevard connects the Syms-Eaton Museum and the Conventions and Tourism Center of Aerospace Park. Courtesy of the Planning Department, city of Hampton

Museum in a room in the Syms-Eaton Academy building in downtown Hampton. This museum displayed various memorabilia concerning the history of Hampton and Elizabeth City County.

The city of Hampton, guided by Mayor Ann Kilgore, began an aggressive campaign to attract tourists to the area in the early 1960s. After a formal study of tourism in Hampton was analyzed, city officials felt confident that travelers who were already sightseeing in the area around Hampton could be persuaded to spend an extra day sightseeing in Hampton itself. The Hampton Tour was initiated in 1964. This "drive-it-yourself, self-guided tour" was based on visiting the important tourist attractions around Hampton such as the Casemate and Syms-Eaton museums by following distinctive scroll-shaped red and white tour-route signs and using a simple travel folder for a guide. The nineteen-year old *Kecoughtan Clipper*, a former oyster workboat, was bought by the city to use for a harbor tour, during which time tourists were encouraged to join "The Hampton Navy." Included in the tour was a brief stop at the historic Fort Wool at the mouth of Hampton Roads. Almost immediately Hampton hotel and motel operators experienced a rise in patronage, and The Hampton Tour was officially given partial credit for improved tourism statistics.

The following year a space-age-looking building opened on Mercury Boulevard, a main thoroughfare of Hampton, and served both as a tour information center and commerce department office. Surrounding the building was a dramatic display of real jet fighters and rockets, and across the road, the newly opened Syms-Eaton Museum continued to display history in a traditional manner.

Andrew D. Greenwell, in his capacity as director of commerce, negotiated the purchase of two red English double-decker buses which were ready for the 1969 tourist season. These buses were credited with a

305 percent increase in number of visitors who took the Langley Field tour that year. Mr. Greenwell also aided the city's receiving a decommissioned Coast Guard lightship from the Baltimore area. *Lightship Hampton*, as it was named, became a floating maritime museum berthed in downtown Old Hampton and a part of the Hampton Tour in 1971.

One of the most significant events in the modern history of tourism in Hampton took place January 31, 1970, when the Hampton Roads Coliseum officially opened. Since that time millions of people, both residents and visitors, passed through its doors to participate in everything from religious conferences to public ice skating and to view everything from tractor-pulls to antique shows. Activities at the Coliseum drew out-of-town people who needed accommodations and places to eat. The section of Hampton near the Coliseum known as Mercury Central experienced a

This double-decker bus is shown on a runway at Langley Field during a Hampton Tour in 1973. Courtesy of the Department of Conventions and Tourism, city of Hampton

The lightship Relief *is being towed to Hampton in 1969 by Capt. Edward Haldeman with his tug* Turmoil. *After being renamed the* Lightship Hampton, *the vessel became part of the Hampton Tour for five years. Courtesy of the* Daily Press, *Inc.*

phenonmenal growth rate for tourist services simply because of its proximity to the Coliseum.

The NASA Visitor's Center opened in 1971, giving The Hampton Tour another boost, but, in general, the economy of the 1970s was slow in Hampton. The Hotel Langley, formerly The Augusta, advertised itself as being in "Historic Hampton, Virginia...truly the cradle of the nation" in the 1972 *Hill's Directory* for the last time. It became part of a downtown redevelopment project and was razed. The New Bay Shore Corporation, led by Charles Williams, had operated a predominately-black amusement park on the same site as the original Bay Shore development since 1940. After the 1960s both the hotel and the amusement park lost money, until finally in 1973 the directors were forced to discontinue the operation. The Bay Shore property was sold to private developers. A bright spot for tourism in the seventies was the sale of the badly deteriorating Chamberlin Hotel by a Richmond-based hotel corporation in 1978 to Mr. and Mrs. Vernon E. Stuart. They began renovating immediately, and by that summer the historic hotel had taken

on some of its former elegance. The Buckroe Beach Amusement Park, then owned by the Stieffen Family, also experienced a decline. The toll-free Hampton Roads Bridge Tunnel encouraged people to go to beaches further south; Busch Gardens, a newer and more elaborate amusement park, drew former patrons of Buckroe; and last, but not least, stinging nettles multiplied to such an extent that bathing in the Chesapeake Bay was no longer a pleasant experience.

The decade closed with the sale of the *Kecoughtan Clipper* and the double-decker buses, leaving The Hampton Tour rather diminished, *Lightship Hampton* was sold to the city of Portsmouth. Fort Wool closed.

In response to a 1982 report on the economic development of the Virginia Peninsula, then mayor James L. Eason initiated several actions to improve the attractiveness of Hampton to the potential tourist and at the same time encourage economic growth. One of the first of these was to have new signs saying "Welcome to Hampton" placed at the city limits along major roads. A concentrated effort was made to beautify interstate interchanges and major road green

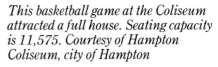

The Coliseum has focused national attention on Hampton via television coverage of special events in addition to information in magazines and newspapers. Courtesy of Hampton Coliseum, city of Hampton

This basketball game at the Coliseum attracted a full house. Seating capacity is 11,575. Courtesy of Hampton Coliseum, city of Hampton

areas. Recognizing that the city was almost centered in Hampton Roads, city officials elected to participate in a coordinated regional tourism marketing program under the Peninsula Chamber of Commerce. "We're in the middle of everything," read a brochure of that time advocating a Virginia Peninsula Vacation.

The City of Hampton celebrated its 375th anniversary as the oldest continuous English-speaking settlement in America in 1985. One of the goals set for the anniversary year was to encourage tourism growth in Hampton. It was intended that the publicity that the celebration events would bring to Hampton would help position the city as an important tourist destination in the Hampton Roads area. A series of events took place throughout the entire year of 1985 using the anniversary theme of "Hampton, First to the Sea, First to the Stars" as a means to emphasize Hampton's strong ties to the sea as well as its importance as the birthplace of America's manned space program.

Amid much fanfare, Fort Wool was reopened for tourists on May 18, 1985. A scheduled tour boat again took visitors to the island during the summer months.

This time guides and new exhibitions were a part of the Fort Wool Tour. The unveiling of a downtown waterfront development plan took place July 9, the official birthday of the city. A luxury waterfront motel was to be complimented with a nearby Visitors' Center, a festival marketplace and the conversion of a post office building into a regional museum.

Hampton Coliseum director, Andrew Greenwell, used the following information as part of the Coliseum's promotional material in 1985:

For a convention site that combines vacation pleasure with modern meeting and exhibit facilities, choose Hampton Coliseum in Hampton, Virginia. Located on the shores of the Chesapeake Bay, Hampton offers excellent swimming, boating, fishing, and golfing facilities as well as historic attractions and fine seafood. Mild temperate weather makes Hampton the ideal setting for year-round activities.

That description of Hampton has a familiar ring to it. Was it used in connection with the Hygeia, the

The NASA Visitor Center at Langley Air Force Base opened in 1971. Courtesy of the Hampton Coliseum, city of Hampton

The Langley Hotel is pictured in approximately 1937. Other businesses nearby are Dominic Fertitta's; Roth Nellie Hat Shoppe; James Carr, barber; Marinello Beauty Shop; and Philip N. Davis, fruit vendor. Courtesy of Charles H. Taylor Memorial Library

The Langley (formerly Augusta) Hotel is pictured in 1960. Businesses, from left, are the Varsity Shop, Sanders Jewelry, Western Union, Hotel lobby, Langley Coffee Shop, Milteer's Typewriters, and Monroe Shop. Courtesy of Syms-Eaton Museum

Originally built as a private residence, this boarding house made way for progress at Buckroe. Courtesy of the Planning Department, city of Hampton

The shoreline in Old Hampton as it was in 1979. By 1985 the bridge in the background on the right had been replaced and a luxury hotel was planned for the site. Courtesy of the Planning Department, city of Hampton

The Chamberlin Hotel is pictured in 1985. Fort Monroe is to the right, and the city of Hampton is seen on the horizon.

The Lightship Hampton, *moored near the center of town, served as a martime museum from 1970 to 1975 as part of the Hampton Tour. Courtesy of the Planning Department, city of Hampton*

In 1985, visitors entering town were greeted by "Welcome to Hampton" signs erected on landscaped medians. Courtesy of the Planning Department, city of Hampton

Mayor James L. Eason, third from left, participated in numerous groundbreakings during his terms of office, which began in 1982. Courtesy of the Planning Department, city of Hampton

Chamberlin or The Augusta?

Whoever said the more things change, the more they stay the same might well have been talking about the state of tourism in Hampton. The years immediately preceding the 1907 Jamestown Exposition marked the first time regional tourism was advocated. The 1980s have brought tourism full circle and once again a regional appeal for tourists is being made.

Albert Walker put it succinctly in 1907 when he wrote in *The Industrial Edition of the Hampton Monitor:*

There is nothing that advertises the advantages of a city more than its hotels. The stranger within her gates is more apt to judge of the town to a great extent by the treatment accorded to him at the hotel where he is entertained and his impressions of the

place are moulded by his host.

In 1985 Hampton visitors were served by many motels, both large and small, as well as the Chamberlin Hotel. One new motel had opened in 1984 and seven more inns were under construction or in the planning stages in 1985. Many restaurants had recently opened along a stretch of Mercury Boulevard frequented by out-of-town travelers. The amount of money spent by visitors during the year of 1984 had increased more in Hampton than anywhere else in southeastern Virginia, indicating that efforts made by the community to promote tourism and conventions in Hampton had been successful.

"Hampton, From the Sea, to the Stars," the 375th Anniversary theme, could have been the theme for the history of Hampton tourism alone.

"To the Stars..." Aerospace Park.
Courtesy of the Planning Department,
city of Hampton

Area Attractions

In 1985 the following attractions, many of them free of charge, could be found within the boundaries of Hampton:

AEROSPACE PARK—a well-developed park-museum exhibiting jet planes, space rockets, and offering a space age playground for children.

BLUE BIRD GAP FARM—has a variety of farm animals, wild animals and fowl, farm equipment, a demonstration garden, and children's playground and picnic area.

BRADDOCK MONUMENT—located at the foot of Victoria Boulevard near the Hampton River. During the French and Indian, War, General Braddock landed in Hampton on his way to the campaign at Fort Duquesne (now Pittsburgh). The monument was erected in 1916 by the Colonial Dames of America to mark this event.

BUCKROE BEACH—a popular family beach on the Chesapake Bay. It has a modern fishing pier and a fine selection of hotels and motels nearby.

CASEMATE MUSEUM—located inside the moat at Fort Monroe, displaying information and objects concerning the histories of Old Point Comfort, Fort Monroe, the Coast Artillery Corps, and the casemate in which Jefferson Davis was held prisoner after the Civil War.

CHAPEL OF THE CENTURION—a center of religious activity at Fort Monroe for more than a century. President Woodrow Wilson was a visitor during his stays at the nearby Chamberlin Hotel. There are a number of historic flags of artillery organizations hanging in the sanctuary. The stained glass windows are also noteworthy.

Bluebird Gap Farm. Courtesy of the
Parks Department, city of Hampton

181

Braddock Cannon Monument at its original location at the foot of Victoria Boulevard and the Hampton River. Courtesy of Charles H. Taylor Memorial Library

Curator Chester D. Bradley at the Casemate Museum, Fort Monroe, in 1973. Courtesy of the Casemate Museum

Sanctuary of the Chapel of the Centurion, part of Fort Monroe's walking tour. Courtesy of the Casemate Museum

EMANCIPATION OAK—selected by the National Geographic Society as one of the ten great trees of the world, this live oak is believed to be the site of where the Emancipation Proclamation was read. It also provided shade for an outdoor classroom serving refugee blacks during the Civil War.

FORT WOOL—a historic fifteen-acre island in the Hampton Roads near Fort Monroe. Abandoned and in disrepair for many years, the fort was leased to the city of Hampton by the state of Virginia. Fort Wool was part of the Hampton Boat Tour in the mid-seventies. After being closed again, Fort Wool was reopened in May of 1985. It was reached by a commercial tour boat leaving downtown Hampton at scheduled times.

GOSNOLD'S HOPE PARK—the largest developed park in the city of Hampton, offering public picnicking facilities, campsites, boat ramp, fitness trail, children's playground and a horse show arena.

GRANDVIEW FISHING PIER—provides the fishermen the opportunity to fish from a pier extending out into the Chesapeake Bay.

GRANDVIEW NATURAL PRESERVE—approximately six hundred acres of marshlands and beach in their natural state and open only to pedestrians.

HAMPTON CENTER FOR ARTS AND HUMANITIES—providing an extensive program of creative arts and cultural enrichment. It sponsors seminars, workshops, historical and archeological research, lectures and discussion groups. Art exhibits changed monthly.

HAMPTON COLISEUM—a multi-purpose indoor recreation arena which hosts professional and amateur sporting events, cultural and civic events, and conventions. Water ski shows can be held on a man-made lake adjacent to the Coliseum.

Emancipation Oak on the grounds of Hampton University was listed as one of the world's greatest trees by the National Geographic Society. Courtesy of the Planning Department, city of Hampton

Hampton Golf and Tennis Center. Courtesy of the Planning Department, city of Hampton

Kecoughtan Indian Village. Courtesy of Syms-Eaton Museum

HAMPTON GOLF COURSE AND TENNIS CENTER—provides a six-thousand yard, eighteen-hole, tournament-play golf course complete with pro shop, locker room and concession stand and a center tennis court with a permanent seating capacity of one thousand. There are also six additional courts whose composition is clay. The Hampton Tennis Center is one of the few clay court facilities on the East Coast.

HAMPTON NATIONAL CEMETERY—initially begun to provide a final resting place for soldiers of both sides who died in the Hampton Hospital, which operated in this vicinity during the Civil War. A granite obelisk monument stands in the center of the older section of the Cemetery adjacent to the grounds of Hampton University due to the efforts of Dorothea Dix, American social reformer. Its dedication was one of the last public appearances of President Garfield before he was assassinated. The two sections of the cemetery hold over seventeen thousand servicemen of every war in which the United States participated from 1812 through Vietnam.

HAMPTON UNIVERSITY MUSEUM—the oldest museum in Hampton. It began its collection of ethnic artifacts in 1868. Located in the historic Academic Building of Hampton University, the museum built a collection of traditional art objects from Africa, Asia, and Oceania, as well as from American Indian cultures. Contemporary work by Africans and African-Americans is exhibited at the museum.

KECOUGHTAN INDIAN VILLAGE—a facsimile of the typical Indian village located in this area at the time the first Englishmen arrived. Wigwams, dugout canoes, ceremonial posts, palisades, and fireplaces are part of the hands-on exhibit.

183

The Bell Tower at Hampton University. Courtesy of the Planning Department, city of Hampton

Friday evenings at Mill Point Park, summer of 1985. Courtesy of the Planning Department, city of Hampton

KECOUGHTAN MONUMENT—located on the waterfront grounds of the Veterans Administration, near where the first Englishmen are believed to have come ashore in 1607. The monument was erected in 1957.

MEMORIAL CHAPEL—an excellent example of Italian Romanesque architecture complimented by an adjoining 150-foot bell tower. The chapel was built on the waterfront campus of Hampton University in 1886. The pews and baptismal font were built by students.

MILL POINT PARK—located in downtown Hampton overlooking Hampton River. An amphitheater with seating for three hundred is used for concerts sponsored by the Hampton Center for the Arts and Humanities during the summer months.

NASA VISITORS' CENTER—located at Langley Research Center on Langley Field Air Force Base. It features an air and space museum which uses films, photographs and exhibits to show in a dramatic manner the progress of America in aeronautics and astronautics.

OLD POINT COMFORT LIGHT STATION—constructed in 1802 and used by the British as a lookout point during the War of 1812, the United States Coast Guard operates this masonry lighthouse on Fort Monroe.

SUNSET CREEK BOAT RAMP—located on Sunset Creek near the Hampton River is this boat launching ramp free to the public. Gas, oil, and necessary boating supplies are sold nearby.

SYMS-EATON MUSEUM—located in a fourteen-acre park connected to the Aerospace Park by an overhead bridge and adjacent to the Kecoughtan Indian Village. The museum displays Hampton artifacts from the earliest recorded times to the present, and also provides guides for the Indian Village.

SAINT JOHN'S CHURCH AND PARISH MUSEUM—located in downtown Hampton. St. John's was built in 1728 as the fourth church of the Elizabeth City Parish, the oldest continuous Anglican congregation in the United States. A small museum in the nearby Parish House contains artifacts and memorabilia of St. John's and its parishioners.

TOURIST INFORMATION CENTER—located in the Aerospace Park on Mercury Boulevard. The Tourist Center provides information about points of interest in the city and state, as well as about hotels and motels, restaurants and cultural or recreational events in the Hampton Roads region, including those at the Coliseum.

REGIONAL ATTRACTIONS: Busch Gardens' The Old Country, Water Country U.S.A., Colonial Williamsburg, Williamsburg Pottery Factory, Jamestown

The National Cemetery, circa 1895. Courtesy of the Casemate Museum

Constructed in 1802, the Old Point Comfort Lighthouse was automated in 1973. Its light was visible out to sixteen nautical miles. Courtesy of Joe Frankoski

Festival Park, Colonial National Historical Park in Yorktown, Waterman's Museum, Mariners' Museum, Peninsula Nature and Science Center, U.S. Army Transportation Museum, War Memorial Museum of Virginia, Norfolk Naval Base, Douglas MacArthur Memorial, Waterside Festival Market, The Hermitage Foundation Museum, Gardens-By-The-Sea, Chrysler Museum and Virginia Beach.

ACKNOWLEDGMENTS

I wish to thank the following people for their assistance: Anna Lee Gordon Abbott, Norma Agee, Kathleen Anderson, Irene Bowman, Casemate Museum, Charles H. Taylor Memorial Library staff, Joan Charles, City of Hampton, Mike Cobb, James L. Eason, Hampton University Archives, Edward J. Haughton, Thornton Jones, William M. Martin III, William C. Matthews, Calvin Pearson, Barbara Richardson, R. V. Richardson, Larry Riggs, Vernon E. Stuart, Susan Tiede, Irene Weston, and Nellie Jo Yannarella.

Frank W. Darling, left, and Robert L.
Howard, charter members of the
Hampton Fire Department, with the
department's first piece of equipment.
Courtesy of the Syms-Eaton Museum,
Cheyne Collection

7
Chapter

Modern Hampton 1900-1985

by Irene Weston

Once the War Between the States, that most devastating of all the wars in Hampton's history, was over, the sons and daughters of the wasted town returned prepared to take up the challenge of rebuilding their lives and homes. With the indomitable spirit inherited from their forefathers, these Hamptonians faced the many problems of Reconstruction as the little town began another phase in its colorful development. The postwar years brought new faces—northern capitalists and educators, such as James Sands Darling, Jacob Heffelfinger, Harrison Phoebus, and General Samuel Chapman Armstrong, many of whom became beloved citizens, adding greatly to the early twentieth century growth of the town.

Of course, the rebirth was not without setbacks. On April 9, 1884, a disasterous fire swept away many of the downtown buildings. Known as the "big fire" for years, it started in the northeast corner of a frame building used as a harness shop and dry goods store on the southside of Queen Street. There was no fire fighting apparatus of any kind, no water supply, and no organized bucket brigade. The Normal School (Hampton University) fire engine, a steam fire engine from the Soldiers' Home (Veterans Administration), and one from Old Point struggled to contain the fire, but it was not stopped until the greater part of the business section was in ashes. A total of thirty-three stores and buildings were destroyed, many of which could have been saved had there been any reasonable fire-fighting apparatus and an organized fire department available. The smoke from the fire had hardly disappeared when a group of citizens purchased a hand pump for about four hundred dollars, and thus the Hampton Fire Department was born. The modern Hampton Fire Company is a direct descendent of the original Hampton Fire Department.

A new war brought the town into the twentieth century. In 1898 the Spanish American War resulted in the mustering of the Peninsula Guards, a state militia company, which went to Cuba but fought in no battles. Hampton citizens loved their Guards, sending them off with great ceremony and welcoming them back with a big banquet. Men from other units were not so fortunate, as noted by C. Taylor Holtzclaw to his wife in a letter dated July 17, 1898: "We have been building quarters for the wounded at Old Point—and had to work 12 hours a day—have about fifty men at work...They have nearly 500 sick and wounded here now and have sent several ships North on account of no place to have them. It was a pitiful sight to see the poor fellows land—dirty and ragged and shot in all kinds of places. Many of them had to be carried on

Seldom has a defeated populace been so desolate as the Hamptonians after Appomattox. Yet from the cinders of their thrice-burned town rose the Hampton of today. This sketch of the ruins of Hampton was made in April of 1862. Courtesy of the Syms-Eaton Museum

litters and in ambulances—the first lot that came had had no attention whatever and were just as they left the Battlefields—but it did not take them long to fix them up and they are now attired in their summer suits (pajamas) and doing well—the ladies and people are sending them lots of stuff of every kind from around here and everywhere—and they are happy. They expect to build a large temporary Hospital in Mill Creek and I hope to get the job!" Mr. Holtzclaw, a contractor, got that job and others as well. He built many homes and buildings in Hampton including the Masonic Temple (which became Wheat Securities), the first Chamberlin Hotel (burned in 1920), Roseland Manor (Harrison Phoebus's mansion which burned in 1985) and Cedar Hall (Frank Darling's home now razed).

The small seaport town at the mouth of the Chesapeake Bay had made a remarkably strong recovery from the desolation and destruction of homes and lives resulting from the War Between the States. On October 29, 1901, the Confederate Monument was unveiled in St. John's Churchyard, both a visible tribute to a lost cause and a break with the past. Hampton was ready for progress and progress came with the new century.

In 1900 there were prosperous crab and oyster plants, but no city water and no gas service. There was a post office and a fire department, but no electricity for illumination and little indoor plumbing or sewage facilities. There was limited streetcar service but no one had automobiles. There was a population of 2,764 but there were no bank buildings. There were at least twenty barrooms and saloons, but no sidewalks and no paved streets. Five or six large stones were placed in

Queen Street upon which ladies would pick their way through the mud. Young ladies were taught to keep their eyes on the ground when passing a saloon, which also undoubtedly helped them avoid the mud. A wooden footbridge was erected at the end of Melrose Avenue (now part of Settlers Landing Road) across the creek to Queen Street so women could by-pass the saloons when shopping.

At the century's turn, Hampton was indeed a "rowboat" town. Once, after a heavy rainstorm, a young Hamptonian, one Frank Lake by name, hitched a mule to a rowboat and rode through the muck from the intersection of Armistead Avenue and Queen Street (called by old Hampton natives "Marsh Market Corner") to Hampton Bridge (replaced in 1985 by the new Booker T. Washington Bridge), smoking a "seegar" and waving to his friends.

During this period Hampton was known as the center of the nation's crab market. James McMenamin had perfected a method of canning crabs, and by 1900 plants in Hampton were shipping the tasty crustaceans all over the world. Hampton was Crabtown, but shellfish also contributed to the economy. One of the most unusual sights shown to visitors was the pile of oyster shells towering several stories high at F. W. Darling's plant.

The first automobile arrived in 1903, the property of oysterman F. W. Darling. The first telephone company was chartered March 16, 1895. C. Taylor Holtzclaw in another letter to his wife dated Sunday, August 14, 1898, wrote "...the old man (Joe's boss) has been drinking some of late. He ordered his telephone out because some girls called up for Joe! I didn't take it out but cut it off at Central as I thought

The Marshall Street home of C. Taylor Holtzsclaw was still standing at number 316 in 1985. Courtesy of the Holtzsclaw collection

Cedar Hall, home of the Darling family, was for many years a gathering place for social, political and philanthropic activities. Courtesy of the Syms-Eaton Museum

Roseland Manor, home of Harrison Phoebus, was built in 1887 by C. Taylor Holtzsclaw and destroyed by fire in 1985. Harrison Phoebus died before the home was complete, but his wife and their seven children occupied it until her death in 1906. Courtesy of the Daily Press, *Inc.*

This is a view of Queen Street looking west in the 1890s. Courtesy of the Syms-Eaton Museum

This is a view of the east corner of King and Queen streets intersection in 1900. In 1985 the building on the left was the oldest surviving commercial building in Old Hampton. It was known as the Sclater Building and housed the law office of David Montague, grandson of the builder. Courtesy of the Syms-Eaton Museum

he would get over his fret and he came around in a few days and was anxious to get it back! so I suppose that will be the end of it."

The first bank, the Bank of Hampton, was established in 1881. Banking as we know it today did not exist in Hampton immediately after the War Between the States. There were no banks; instead, merchants performed financial services. People who had enough money to bank sent or carried it to Barnes Bank in Portsmouth, and others relied on a shoe merchant in Norfolk for banking matters. After Barnes Bank failed, there was a definite need for a bank in Hampton. The Bank of Hampton was established with a desk, a counter and a safe at 25 South King Street. It was a prosperous, popular and progressive institution, and became the largest bank in the city until 1933. The first permanent home of the Bank of Hampton was 36 East Queen Street, but a large, impressive building was erected on the southeast corner of Queen and King Streets in 1901. This building was to stand for almost seventy-five years, changing names several times, but always a banking institution. The building was torn down in 1975, and a new bank building was erected which in 1985 was occupied by the United Virginia Bank.

In October of 1885, the Schmelz brothers, George and Henry, decided to open a small privately owned bank in the rear of Henry's King Street Bakery. "The back room bank" flourished and the brothers opened their first full bank in 1902 on the northwest corner of King and Queen streets. This bank merged with the Bank of Hampton in 1903.

When the Schmelz brothers bank consolidated with the Bank of Hampton in 1903, a new bank, the First National Bank, was established and moved into the old Schmelz Brothers building. Both the Bank of Hampton and the First National Bank closed during the 1933 "bank holiday." They opened later as Citizens National Bank. The building on the northeast corner became Woodwards Drug Store, for many years a favorite spot for friends to gather until it was torn down. A third bank, the Merchants National Bank, opened for business on June 1, 1903 because of the demand for 6 percent loans. It flourished and was the only bank to reopen without changes after the "bank holiday." It occupied a building on the northeast corner of King and Queen streets, remodeling several times. Eventually the Bank of Phoebus and the Merchants National Bank consolidated. Later they became a part of the Virginia National Bank system, and in 1985 the Sovran Bank. In 1970 a beautiful new building located on the southwest corner of King and Queen streets became the first to lead the rebirth of "Old Hampton." The northeast corner building was demolished and the site became a part of Kings Way Mall.

The Old Point National Bank, which was chartered in November of 1922 and opened for business in January of 1923, was unique in that it continued in business under its original name. All the other banking institutions had either merged with other banks or gone out of business. The bank, located in Phoebus, opened in a part of a building occupied by Cooper Confectionery on Mellen Street. Later a one-story building was constructed on the corner of Mellen and Mallory Streets. The present main office building was erected on the same site in 1971, and was enlarged in 1977 to meet the expanding needs of the growing bank.

190

In this view of South King Street about 1910, on the left side of the street is the Bank of Hampton, part of the Barnes Hotel, and the Kecoughtan Building. On the right side is a "Jamestown Exposition restaurant," Dobson's Saloon (later Apollo Theater), George W. Phillips office, "Idle Hour" moving picture theater, and the YMCA building. In front of the Powhatan Dining Room is a drinking fountain presented to the city by the Women's Christian Temperance Union. Courtesy of the Syms-Eaton Museum

The Bank of Hampton building, as it looked in 1915, was designed by Samuel Gordon Cumming, an attorney who had his office here. Courtesy of the Syms-Eaton Museum

In 1915 the view of King Street looking north included the newly-renovated Elks Hall, formerly the YMCA building. Courtesy of the Syms-Eaton Museum

This view is toward the Queen Street Bridge from the intersection of King and Queen streets in 1915. Courtesy of Syms-Eaton Museum

In 1923 the First National Bank occupied the northeast corner of the intersection of King and Queen streets. Before the Civil War, the site was the home of Robert A. Armistead. After the First National Bank closed in 1933, Woodward's Drugstore occupied the building until it was torn down. Courtesy of the Syms-Eaton Museum

The Merchants National Bank occupied the northeast corner of the intersection of King and Queen streets in 1923. It had replaced Elisha Darden's dry goods store on the site in 1903. The spire of Hampton Baptist Church can be seen in the background. Courtesy of the Syms-Eaton Museum

In January 1889 a group of black men met to discuss the advisability of organizing a building and loan association to aid minorities in securing homes and other properties. A charter was granted and the association started in a room in the Excelsior Hall on Howard Street, moved to King Street and in 1971 built a modern building on Armistead Avenue. The People's Building and Loan Association performed a dual service to the community—borrowers and investors got together for their mutual benefit and convenience for home buying and home building.

There were two other pre-World War I banks.

Boyenton's Bank was one and the Galilean Fisherman's Consolidated Bank near Marsh Market Corner was another. Both were gone by 1910. Boyenton encountered financial difficulties and the Galilean Fisherman's was absorbed by Richmond insurance combines.

Hampton life in the first decade of the new century was characterized by a leisurely pace and colorful citizens. The railroads and streetcars were increasing service to a greater area because of the demands of progress. A Hampton native wrote of this period, "All in all, Hampton was a nice quiet place in

This is how the Old Point National Bank looked in the 1940s at the corner of Mellen and Mallory streets. Courtesy of Old Point National Bank

Built in 1885, Boyenton's Bank building became the first permanent home of the Bank of Hampton. The building was occupied by Howard Saunders Insurance Company by 1915, and later by a soda shop. Courtesy of the Syms-Eaton Museum

The twenty-third Annual Convention of the Virginia State Fireman's Association met in Hampton in August of 1909. Courtesy of the Syms-Eaton Museum

The Galilean Fishermen's Printing Office was located at 186 West Queen Street near the Queen Street Baptist Church. The Rev. T. Shorts, pastor of the Queen Street Baptist Church, was the bank president. Courtesy of Charles H. Taylor Memorial Library

The Chautauqua brought literary and cultural knowledge to the town on its summer visit. A large tent was set up at the foot of Victoria Boulevard on the corner at Bridge Street. The name comes from Chautauqua, New York, where in 1874 Bishop John Heyl Vincent of the Methodist Church and a co-worker, Lewis Miller, gathered people to study and learn in preparation for winter study at home. The Kecoughtan Literary Society was formed in the early 1890s as a result of a winter reading course suggested by the Chautauqua. The society was active in 1985, contributing moral and monetary support to the new Hampton Public Library. Courtesy of the Syms-Eaton Museum

which to live. Anyone with an income of $100 a month could really live the life of Riley."

By 1908 the population had increased to five thousand. Hampton became a city of the second class. This was a golden period with parades, minstrel shows, fireworks displays, brass-band competitions and concerts, tournaments, picnics, barbershop quartets, Chautauquas, and other trappings of the "good old days." Visitors to the Jamestown Exposition in Norfolk became aware of the other side of the water. The Virginia Yacht Club was established in 1907; it was renamed the Hampton Yacht Club in 1926. In February 1909 a whale which had washed up on Buckroe Beach brought sightseers from Richmond on a special excursion train. There was a state championship football team in 1912. A new Dixie Hospital on East Queen Street in 1913 replaced the original built in 1892 on the Hampton Institute grounds. A merger of existing companies became the Newport News and Hampton Railway Gas and Electric Company, and the Post Office was built on Queen Street in 1914. Battery D, a Militia Company, came into existence on November 19, 1915.

There are many people who consider December 30, 1916, as the beginning of the end of this slow-paced living in Hampton. On that date the United States

government bought the 1,659 acres which, less than a year later (August 7, 1917), became Langley Field. An interesting sidelight to the Langley story was recorded in the *Richmond Times Dispatch* for January 13, 1935, told by Mr. Harry H. Holt, clerk of courts of Elizabeth City County and one of the three men responsible for the purchase of the land. He told the story in this fashion:

Every Virginian has the right to be proud of Langley Field. And probably nothing in these modern days has carried the fair name of the Old Dominion and its fame into the far corners of the earth more than have the boys Uncle Sam has quartered at this same Langley Field.

But such far reaching results were not the glorious vision of Langley Field's foster fathers. Their perspective was small indeed compared to the results which their efforts have achieved.

It was in those days—those first arid days—when old Virginia went dry that Langley Field was first conceived. With a population of only around 5,000, Elizabeth City County had an abnormal number of its citizens receiving their livelihood from the liquor industry and its many varied phases. The cutting off of this source of support seemed certain

In 1913, a new Dixie Hospital was erected at the former site of Villa Margaret on East Queen Street. It provided facilities for the care of sixty-five patients and living quarters for student nurses. This picture shows the side facing the water. Courtesy of the Syms-Eaton Museum

Miss Alice Mabel Bacon, an instructor at Hampton Normal and Agricultural Institute, established a hospital and a training school for nurses which she named Dixie, after the faithful horse which carried her to visit the sick. Courtesy of the Hampton University Archives

Hose races were part of the fireman's parade in 1909 on South King Street. Courtesy of the Syms-Eaton Museum

In 1918, this was the view of Queen Street looking west. The church next to the Post Office is the First Methodist Church, where the wedding of Miss Carrie Wood took place during the flu epidemic. Courtesy of the Syms-Eaton Museum

to doom our community. In the city of Hampton alone hundreds of families emigrated to other sections, scores were made jobless, houses were empty and business generally suffered. Most severely the blow fell upon real estate.

At the same time Congress had conveniently passed an appropriation of $300,000 for establishment of an experimental aviation station. The thought came to me: Why couldn't Hampton secure this air post and it would be sure to improve the realty values here and with the incidental purchases such a project would entail all lines of business could look to it as a boon?

I went to my closest associate, Nelson G. Groome, and laid my plan before him. He agreed that it offered a feasible way out of Hampton's dilemma. Then we consulted with H. R. Booker and together we worked out our plan.

The plan as conceived by Mr. Holt resulted in securing the air post. It was indeed a boon to Hampton's economy.

The flu epidemic in 1918 reached a peak in October with thirty deaths recorded from pneumonia and seventy-one from Spanish Influenza. Social life suffered, as witness these items from the last issue of the *Hampton Monitor*, dated October 18, 1918:

Captain W. A. Wood yesterday announced the withdrawal of the invitations to the marriage of his daughter, Miss Carrie Wood, to Captain Alvin Massenburg, because of the influenza epidemic. The wedding will take place Saturday in the First Methodist Church, but will be witnessed only by the members of the families and a few close personal friends.

Invitations to the shower given by Mrs. Richard Gaston in honor of Miss Carrie Wood, who is to be married to Capt. Alvin Massenburg tomorrow, had to be recalled owing to the illness of Mrs. Gaston.

Mrs. Gaston still continues quite ill at her home with Spanish influenza.

After World War I, Hampton began to consider some needs for "the better life" and to replace the old with the new.

A high point in the educational progress was the erection of the Hampton High School building in the early twenties. The school children, many of whom themselves would be Hampton High School graduates, little realized that day in 1922 as they marched down Victoria Avenue to Jackson Street and Kecoughtan Road toward the dedication of the long-desired building, that progress would catch up to it, too. During the seventies it would stand boarded up, be razed and by 1985 the site would once more be a grassy field.

More progress in community education came with the development of libraries. Many people have fond memories of The Esther Burdick Library which started with forty-five books in 1922 and was housed in Syms-Eaton School until the school closed. Mr. and Mrs. F. L. Burdick started the library in memory of their daughter, a former pupil of the school. It was dedicated on December 15, 1922, and was a success from the start. The books were placed on shelves and cases built on the landing in the hallway. As the demand grew, a larger place was needed so, with funds

This is the view of Queen Street looking west in 1957. Courtesy of the Syms-Eaton Museum

appropriated by the city, a large room in the basement was made an attractive place for adults and children alike. Many people in Hampton contributed books. The library was dismantled in 1938, and the books were given to the Willis School Library, Charles Taylor Library and Hampton High School Library, each with a special bookplate in recognition of the gift.

Mrs. M. C. Armstrong donated funds for the grounds, buildings and equipment for a free library which opened on July 12, 1926. Called the Charles H. Taylor Memorial Library for her father, General Charles H. Taylor, editor and owner of the *Boston Globe*, it was the first free county public library in Virginia. Miss Bessie Lee Booker was the first librarian. Soon after the library opened, a mobile library began, serving residents of Back River and Sawyer's Swamp roads. At first, Mrs. Armstrong sent out her car and chauffeur to take books to outlying areas. Reportedly, books were placed in square clothes baskets and fitted into the rumble seat. Each basket held about 85 books. When the car stopped, the librarian would ring a large bell to call the neighborhood to the bookmobile. Many Hamptonians experienced great pleasure as youngsters from the visit of the bookmobile to the country in the summertime. The author of this chapter, as a teenager, often accompanied Miss Mary Lee Daniel on the bookmobile route.

In 1942 the first branch library was opened at College Court for dependents of servicemen in Phoebus. This was the first service of its kind in the state of Virginia. Later, a branch was opened at Langley View School. These libraries performed a service during the war years but eventually were absorbed in other libraries. Other branches included the Northampton Branch (1969), Phoebus Branch (1973), Willow Oaks serving Fox Hill Area (1974), Pine Chapel (1976) and the Subregional Library for the Visually Handicapped in Phoebus (1982). On March 6, 1985, ground was broken for a much-needed new Hampton Public Library situated on Victoria Boulevard on the site of the 1899 West End Academy last known as John M. Willis Elementary School.

The beautiful Collis P. Huntington Library at Hampton University, a gift of Mrs. Collis P. Huntington as a memorial to her husband, was constructed in 1903 at a cost of sixty thousand dollars. It became the repository of one of the largest and most valuable collections on black history and culture in the country.

In March 1920 the first Hotel Chamberlin burned; in April 1928 the new Chamberlin-Vanderbilt Hotel (now the Chamberlin) replaced it. On July 4, 1928, the Hampton Yacht Club held the first annual regatta. The Hampton Horse Shows began in 1929. The twenties in Hampton were not-so-roaring perhaps, but the average citizen felt that Hampton was a real "live"

Two months after the library opened, it had a circulation of sixty volumes per day. This bookplate appeared in every library book. Courtesy of Charles H. Taylor Memorial Library

The Esther Burdick Memorial Collection was made part of the Charles H. Taylor Memorial Library. A few of the collection's books remained in circulation in 1985. Courtesy of Gerry Lassiter

The new Hampton Public Library was under construction in 1985 at the former location of John M. Willis School on Victoria Boulevard east of the present Charles H. Taylor Memorial Library. Courtesy of Rancorn, Wildman and Krause, architects

A quiet scene on Hampton Creek shows Cedar Hall in the background and the yacht club docks to the right. Courtesy of the Syms-Eaton Museum

town.

The 1930s, those Great Depression years, left a lasting impression with those folk who lived through the times. Money was scarce in Hampton, but there were no soup kitchens, no pencil or apple sellers on the streets. Citizens made do, did over, did without, and helped each other. No one in Hampton signed up for a Reconstruction Finance Corporation Loan; the city did not request relief funds from the state. Serious unemployment did not seem to exist in Elizabeth City County. The "bank holiday" of March 6 through 19, 1933, closed two banks permanently, but a new bank opened the following summer. Funds were obtained from President Roosevelt's new alphabet agencies to employ men to repair city streets and to provide jobs for projects such as the National Guard Armory and a new city hall on King Street, the Darling Stadium, George Wythe Junior High School (now an elementary school) and the Fort Monroe Bandstand. Eggs were 21 cents a dozen, bread 8 cents a loaf, a boy's shirt was 59 cents and a beginning school teacher fresh out of Farmville State Teachers College (Longwood) was happy to get $630 a year—$63 for each of ten months.

A memorable event in the thirties was the great August 1933 hurricane. Later, after names were given to such storms, Hazel in October 1954, Flossie in September 1956, and the Ash Wednesday Storm in March 1962 also did much damage, but in the nameless 1933 storm Buckroe Beach, Bayshore and Grandview suffered great destruction to homes, hotels,

amusement parks and beach erosion.

Other thirties happenings, good and bad, also brought Hampton into the limelight. In the early thirties Vincent Serio originated the Hampton One Design, a fast inexpensive sailboat which revolutionized small boat racing. His Hampton Roads Boat Works built the first one at a cost of $325, and sold it to Sydney Vincent in February 1935, who christened it *Jasyto* for his three sons, James, Sydney and Thomas. The first of many Hampton Ones, *Jasyto* rests in the Mariners Museum in Newport News, Virginia. Others may yet be seen sailing on the bay any pretty day in the year.

The city of Hampton also received national notoriety during the fall and winter of 1931. It was called the city's "Trial of the Century." Dr. Elisha Kent Kane, III, professor of romance languages at the University of Tennessee, was arrested September 13, 1931, and charged with the murder of his wife. She had drowned while swimming with him at Grandview Beach on September 11, 1931. The trial, which attracted nationwide attention, was held in the Hampton courts, and Dr. Kane was found not guilty. At the fiftieth reunion of the 1934 class of Hampton High School several in attendance laughingly recalled the day they played hookey to attend the trial and their chagrin when their pictured appeared in the paper the next day!

On the plus side, the Crusaders, a male chorus from the Hampton Institute (Hampton University,

This very early picture of Hampton High School in 1924 shows the original building before additions. The building was demolished in 1984. The Darling Stadium was later built to the west. Courtesy of Charles H. Taylor Memorial Library

1984) was organized February 12, 1938. It brought a bit of Hampton wherever it toured, singing up and down the East Coast. When Hampton began its 375th Anniversary celebration on February 23, 1985, the Crusaders supplied the musical selections.

From the time of the Spanish-American War, wartimes have brought prosperity to Hampton. World War II was no exception. Along with the nation as a whole, World War II provided the catalyst for greater progress. Langley Field, Fort Monroe, Fort Eustis, and the Newport News Shipyard brought an influx of people needing shelter, food, clothing, and services. The little town bulged at the seams, but did its best to fulfill the demands. Copeland Park opened in 1940 on eight hundred acres with 3,850 housing units. The building boom was on and with it evidence of "progress." Buses replaced the last streetcars on January 13, 1946.

After the war, to the surprise of many, Hampton continued its intense growth. In 1948, realizing the need for a radio station in Hampton, a voice of its own, Mr. Thomas Chisman, a Hampton native son, began station WVEC. It was a success from the start. In 1953, having faith in a dream, he opened television station WVEC, UHF Channel 15. For six years, it barely made it. In fact, the radio station supported the television station for some time. When the television station became VHF Channel 13, things began to improve. The station was sold in 1980 to Dun and Bradstreet for $32 million but it continued to be the voice of Hampton. Also in 1948 the Hampton Junior Woman's Club initiated a National Seafood Festival. It was quite an undertaking and became an annual club affair for the next several years. Mitzi Gaynor, then a relatively little-known starlet, was Queen Lorilei III in 1950.

Hampton was not isolated; the entire Peninsula area was growing. Unavoidably, there was postwar talk of Newport News annexing Elizabeth City County. Equally unavoidably, Wythe District, Phoebus, and Hampton voiced strong opposition to any such annexation. To understand the opposition and the relationships among the separate governments and localities, it is helpful to skip back in time. From the very beginning, Elizabeth City County and Kecoughtan meant the same thing to many people. Kecoughtan, the original name of the settlement of 1610, was changed to Elizabeth City in 1620. Elizabeth City County was one of the eight original shires incorporated in 1634, and included areas that came over time to be known as the Buckroe, Wythe, Fox Hill, and Chesapeake districts.

Each of the districts, and the towns that grew up in them, has its own unique history. Buckroe, with its famous beach, was a popular tourist attraction for many years. Its history goes back to 1610 when Lord Delaware established the first health resort and quarantine station nearby. In 1894, Mr. Edward B. Chiles of Hampton built the first public bath house; hotels were also erected, and by the early 1900s Buckroe was the favorite seaside resort on the Chesapeake. The August 1933 Hurricane and the Depression did severe damage to the beach from which it did not recover until the 1980s, when beachfront houses and condominiums sprang up. Fox Hill, which was called Rip Raps at the turn of the century, also has a long history. It is mentioned in 1625 records as a fishing settlement. It, too, was a resort with Grandview Beach, which fell to Hurricane Hazel in 1954. The Back River Lighthouse, long a local landmark, was destroyed by Flossie, the 1956 storm. Wythe took its

At the Fort Monroe Bandstand on Thursday evenings during the summer, people gathered to hear the Continental Army Band. Before the Old Point Wharf was demolished, passengers on the steamers were often welcomed by the music. Courtesy of the Casemate Museum, photo by Sp6 Russel Shipley

The Hampton Crusaders Male Chorus grew out of the Phenix High School Choir directed by Charles H. Flax in the early 1930s. Courtesy of the Daily Press, Inc.

The Hampton One Design sailboat won a prominent place in racing and captured numerous trophies for sailors. In the summer of 1937, Jack Vincent sails the Jasyto II HOD No. 40 in Hampton River. Courtesy of the Vincent Collection

East Queen Street filled with water during the 1933 hurricane. Courtesy of the Syms-Eaton Museum

Elizabeth City County Court House.
Hampton, Va.

Hampton's Courthouse dates from 1876. It was remodeled by C. Taylor Holtzsclaw in 1910, and had several subsequent additions. The horse trough was on the sidewalk for some time after World War II. Courtesy of Elizabeth Brauer

In 1905 the Buckroe Beach Fishing Pier was one of many attractions at Buckroe Beach. Courtesy of Syms-Eaton Museum

name from the family which produced George Wythe, lawyer and signer of the Declaration of Independence.

The towns also claimed rich legacies. In 1680, fifty acres were allocated by the House of Burgesses for a town to be incorporated in the county. The town, of course, is Hampton, and is the subject of this book. The town of Phoebus, incorporated in 1900, also has had a colorful and exciting past. Few people realize that the area was variously known as Mill Creek, Camp Hamilton, and Chesapeake City before it became Phoebus, named after one of its most unusual citizens. Harrison Phoebus, a truly self-made man, young and dynamic, played an important role in having the Chesapeake and Ohio Railway extended from Newport News to Chesapeake City. The C&O named its station after him, and when the town incorporated it assumed the name as well. A Phoebus native, Inez Knox, wrote

this about her town: "We always thought of the town of Phoebus as having faithful friends and being a friend to all. Togetherness was the motto if we had one." Roberta Nicholls calls the town a "survivor." In an article for the *Daily Press*, July 31, 1977, she talks about the town and its people, noting that Phoebus kept its identity and close community spirit even in the face of consolidation.

In addition to the towns of Hampton and Phoebus, the county once had a third town within its boundaries—the town of Kecoughtan. Kecoughtan was a town for just ten years from June 19, 1916, to midnight, December 31, 1926. It extended from the waters of Hampton Roads down the mid-point of Pear Avenue to the end of Pine Avenue, down Salter's Creek, and back to Hampton Roads. In 1923, a petition with seventy-nine signatures was presented to the courts requesting

For more than a century the Back River Lighthouse cast a warning light eleven miles into the Chesapeake Bay. It was built in 1829 and continued in use until 1936, when its signal was replaced by the buoys in the bay. Courtesy of Irene Weston

The summer home of President John Tyler and his second wife, Julia, was named Villa Margaret after Julia's sister. It was painted green and had a high verandah. Pearl, the youngest Tyler child, was born in this house. Courtesy of the Syms-Eaton Museum

that the town of Kecoughtan be annexed to the city of Newport News. This annexation became a controversial matter, and it took two years to come to a settlement, after which the fifteen hundred inhabitants of the "thriving village of Kecoughtan" became residents of Newport News.

All of this points to a definable difference between Elizabeth City County and Newport News, which had grown gradually since the turn of the century with the expansion of Collis P. Huntington's shipyard and then had exploded during World War II. The feeling of the three areas, Elizabeth City County, Hampton, and Phoebus, was clear enough that residents of the areas voted to consolidate and on July 1, 1952, they merged to become, in Virginia legal terminology (and in the hearts of the citizens) a city of the first class. All attempts to consolidate Hampton and Newport News failed.

Without doubt, 1952 was a critical point in Hampton's progress. With the consolidation of Hampton, Phoebus, and Elizabeth City County, it became in area a city of 57 square miles. The transition from three governments to one municipality involved cooperation and patience. The farms, though some still exist, have largely disappeared; shopping centers are abundant. The changes have been gradual and inevitable, one hopes, along the lines of progress and enterprise.

Other factors such as transportation entered into the changes. The last passenger train rolled over Hampton tracks on November 15, 1954, and on December 30, 1954, the Old Bay Line steamer *City of Richmond* made its final call at the Old Point Wharf.

However, on November 1, 1957, the Hampton Roads Bridge Tunnel opened, the longest trench-type tunnel built to that time. The National Advisory Committee for Aeronautics became the National Aeronautics and Space Administration; the original seven Mercury astronauts became part of the Hampton story in the 1960s. Military Highway, built during World War II to ease troop and supply movements, emerged as the main business throughfare. Military Highway became Mercury Boulevard after the space program started. At the same time, the city named the seven bridges over Newmarket Creek for each of the seven original astronauts.

Providing adequate health facilities was also vital for a progressive city. The first hospital was built in 1892 and was named "Dixie" after Miss Alice M. Bacon's horse, "Dixie." Miss Bacon was instrumental in starting the hospital with two wards of five beds each in June 1892 on the Hampton Institute grounds. On June 24, 1913, the Dixie Hospital moved to new quarters on land where John Tyler once had his summer home, Villa Margaret. This house was on a point of land opposite the town of Hampton on the east

Hampton General Hospital was built in 1957 on Victoria Boulevard and opened a $10 million new wing in 1984. Courtesy of Hampton General Hospital

In February of 1978 construction on the Queensway Mall unearthed street-car tracks. Courtesy of the Syms-Eaton Museum

side of Hampton Creek; therefore, it escaped the flames that destroyed the town in 1862. It was used by Union forces and in 1866 by white teachers sent by the Freedmen's Bureau. Julia Tyler sold it in 1874. Eventually it became the property of the Hampton Normal and Agricultural School, and later the site of the hospital. Villa Margaret was razed in the early 1900s. The hospital had constant growing pains as the city expanded, and in 1932 and 1943 additions were necessary. In 1959 the hospital was relocated to Victoria Boulevard, and the name was changed in 1973 to Hampton General Hospital.

On May 4, 1958, the Hampton Redevelopment and Housing Authority was born. It was to have a tremendous effect on the town and its people bringing about radical changes in the name of progress. The first project in 1962 extended Bridge Street to meet Queen Street. Portions of Phoebus and Buckroe areas were redeveloped next. Old downtown Hampton received a complete face-lift, Queen Street became Queens Way Mall, and King Street became Kings Way Mall with pedestrian traffic only and a Kiosk where

the streets cross. The Westhampton housing project plus two community centers have been successful. HRHA is currently providing housing opportunities for over sixteen hundred families. The redevelopment projects tied the ring road system into the new Booker T. Washington Bridge which opened January 11, 1985.

Citizens of Hampton have taken great care to remember the place in history of the city and the area. There was quite a celebration in the city for the 350th anniversary of the settlement at Jamestown. Hampton Day, May 1, 1957, began at 9:30 A.M. on the Veterans' Administration grounds overlooking Hampton Roads near what is traditionally believed to be the original landing place of the colonists. A band concert by Hampton High School students was followed by the dedication of the monument and a pageant, "The Landing at Kecoughtan," lunch, and an air show at Langley Field. The full day ended with a parade and dance in Old Hampton. Hampton celebrated its own 350th birthday three years later with a series of events using the theme *Out of the Past...the Future.* A special seal was adopted for the year depicting the silhouette of three halberdiers with a sailing vessel in the background symbolizing the 1607 landing at Kecoughtan. The next year, on May 10, 1961, a seal designed by the British College of Heralds became the new seal for the city. Hampton became the only place outside the British Commonwealth to possess a seal prepared by the College.

The crest of the new seal depicts a Chesapeake Bay crab holding aloft in its claws a Mercury space capsule while standing on a wreath of the colors. This rests on a casque which, in turn, surmounts a shield embracing four crowned and tethered buffaloes from the arms of the third Earl of Southampton, for whom the city was named, divided by the Cross of St. George from the flag of England. Above the cross are three fleurs-de-lis from the arms of the Princess Elizabeth, eldest daughter of King James I, for whom was named Elizabeth City County, which consolidated with the City of Hampton in 1952. Supporting the arms are a

This seal was designed in 1920 and placed over the entrance to the 1938 City Hall. However, historians found the depiction of the teepee and the log cabin to be inaccurate. Courtesy of Charles H. Taylor Memorial Library

Hampton was established as a town and port in 1705. It was incorporated as a city in 1852 and again in 1887. These photos depict three of the city's seals since its incorporation. Courtesy of the Syms-Eaton Museum

halberdier of the reign of King James I, much like those who accompanied the colonists who settled Hampton, on the right and Chief Pochin, of the Algonquin village of Kecoughtan which then occupied the site, holding his longbow on the left. Under all of these the scrolled city motto, *E praeteritis futura,* "Out of the past, the future."

The basic seal consists of these arms within a ring inscribed simply "Hampton, Virginia, July 9, 1610." The new seal departed radically from the 1887 seal which "shall be in the shape of a circle, with a double border; around this circle shall be the following inscription: Hampton, Virginia, Incorporated May 1887. In the centre of the circle shall be the figure of a crab."

Anniversaries were not the only reason for having fun. The Hampton Exchange Club initiated "City Employees Day" in 1963 which later became Hampton Fair Day, a day that captured the spirit and traditions of the county fair. This became a very popular event every year held at Gosnold's Hope Park. Another festival, Bay Days, was first presented in October 1979 by the old Hampton merchants and the Citizens Program for Chesapeake Bay. Held in downtown Hampton, the program offered something for everyone. By 1985, the two events were combined and, from all reports, a good time was had by all! Seafood, craft exhibits, carnival rides, art shows, races, music, dances, shows, and of course, fireworks for a grand finale combined to make great things happen in the old downtown with its King's Way and Queen's Way pedestrian malls.

The story of education and schools of Hampton has its own chapter in this history. Yet, there is an event that bears emphasis. In 1960 the first black student entered a previously all-white school in Hampton. Cities and towns elsewhere in the South were fighting integration. In Hampton, however, things moved calmly and deliberately. While some tension, frustration, and difficulty arose, cool heads and careful planning, under the direction of C. A. Lindsay, superintendent of schools, made the transition from segregation to integration fairly smooth. Luther Santiful, president of the Hampton NAACP, wrote in 1973:

Construction began on the Hampton Coliseum in early 1969. Courtesy of the Hampton Coliseum, city of Hampton

The race question has caused a lot of turmoil in Virginia. But we haven't been making headlines in Hampton, we've been making progress. Instead of lying back and then griping when we didn't get results, we've worked to shape things as they're being planned. We've integrated the government, the businesses, and the schools—and we did it quietly. When the School Board came up with a desegregation plan that called for extensive busing, City Council gave its support. We never had to go to court. I don't think there is another major city in Virginia that can make those claims.

A plaque, dated December 1972, was awarded by the NAACP to the Hampton School Board for "its steadfast adherance to the mandate of the American people that segregated schooling must end; and for its maintenance of principle in the face of continuing and formidable pressure." There is no doubt that smooth integration in Hampton was aided by the influence of Hampton University. The city and the college always had a close "family" relationship, a mutual respect for each other and an awareness of the dependence of each to the other. Hampton city folks worked, taught, and attended events at the Institute. The students shopped downtown. General Armstrong's influence for good was at work from the beginning of Hampton Institute and almost a hundred years later.

In 1963, Mrs. Ann Kilgore became the first woman to be mayor of the city. The population was 89,258, the city was fifty-seven square miles in area with some areas totally undeveloped, still some pasture and farming land; the baby boom was in the schools, enrollments totalled 17,978, and were steadily increasing. The need for urban renewal was urgent, and some problems resulting from the consolidation remained unresolved. A decade later, in 1973, two years after her administration ended, Hampton was selected an All-American City. Mrs. Kilgore, a former school teacher, combined optimism with a clear-headed analysis of Hampton's needs, and proceeded to do something about the problems which faced the city. That she succeeded was evident. She was selected to make the presentation for the city in the All-America Cities Award competition.

December 1, 1969, provided another milestone and another first for Hampton. The Coliseum, the first such cultural and sports center in Virginia, held its first, albeit unofficial, event on that date—The College of William and Mary vs. North Carolina State in basketball. Built at a cost of $8,500,000, seating eleven thousand, the building offered an impressive sight from Interstate 64. Its faceted construction resembled an architectural jewel, its reflection sparkling in the freshwater lake, pleasing to the eye of the beholder. A wide variety of quality events used the new arena: top entertainers of all kinds, sports and sports figures, the circus, rodeo, ice skating, conventions, concerts, and special shows such as antique, boat, craft, and art. The Hampton Institute Kool Jazz Festival, begun at the college in 1968, moved to the Coliseum. Jack Benny officially opened the Coliseum on January 31, 1970. Not only did it provide an economic stimulator, it also served as a metaphor for progress in the community,

206

City Hall is seen from the Hampton waterfront. Courtesy of the Hampton Planning Department, city of Hampton; photo by Barbara Dorr

On July 9, 1985, Hampton celebrated its 375th anniversary with a birthday cake, parade, church service and fireworks. Courtesy of Jack Johnson

In 1985, a luxury hotel was planned as a focal point for the downtown waterfront. Courtesy of the Planning Department, city of Hampton

City Councilwoman Brenda Wharton, left, and Anniversary co-chairman Elizabeth Brauer cut the city's five-tier birthday cake. Photo by Jacquelyn A. Johnson

207

taking Hampton from the horse and buggy age to the jet age of entertainment.

The years of the Vietnam War, 1965 to 1973, left a legacy to the United States in general and to Hampton in particular in the form of refugees seeking freedom and a better life. The people of Hampton opened their hearts, homes, churches and pocketbooks to hundreds of Asians. In turn the Cambodians, Laotians, Vietnamese and others added new dimensions and new insights to the culture and life style of the town. Many opened restaurants serving oriental food; the children rubbed elbows with the students in Hampton schools; some found jobs in service stations, in fish and crab plants, as seamstresses and tailors, and in the professions. They attended classes in English and learned skills necessary to obtain other jobs. They used the Social Service and Health Departments and when necessary, came in contact with other agencies also. Hampton became their hometown.

The Bicentennial of the United States was celebrated in Hampton with events concerning Hampton as a Revolutionary War port town. Because of Hampton's strategic location on the water it was an important port and during the Revolution it was the home of Virginia's State Navy. The Battle of Hampton which occurred in October 1775 was the first battle of the Revolution in Virginia. The British were turned back after a two day confrontation. This was re-enacted on October 26 and 27, 1975, at the foot of King Street and on Kings Way Mall. Other events included a band concert by Hampton City School's All-City Band, an arts festival, an exhibit depicting Hampton as a port town, a twelve-hundred-dollar contest for Hampton Roads artists dealing with the "Hampton Heritage," and a special celebration on Hampton Fair Day September 13, 1975, in Gosnold's Hope Park.

As Hampton continued to grow so did commercial and shopping opportunities. Coliseum Mall, the largest retail shopping center between Norfolk and Washington, D.C., opened in 1973. Newmarket North Mall opened next and by 1985 at least twelve large shopping centers existed in the area. An ultra-modern nine-story Hampton City Hall can be seen from many vantage points. It was dedicated on January 8, 1977; it is expected to serve the needs of the city government into the next century.

"The Hampton Spirit" was the theme of the All America City presentation which led the April 1973 announcement that Hampton, Virginia, was named as All-America City for 1973. What defined this Hampton spirit? In his address May 1, 1957, at the unveiling of the Kecoughtan Monument presented by the Hampton Historical Society, E. Sclater Montague said, "There is something intangible, undefinable, and unexplainable about Hampton: It is a spiritual quality. In many respects, citizenship in Hampton is synonymous with a philosophy of good living and a way of life, which I consider unsurpassed by any community in which I have ever resided. Though I have travelled upon every continent of the world, I have never discovered Hampton's equal." Elbert Hutton, known to all as "Tiny," in an address at Hampton Landing Day Ceremony on May 5, 1968, described Hampton's spirit in this manner: "Hampton has her firsts, far more than any other community I know. But there is a great deal more to Hampton than just being the first to do anything; that is the lasting quality that Hampton has. It is this lasting quality built on vision, understanding and courage begun by those men who stopped here in 1607, followed by those of every generation, and being carried on by those around us past 1968, that has made Hampton the proud community that it is today and the greater community that it will be tomorrow." On April 16, 1973, David Montague, mayor when Hampton earned All-America City honors, expanded on his father's (E. Sclater Montague) words: "It is now time to look toward the future, with a new sense of purpose mingled with pride, to seek areas for greater cooperation, to plan for further improving the quality of life for all our citizens."

In 1982, thirty years after consolidation, the population had more than doubled from 60,994 in 1952 to 130,000. Once Hampton was a segregated, Democratic community; by the mid-1980s it had become an integrated, bi-partisan multicultural city. By all accounts Hampton faced an expansive future into the twenty-first century.

Hampton waterfront looked like this from the 9th floor of City Hall in 1980. Courtesy of the Planning Department, city of Hampton; photo by Barbara Dorr

ACKNOWLEDGMENTS

In my effort to get accurate and interesting facts about Hampton's last eighty-five years, I have talked to many people. I wish to thank the following: Mr. Thomas Chisman (WVEC); Mrs. Nan Holtzsclaw, Carolyn Hawkins, Rick Piester (Hampton General Hospital); Carol Booth (Daily Press); Ed Haughton and John Sharp (Hampton Planning Department); Gerry Lassiter (Charles H. Taylor Memorial Library); Mike Cobb (Syms-Eaton Museum); Andy Greenwell (Coliseum); Mary Jackson (Old Point National Bank); the staff of the Hampton University Archives; Neva Smith, Joanne Dotson, and Karen Hall (Hampton Redevelopment); Wallace Hicks (Hampton Fire Department); Thomas H. Daniel (Parks Department); and Mary Richardson (Typist).

Five, four, three, two, one, Liftoff! The Space Shuttle ascends from Cape Canaveral, Florida. Langley engineers and technicians proved that the *Shuttle's tiles were flight worthy as both a thermal protection and a structural system. Courtesy of NASA*

8
Chapter
To the Stars—
the Development of NASA

by James R. Hansen

One might have thought that the cosmopolitan character of modern science and technology called for locating America's first, and, until after World War II began, *only* aeronautical research center in the industrialized northeast, in the nation's capital, or perhaps on the campus of a major university. Instead, the National Advisory Committee for Aeronautics, or NACA, selected a tract of farm land just north of Hampton, Virginia, a small and rather isolated town on the southwestern shore of the Chesapeake Bay, as the site of its first laboratory. With 20/20 hindsight, knowing what we know about the many historic firsts in aeronautics and space technology that would be accomplished at Langley in the next seventy years, the selection of Hampton as the site of the nation's research center seems clairvoyant. But in the early years of NACA Langley, many people had good reasons to consider the selection of Hampton a fatal mistake.

How and why was this site selection made which has had so much influence on the course of Hampton history since 1917? Why was a sprawling complex of modern laboratories, wind tunnels, and offices built near this town, of all places, where crops of wheat and alfalfa had recently grown, and watermen farmed oysters in the waters of nearby Back River? How and why was this area, which was then known to some as "the Asia Minor of Virginia," chosen by the federal government as the place for constructing a facility that was to become one of the most important research centers in the world?

In its early years the NACA was an obscure, small potatoes operation. Conceived in 1915 by a few far-sighted men who feared that the homeland of the Wright brothers might fall hopelessly behind the European belligerents in aviation, the fledgling agency began with a meager five-thousand-dollar budget and the unpaid services of twelve presidential appointees. Faced with such limitations, the NACA slowly came to realize that its best chance to obtain enough land for even a small laboratory was to cooperate with an Army project. In 1915, as aerial combat over France intensified, Congress had directed the War Department to identify an American military reservation already suitable for housing an experimental aeronautics facility. When that quest failed, the secretary of war authorized $300,000 for the purchase of a new site. The Chief of Army aviation appointed a board of officers to investigate new locations for the proving ground, and agreed to give the NACA the benefit of its inquiries and conclusions and to make available any land chosen.

The center's original name was the Langley Memorial Aeronautical Laboratory, after Prof. Samuel Pierpont Langley (1834-1906), above left, *who had been a leading American scientist of flight and head of the Smithsonian Institution in Washington, D.C. In 1948, its name was shortened to the Langley Aeronautical Laboratory. Ten years later, when the center was transferred from NACA to NASA, it became the Langley Research Center.* Above right, *five biplanes parked outside of the NACA hangar in 1924. Courtesy of NASA*

After considering fifteen tracts of land (six in Maryland, four in Virginia, and one each in West Virginia, Tennessee, Ohio, Illinois, and Missouri), the board's president informed the NACA of the Army's choice—1,650 acres in Elizabeth City County, Virginia, just north of the town of Hampton. Following an inquiry to the surgeon general concerning health conditions in the Hampton area and an inspection of the site by one of its subcommittees, the NACA recommended that "this site be obtained for the use of the Government at as early a date as practicable." The chairman of the NACA summarized the rationale behind his endorsement of the site for Langley Field in the NACA's *Annual Report* to Congress for 1916: Hampton, close to the Chesapeake Bay but reasonably immune from attack, stood in relative proximity to Washington, D.C., (an overnight steamer ride) and to the shipbuilding and repair industries at Newport News, Norfolk, and Portsmouth. Temperate but changeable climate, plus location alongside a tidal river, permitted experimental flying above both land and water and under nearly all conditions that aircraft would meet in service.

Climate and topography seemed to bless the site, but shrewd Hampton businessmen sold it. Harry H. Holt, clerk of the court of Elizabeth City County; Hunter R. Booker, president of the Hampton-Phoebus

Harry Holt was county clerk and head of the local committee that brought the site near Hampton to the government's attention. Courtesy of Hampton Center for Arts and Humanities

Members of the United States Army Corps of Engineers surveyed the site of Langley Field in the fall of 1916. Courtesy of NASA

Merchants' Association; Col. Nelson S. Groome, executive officer of the Hampton Bank; and Capt. Frank W. Darling, vice-president of two local banks and head of J. S. Darling and Son, the third largest oyster packer in the United States, saw a chance to revive a struggling economy while making a profit for themselves. This local committee brought Hampton to the government's attention.

Elizabeth City County had a population of around five thousand during World War I. Until a referendum in December 1914, a significant number of its citizens had earned their livelihood from the liquor industry. Then the Commonwealth of Virginia went dry. Harry H. Holt recalled the parching effects of Prohibition:

The cutting off of this source of support seemed certain to doom our community. In the city of Hampton alone, hundreds of families emigrated..., scores were made jobless, houses were empty and business generally suffered.

The most severe blow fell upon holders of real estate. Holt approached banker Groome, his closest associate, with news of the government's interest in buying land for an airfield. "There were ideal sites," Holt assured him, "in the plantations of the Sherwood, Lambington, Pool, Morefield, Blumfield and Shellbank properties."

Quietly, so as not to attract attention to the speculation, the two proceeded quietly to secure cheap ninety-day options on large parts of these properties.

From Halloween to Thanksgiving 1916, the Hampton committee, spearheaded by Holt and Groome, met once at home and once in Washington with the army's site selection board. "We had just the right place to offer," Holt recalled in 1935, "and after repeated visits here, and agreements by us to build a railroad line onto the property, a price of $290,000 was finally agreed upon." The entrepreneurs were forced to sink $17,000 into some unexpected purchases of right-of-way—$3,000 of which was defrayed by a stock subscription by the Newport News, Hampton, and Old Point Railway—but they had walked off with all but $10,000 of the $300,000 authorized by Congress and the War Department for the land purchase.

The land gamble paid off handsomely for Holt and confreres, but it also benefitted the entire northern shore of Hampton Roads. A small group of men had made about $175 an acre on typical Tidewater fringe land—low-lying next to shallow water. (By April 1918, in fact, when the Atlantic, Gulf, and Pacific Company concluded dredging a channel in Back River to allow larger boats to dock, it had deposited 1,791,320 cubic meters of fill onto Langley Field at a cost of half a million dollars.) The entire community cheered the

These aerial views of Langley Field were taken in 1938. In the foreground of both pictures stands the NACA's 2,060-foot long towing tank, which was used to study the hydrodynamic performance of water-based aircraft. Courtesy of NASA

venturesome heroes and the expected business boom: the Newport News *Daily Press* announced a "fine Christmas for the entire Lower Peninsula...the future of this favored section of Virginia is made." Public works—road, bridge, and electric railway construction—reverberated around Langley Field for many years to come. Prior to these projects, it had been "almost impossible to get...to Newport News, or for that matter, to get anywhere" from Hampton. Many residents were not exactly sure what was going on at Langley Field (even today, many do not differentiate between Air Force and NASA activities there), but all recognized the life-giving energy of the thousands of federal dollars poured into their midst.

But the reality of Langley Field was hardly as pleasant to the laborers who built the government installation as was the promise of the field to the local citizens who were bound to benefit materially from living close to it. The construction of the flying field was an ordeal. One of the first soldiers to arrive at the site recorded that it was

> Nature's greatest ambition to produce in this, her cesspool, the muddiest mud, the weediest weeds, the dustiest dust and the most ferocious mosquitoes the world has ever known. Her plans were so well formulated and adhered to that she far surpassed her wildest hopes and desires...

Forty-six Langley workers died of influenza between September 1918 and January 1919. So severe was the epidemic that the undertaker who had the contract for burying the government dead was unable to secure enough coffins to take immediate care of the bodies.

One person who experienced the ordeal of con-

structing Langley Field was Thomas Wolfe, who, in his autobiographical novel *Look Homeward, Angel* (1929), described how young Eugene Gant (Wolfe in fictional clothing) spent the summer of 1918. From Norfolk

he went by boat once more to Newport News, and by trolley up the coast to Hampton. He had heard, in the thronging rumor of Norfolk, that there was work upon the Flying Field, and the worker was fed and housed upon the field, at company expense.

In the little employment shack at the end of the long bridge that led across into the field, he was signed on as a laborer and searched by the sentry, who made him open his valise. Then he labored across the bridge...staggered at length into the rude company office and sought out the superintendent....

He was given a job as a personal checker, a horse to ride, $80 a month, and room and board.

Three times a day he rode around the field to check the numbers of two dozen gangs who were engaged in the work of grading, levelling, blasting from the spongy earth the ragged stumps of trees and filling interminably, ceaselessly, like the weary and fruitless labor of a nightmare, the marshy earth-craters, which drank their shovelled toil without end. The gangs were of all races and conditions:...part of the huge compost of America.

Conditions were so difficult for the NACA at Langley in the early years, and its relations with the military authorities so poor, that the NACA seriously considered moving its research center somewhere else. In December 1916, the NACA had asked the Army for an official designation of property on which it could construct its own laboratory buildings, but the Army had failed to respond. Air Service commanders wanted to maintain control not only over the field but over all experimentation that was to take place there, including that to be conducted by the NACA. (The chief of the Air Service Technical Command opposed the idea of dual military-civilian control so much that, in January 1919, he recommended to the Army's director of military aeronautics that all NACA personnel at Langley Field "be subject" to his orders.) The NACA repeated its request three months later, but the Army answered that formal assignment of land would be postponed "until the work of preparing Langley Field [was] in a more advanced state." The Army used the same delaying tactic to ward off similar appeals made by the NACA in August 1917 and December 1918.

After the war ended the military could continue to put off the NACA for only so long. In April 1919 the acting secretary of war approved an Air Service recommendation that "the portion of Langley Field known as Plot 16 be definitely set aside for use by the NACA for their purposes in constructing laboratories or other utilities in the problems of flight." Although welcomed by the NACA, the Army's offer was hardly generous. The NACA had already acquired Plot 16 unofficially in 1917. By the end of 1918, the NACA's first building on this land had been erected, and work on its first wind tunnel had been started. And there was another problem with this tardy token of Army generosity: it was too small to accommodate the building of any living quarters for NACA employees. Suitable housing close to work was for the NACA a major problem that only the military could remedy. In

July 1919, after repeated requests from the NACA chairman, the Army did agree reluctantly to make primitive housing, along with heat, light, and telephone services, available to a certain number of civilian Langley employees. This arrangement, though unpleasant, was better than nothing, but it lasted only a short time. In the fall of 1919, based on a ruling by its judge advocate general, the Army informed the NACA that it could no longer furnish Langley's civilian employees with housing or utilities.

Isolation, mosquito bites, flu, inadequate housing, and poor relations with the military—where but Langley Field could things be so bad? This question began to plague one NACA employee after another early in 1919 until feelings against the place festered into a mutiny. In July of that year, the NACA's engineer in charge of building and construction complained to NACA headquarters in Washington that "Langley Field can never be an efficient or satisfactory place for the Committee to carry on research work." Headquarters agreed, and in its *Annual Report* for 1919, the NACA formally requested congressional approval to move the laboratory from Langley to Bolling Field, a base under construction in the District of Columbia.

But the reluctance of Congress to change the lab's location and its cutting of the NACA's postwar budget requests forced the Langley staff to make the best of a bad situation near Hampton. In 1919 and 1920, the staff pushed to finish the wind tunnel, dynamometer lab, administration building and small warehouse, and began preliminary research—a flight investigation of the lift and drag characteristics of the Curtiss Jenny airplane. The full-time Langley complement grew from three to eleven persons. Meanwhile, an inquiry by the Committee revealed that Bolling Field had serious shortcomings of its own.

Formal dedication of the Langley Memorial Aeronautical Laboratory on June 11, 1920, guaranteed that the NACA would remain near Hampton. Ceremonies included an aerial exhibition highlighted by a twenty-five plane formation led by Brig. Gen. William "Billy" Mitchell, addresses by prominent military and civilian officers congratulating the NACA and giving it best wishes, and a tour and demonstration of the wind tunnel—all of which improved morale. As a result of this fine occasion, relations between the NACA and the Army improved immediately. Ten days after the

dedication, the NACA chairman sent a warm letter to the commanding officer of Langley Field, thanking him for courtesies extended the Committee at the ceremonies. "The efficiency of our work at Langley Field," wrote the chairman, "depends in the end to a great extent upon the degree which you give us your support, and I feel that if your cooperation on June 11 was an indication of your attitude toward us, we can rest assured as to the future."

Although relations with the military grew more cordial after the lab's formal dedication in 1920, relations between the NACA laboratory and Hampton still needed much improvement. For over three hundred years, the life of the town had been shaped predominantly by people whose everyday business and lifelong passion involved moving through the water. Now, the life of the town was being influenced significantly by people whose everyday business and lifelong passion involved flying through the air. For a period of time, then, until they discovered their common ground, the watermen and the airmen of Hampton were to be divided into two distinct parties that did not always get along.

In the mind of one Langley veteran of the 1920s, "there is no question" that, in the early years of the NACA, the professional employees of the Langley Memorial Aeronautical Laboratory "were not, on the whole, warmly welcomed into the community." This fact, he believes,

> was due only in part to the natural reluctance of the local people, who had had Hampton completely to themselves for so many years, to accept strangers into their social and civic circles. I believe it was due in part to the misguided and somewhat "smart-alecky" behavior of some of the Langley professionals, who regarded themselves as intellectually superior to the natives.

When asked to make a few remarks to the Hampton Rotary Club in 1923, Langley's first engineer-in-charge, for example, used the opportunity to tell everyone what he thought was wrong with the town.

The great majority of NACA scientists and engineers working at Langley had come there from great distances beyond Hampton, mostly from the northern states that possessed the major universities and technical schools. Many of these research profes-

Curtiss JN4H "Jenny" prepares to take off from Langley Field for NACA flight research, 1919. Courtesy of NASA

The first wind tunnel, called the Atmospheric Tunnel, was dedicated in June 1920. Courtesy of NASA

sionals left Langley in the 1920s—not because they were unhappy with the NACA per se, but because they were unhappy in Hampton. In the eyes of many college-educated northerners, the community appeared a cultural backwater, an isolated place surrounded by large bodies of water on three sides and a wilderness of marshes and tall pines on the fourth. With the exception of regular steamboat lines on the Chesapeake Bay and a few river ferries, travel into or away from the Peninsula was difficult. Unlike today's citizens, Hamptonians then enjoyed neither a tunnel under Hampton Roads to Norfolk nor bridges spanning the wide James River at Newport News or the York River at Yorktown. Langley Field itself rested at the northern frontier of Elizabeth City County as an island within an island. A few miles of farms and swampland separated the airfield from the small town. Only bad roads—some made from crushed oyster shells—linked laboratory to living room. The most attractive residential areas were the farthest from Langley, along the boulevards paralleling Hampton Roads, the James River, or Buckroe Beach on the Bay. And the old families who lived in these established neighborhoods did not welcome strangers from the north into their midst. One young Langley arrival, after failing to find a room-for-rent sign in a

pleasant neighborhood, went to the door of a private home in order to ask advice of its owner. The homeowner, besides informing him that he knew of no rentals, growled that the newcomer was the first "Yankee" ever to come through that gate.

Langley management was very aware of this and other housing problems. A number of the earliest employees had had to sleep on cots in the Research Laboratory Building. Several unmarried men had herded together in boarding houses while others had slept at hotels. Some NACA recruits had even turned down job appointments because they could not find suitable residences for themselves and their families in Hampton. Late in the 1920s the lab endeavored to influence some local businessmen to finance the building of new houses and apartments for its employees and even took surveys on what rent its employees would be willing to pay, how many rooms and what kind of furnishings were required, etc. This effort to motivate the local construction industry met with some success, but the problem of finding satisfactory housing remained severe for Langley employees into the 1950s.

The environment oppressed the newcomer in at least one other way. One aeronautical engineer who reported to work at Langley from Michigan arrived in Hampton on a humid summer day in 1927 when the temperature was ninety-five degrees. People told him that it was unseasonably hot, but the young man subsequently discovered that it was unseasonably hot there almost every year at that time. What was worse, Prohibition was in effect!

In many individual cases, of course, there were friendly relations between NACA employees and Hampton natives even in the beginning. It simply took time for the newcomers and natives to get to know each other through church, school, or business contacts. As another Langley oldtimer remembers:

Among the important factors contributing to improved relations over the years have been the marriage of local girls to Langley men, the active participation of Langley employees in civic and other community activities, and the increasing economic importance of the government laboratory to the community as a whole.

There were a few aberrations in this steadily improving picture, however. In the 1930s, for example, some of the townspeople resented a prominent member of the NACA laboratory for becoming deeply involved

Langley's staff of young engineers wore shorts to beat the Tidewater heat in 1930. Courtesy of NASA

In 1937 major parts of Langley's Nineteen-Foot Pressure Tunnel were built by area construction workers. Courtesy of NASA

NACA nuts are shown supervising cleanup operations after the 1933 hurricane. Courtesy of NASA

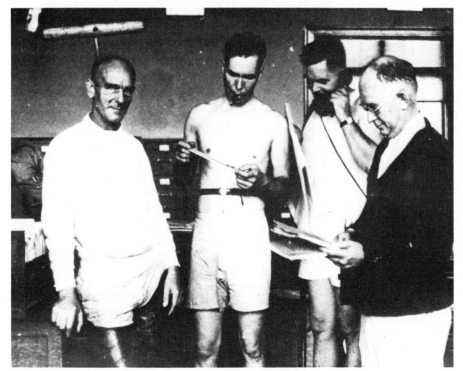

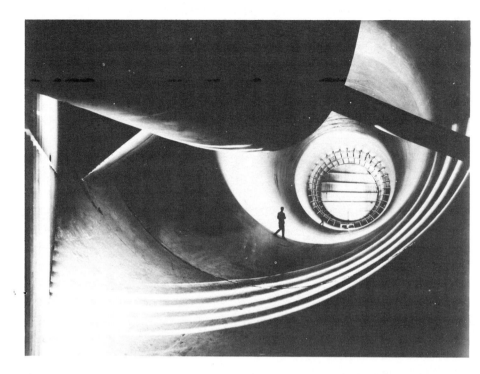

In the public mind, the wind tunnel is the shadowy domain of many NASA wizards. Courtesy of NASA

in local politics. Another aberration was caused by the general exemption from military service of Langley professional employees during World War II. One Langley engineer recalls his children being "ostracized" by schoolmates because their father was regarded as a draft dodger.

Such instances were the exceptions, though, and the general picture to be drawn is one of cool initial reception of the NACA outsiders followed by a slow but steady improvement in community relations over the years until nearly all NACA employees felt completely accepted by and part of the Hampton society.

This is not to say that longtime Hampton natives stopped distinguishing between themselves and other people altogether. There are many tall tales still being told in the city's barber shops and garages about "NACA Nuts"—eccentric Langley employees who wanted to know the RPM of their vacuum cleaners and asked that their lumber be cut to the sixteenth of the inch. In local lore, this technical sophisticate was the dreaded figure of every hardware salesman in Hampton and nearby Newport News. One local Ford dealer, in fact, employed a special salesman who understood automotive engineering just to take care of customers from NACA.

This interesting period in the social history of Hampton changed dramatically beginning in late 1957 as a result of the Sputnik crisis. In step with the nation's growing awareness of the importance of space

exploration for American prestige and security, many Hampton residents stopped perceiving Langley's scientists and engineers so much as "nuts" and began seeing them more as "wizards"—the technological magicians who could not only explain to them the meaning of the foreign objects orbiting ominously overhead but who could also answer whatever challenges to the nation's security those objects implied, conjuring the scene from *The Wizard of Oz* where the wicked witch flies over the city spelling out "Surrender Dorothy," and all the terrified citizens of Oz rushed to the wizard to find out what it meant. In the early 1960s, when nearly every NASA mission received national television coverage complete from liftoff to splashdown, and Langley was the home of the Space Task Group which ran Project Mercury, the city of Hampton showed its appreciation for the activities of Langley Research Center as it had never done before, changing the name of "Military Highway" to "Mercury Boulevard" and dedicating the town's numerous bridges in honor of the original astronauts.

Since that time nearly twenty-five years ago, Hampton and NASA Langley Research Center have grown closer together until they are now united in a community of mutual respect. Where two human passions—one for water, and one for air—had once separated neighbors into parties with little in common, a new passion—for space—helped bring them together.

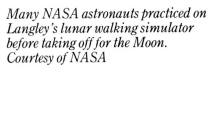

The Mercury astronauts received their original spaceflight training at Langley in 1959. Front row (from left) are Virgil "Gus" Grissom, Scott Carpenter, Donald "Deke" Slayton, Gordon Cooper; rear (from left) are Alan Shepard, Walter Schirra, and John Glenn. Courtesy of NASA

Many NASA astronauts practiced on Langley's lunar walking simulator before taking off for the Moon. Courtesy of NASA

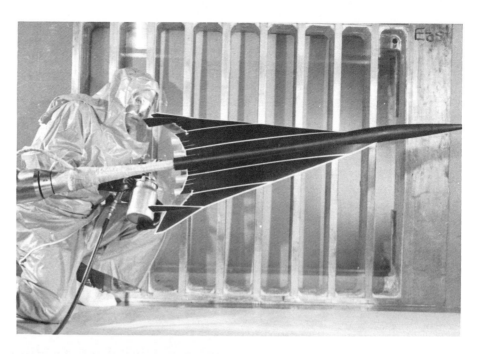

In 1970 this NASA wizard, clothed head to foot in protective plastic clothing, applied a toxic solution to a model of an advanced supersonic tunnel transport for wind-tunnel testing. He then knew wherever turbulent airflow occurred on the model, because the chemical evaporated at that point. Courtesy of NASA

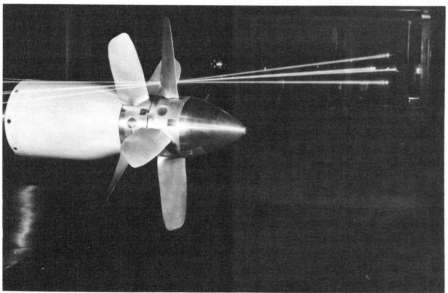

An example of NASA's technological prestidigitation from 1983: a laser velocimeter explores the characteristics of an advanced counter-rotating turboprop concept in Langley's four-by-seven-meter Wind Tunnel. Courtesy of NASA

This is one of NASA's concepts for a permanent space station. Courtesy of NASA

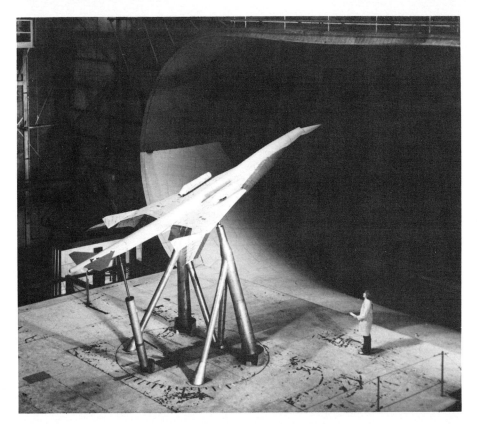

The busy west area of NASA Langley Research Center is seen here in 1984. Forty-five years earlier, before World War II, there was nothing here but trees and farmland. Courtesy of NASA

Today there is renewed interest at the center in a concerted national effort to ready technology for the development of an American super SST, a 250-passenger supersonic transport capable of cruising speed in excess of Mach 2.5! In this photo from 1975, a 1/7th-scale model of an advanced SST concept is being tested in Langley's Full-Scale Tunnel. Courtesy of NASA

EPILOGUE

by Elizabeth H. Brauer and Harrol A. Brauer, Jr.

Hampton, the oldest continuous English-speaking settlement in America, celebrated its 375th Anniversary in 1985.

Since its founding on July 9, 1610, Hampton has played an important role in the critical events that have shaped our nation's growth. To commemorate this milestone in our heritage, the entire year of 1985 was devoted to observing, honoring and celebrating Hampton's significant contributions to the past, as well as recognizing its potential in years to come.

The anniversary celebration's mission and challenges to promote a sense of civic pride, to encourage economic development and tourism, and to leave legacies for future generations were accomplished beyond expectations.

Events and activities for the year-long observance were segmented into five periods of emphasis: Celebration Premiere, Celebration of the Mind, Celebration Birthday, Celebration of the Spirit, and Celebration Reflections and Challenges.

The plan was designed to celebrate and commemorate the character and significance of Hampton, with something to involve each and every citizen. Beyond the numerous activities during these periods of emphasis, a special twelve-week activity was "In Pursuit of Hampton," our popular and enlightening history trivia game.

The legacy contributions included presenting to Hampton: a historical landmark sampler, a numbered 375th commemorative pewter plate and a city flag, all of which traveled aboard the recreated *Godspeed* and then into space via a space shuttle, carrying through our theme, "First from the Sea—First to the Stars"; a bronze sculpture depicting the anniversary theme; scrapbooks with anniversary memorabilia; and this pictorial history book.

The overwhelming success of the 375th Anniversary year was the direct result of many citizens who gave of their talents and time to share our Hampton, a city worth knowing.

> Elizabeth H. Brauer
> Harrol A. Brauer, Jr.
> Co-chairmen
> Hampton 375th Anniversary Committee

HAMPTON HISTORICAL CALENDAR

Jan. 1, 1829   Edgar Allan Poe is promoted to sergeant major at Fort Monroe

1863   Lincoln issues Emancipation Proclamation

1923   *Daily Press* advertises Florsheim shoes for $10 at Wyatt Brothers

Jan. 4, 1896   First issue of *Daily Press* is published

1921   Wythe and Hampton schools authorize use of standardized tests

Jan. 6, 1609   Capt. John Smith and company end lodging with the Indians at Kecoughtan after severe winter weather

1921   Hampton police move to new quarters on Court Street

Jan. 7, 1846   Hampton justices order family at Little England quarantined for smallpox

Jan. 8, 1830   St. John's Church is consecrated

1977   City Hall is dedicated

Jan. 9, 1921   Mrs. H. L. Schmeltz heads $3,000 campaign to feed starving Armenians

Jan. 12, 1805   Syms and Eaton properties sold to establish new school called Hampton Academy on Cary Street

1922 $100,000 authorized to build Queen Street Bridge

Jan. 14, 1898   Citizens ask legislature for $100,000 bond issue for sewer and paving

Jan. 16, 1898   Fire destroys 80-year-old Sewall mansion in Phoebus

1925   Phoebus Chamber of Commerce proposes ferry to Willoughby Spit

Jan. 17, 1873   Capt. P. T. Woodfin assumes charge of National Soldiers' Home

Jan. 18, 1922   Crabbers oppose ban on winter crab dredging

1925   Diary entry printed describing burning of Hampton

1925   Old Point Improvement Co. given permission to rebuild 315-room Chamberlin Hotel after fire

Jan. 22, 1922   Police announce 63 arrests in prohibition crackdown

Jan. 24, 1828   Hampton and Mill Creek Bridge Co. granted permission to build toll bridges on ferry routes

1925   Army Air Force photographers from Langley Field photograph eclipse from the air

Jan. 25, 1780   Regimental Hospital established at Hampton

1921   Thief steals money box from Bank of Hampton lobby holding contributions for starving Armenians from Hampton children who gave up Sunday dinner

Jan. 27, 1924   Kecoughtan Literary Circle gives portrait to Ft. Monroe

Jan. 27, 1925   Oystermen counter nationwide scare of contaminated oysters, charging "yellow journalism"

Jan. 29, 1925   Mrs. M. C. Armstrong donates funds for free library on Victoria Boulevard

Jan. 30, 1924   Delegation urges state legislature not to regulate rates charged by harbor pilots

Jan. 31, 1970   Hampton Coliseum is dedicated with Jack Benny performing

Feb. 1, 1906   Town Council bans overhead signs on streets and sidewalks

1933   Women's Club of Phoebus asks for additional contributions due to "widespread unemployment"

1955   Fort Monroe is made headquarters for Continental Army Command

Feb. 2, 1909   Citizens adopt resolution seeking construction of Bridge Street bridge

Feb. 3, 1941   111th Field Artillery of Virginia National Guard is called into federal military service

1865   Three representatives of Confederacy meet Pres. Lincoln aboard steamer in Hampton Roads in effort to negotiate peace

1898   J. S. Darling wins right to build streetcar line on King Street

Feb. 10, 1634   Benjamin Syms bequeaths property to establish first free school in the country

Feb. 12, 1635   Elizabeth City County Council creates first free school through Syms bequest

1905   New choir sings first service at First Methodist Church

1905   Fire destroys home of keeper of National Cemetery

Feb. 13, 1902   Parade and holiday mark opening of Syms-Eaton Academy, the new elementary school

Feb. 17, 1911   Power plant failure causes 45-minute blackout city-wide

Feb. 19, 1957   Ground is broken for new Dixie Hospital, later Hampton Hospital, on Victoria Boulevard

Feb. 21, 1922   Dirigible *Roma* crashes after takeoff from Langley Field

Feb. 24, 1905   "Frogs" social club celebrates 1st anniversary with dance at Pythian Castle

Feb. 25, 1886   Harrison Phoebus, proprietor of famous Hygeia Hotel, dies

1909   Sightseers fill special trains to Buckroe to see large black whale caught by Taylor Dixon in nets offshore

March 1, 1935   Langley Field becomes center of tactical aviation for the United States Army

March 2, 1755   Two transport ships carrying two hundred Redcoats anchor at Hampton, where five deserters were caught and whipped in view of townspeople

March 2, 1941   High-powered electric transmission line from Richmond to Peninsula is completed

March 4, 1892   Virginia General Assembly grants charter for Hampton Training School for Nurses, later Hampton General Hospital

March 5, 1623	Virginia General Assembly orders court to be held each month in Elizabeth City
March 6, 1830	Reconstructed St. John's Church is consecrated
1962	Ash Wednesday Storm begins, causing great damage
March 7, 1920	Fire destroys Hotel Chamberlin, causing $4 million damage
March 8, 1781	Col. Frances Mallory of Hampton dies fighting British at Big Bethel in last skirmish of Revolution near Hampton
March 9, 1862	Confederate ironclad *Merrimack* and Union ironclad *Monitor* dual off Hampton Roads
March 16, 1895	Telephone service begins in Hampton
March 18, 1879	Presbyterians meet and pass resolution to form church
March 20, 1629	Eight court commissioners for county are appointed
March 30, 1629	Virginia General Assembly passes act to erect new fort at Point Comfort
1908	Hampton reaches population over five thousand and is designated "city of the second class"
April 1, 1900	Phoebus is named in honor of Harrison Phoebus and incorporated as a town
April 6, 1868	Hampton Normal and Agricultural Institute (later Hampton University) opens
1879	First Presbyterian Church is founded
1972	First National Bank in downtown Hampton is demolished for urban renewal
April 9, 1884	Fire destroys Queen Street businesses and homes
April 15, 1623	Buckroe resident reports good prospects for silk industry
1878	Indians are enrolled at Hampton Institute
1942	Twenty-nine German sailors from U-2 sunk off North Carolina are buried in secret at National Cemetery
April 17, 1879	Bethel African Methodist Episcopal Church hosts thirteenth annual state conference
April 21, 1827	Parish vestry name church St. John's
1905	County pest house burns to ground. Two quarantined occupants escape injury
April 26, 1849	James Barron Hope and John Pembroke duel at Buckroe Beach
April 26, 1872	Hampton court institutes public schools
April 29, 1700	Peter Heyman, collector of customs, is killed aboard British ship in combat with pirates
April 30, 1607	Settlers meet Indians at Kecoughtan en route to Jamestown
May 2, 1861	Hampton ratifies vote to secede from Union
May 6, 1862	President Abraham Lincoln arrives at Fort Monroe expecting to see capture of Norfolk by Federals
May 7, 1831	Robert E. Lee reports for duty at Fort Monroe
May 13, 1867	Jefferson Davis, President of the Confederacy, is released from confinement at Fort Monroe
May 14, 1861	Fifty-one member cavalry mustered, named Old Dominion Dragoons
1871	National Cemetery established for soldiers
May 15, 1923	Headquarters for Third Coast Artillery is transferred to Fort Monroe
May 19, 1865	Jefferson Davis is imprisoned at Fort Monroe in Casemate No. 2
May 23, 1861	Federals from Fort Monroe march into Hampton but Hampton's Major Cary and Federal Colonel Phelps make peace pact and

	troops return without bloodshed
May 24, 1861	Three runaway slaves are given sanctuary at Fort Monroe, thus establishing the fort as a refuge during the war
May 28, 1865	Jefferson Davis' ankle irons removed due to public outcry
May 29, 1852	Adelphi Debating Society holds forth in grand jury room
June 1, 1903	Merchants National Bank opens in temporary building
June 4, 1870	One-hundred-thousand-dollar bequest of Horatio Ward of London is awarded to build National Soldiers' Home
June 4, 1918	Thomas Wolfe signed on as laborer at Langley Field, using experiences in his novel *Look Homeward, Angel*
June 10, 1861	Hannah Nicholson Tunnell at early dawn warns Confederates at Big Bethel that Federal troops are approaching
	Virginia forces defeat Federals in first land battle of Civil War despite being outnumbered by nearly four to one
June 20, 1897	Buckroe Beach Hotel opens with large pavilion for dancing
June 24, 1813	Failing to take Norfolk, British land at Indian River
1913	New Dixie Hospital opens on East Queen Street
June 25, 1813	Twenty-five-hundred British land at Hampton
June 28, 1851	Methodist Church is allowed to hold services in courthouse building
July 1, 1715	Governor Spottswood gives permission to erect new courthouse for Elizabeth City County in Hampton
1943	Copeland Park's 3,850 housing units are completed
1952	Hampton consolidates with Elizabeth City County and Phoebus to become city of first class
1973	Dixie Hospital changes its name to Hampton General
July 4, 1837	Dispute over school administration leads to murder of Thomas Allen by Major Cooper, schoolmaster at Hampton Academy
1928	Hampton Yacht Club holds first regatta
July 9, 1610	English capture Indian village at Kecoughtan, driving out inhabitants
1890	Virginia Oyster Planters Association meets in Hampton
July 11, 1920	Langley Memorial Aeronautical Laboratory is dedicated
July 12, 1926	Charles Taylor Memorial Library opens
July 19, 1905	Thunderstorm kills man struck by lightning and injures another
July 27, 1867	County court reopens for first session after Civil War began
July 30, 1619	Legislative Assembly votes to change name of Kecoughtan to Elizabeth City
	Captain William Tucker and William Capps were city's two delegates
Aug. 7, 1861	Gen. John B. Magruder, commander of Virginia Peninsula, orders Hampton resident Capt. Jefferson C. Phillips to set fire to Hampton after reading newspaper report that Federals would quarter troops and former slaves here. Old Dominion Dragoons burn thirty businesses and one-hundred

	houses
1917	Langley Field opens as National Advisory Committee for Aeronautics experimental field
Aug. 19, 1885	Five-thousand people witness Old Point Regatta followed by ball at Hygeia Hotel
Aug. 20, 1952	Syms-Eaton Museum opens
Aug. 23, 1933	Hurricane and tidal wave bring severe damage to Buckroe and other low-lying areas
Sept. 2, 1775	Elizabeth City County residents burn British ship *Otter* after storm drives her into Back River
Sept. 11, 1931	Wife of Dr. Elisha Kent Kane, III, drowns while swimming with him at Grandview Beach
Sept. 12, 1570	Spanish arrive at Kecoughtan
Sept. 13, 1931	Dr. Kane arrested and charged with murder
Sept. 15, 1887	James Barron Hope dies
1899	Quarantine ends after yellow fever kills twelve of forty-three stricken residents of Soldiers' Home
Sept. 17, 1861	Mary Peake begins school to teach blacks to read
Sept. 19, 1659	Thomas Eaton bequeaths land and property to educate children of the county
Sept. 24, 1853	Every white male adult is taxed three dollars to support schools
Oct. 1, 1609	Fort Algernourne is constructed at Point Comfort
1958	National Advisory Committee for Aeronautics becomes National Aeronautics and Space Administration
Oct. 4, 1956	First supersonic "Supersabre" plane is christened *Miss Hampton* at Langley AFB
Oct. 10, 1624	Town council orders construction of church
Oct. 12, 1956	Ground is broken for new Hampton High School
Oct. 18, 1918	Hampton *Monitor* ceases publication
Oct. 24, 1775	British, commanded by former *Otter* captain, attack Hampton but are repulsed by minute-men. Cannonade damages St. John's Church
Oct. 26, 1768	Norborne Berkeley, baron de Botetourt, first full royal governor of Virginia, lands at Little England on the Hampton River on his way to take office in Williamsburg
Oct. 29, 1901	Confederate Monument in St. John's Cemetery is unveiled
Nov. 1, 1918	Work is begun on 40 buildings at Fort Monroe
1957	Hampton Roads Bridge Tunnel opens
Nov. 6, 1956	Hampton votes against consolidation with Newport News and Warwick County
Nov. 15, 1919	Red Cross gains 2297 in Membership campaign
Nov. 15, 1954	Last scheduled passenger train rolls over Hampton tracks
1921	410-foot airship *Roma* makes maiden American flight from Langley Field
Nov. 18, 1619	Virginia Company's London council divides colony into four incorporations, one of which is Kecoughtan
Nov. 19, 1919	Phoebus Men's Club launches two-hundred thousand-dollar campaign for road from Phoebus to Grandview
Nov. 21, 1919	LaSalle Improvement Association begins project to widen stone road
Nov. 21, 1718	Lt. Robert Maynard, British sailor commissioned by Gov. Alexander Spotswood,

	discovers pirate Blackbeard at Ocracoke Inlet, kills him, and in following days brings his head to port of Hampton, mounting it on a pole at mouth of Hampton River as warning to pirates
Nov. 23, 1829	Jame Barron Hope, poet laureate of Virginia, is born
Nov. 27, 1919	Blacks raise twenty-five hundred dollars for school in Wythe
Nov. 30, 1919	Apollo Dance Castle opens in Pythian Hall
Dec. 2, 1919	Leading Hampton men meet to promote change to city manager form of government
Dec. 3, 1910	Conrad Wise Chapman, eminent Civil War artist, dies
Dec. 6, 1884	First issue of *The Home Bulletin* printed for residents of The National Soldiers' Home
1919	Hampton Institute begins cutback in coal use in response to nationwide coal strike
Dec. 18, 1919	John M. Willis resigns after thirty years as head of city schools
Dec. 19, 1606	One hundred five men embarked in vessels under command of Christopher Newport to form first colony of Virginia
Dec. 27, 1884	Round trip steamer fare between Old Point, Virginia and New York is sixteen dollars
Dec. 29, 1919	Hampton Roads Hunting Club established, Capt. H. M. Gallop, president
Dec. 30, 1608	Capt. John Smith begins lodging with Indians due to extreme cold weather
1959	Old Bay Line Steamer *City of Richmond* makes final call at Old Point Comfort

GENERAL BIBLIOGRAPHY

BOOKS

Armstrong, Mary Frances and Helen W. Ludlow. *Hampton and Its Students*. Freeport, New York: Books for Library Press, 1971. (Reprint of 1874 edition).

Armstrong, Mrs. F. M. *The Syms-Eaton Free School*. Hampton: N.p. 1902. (Published for the Benefit of the Daughters of the American Revolution and the Association for the Preservation of Virginia Antiquities).

Brown, Alexander Crosby. *Steam Packets on the Chesapeake: A History of the Old Bay Line Since 1840*. Cambridge, Maryland: Cornell Maritime Press Inc., 1961.

Brown, Alexander Crosby. *The Old Bay Line, 1840-1940*. New York: Bonanza Books, 1977.

Brown, Alexander Crosby. *The Old Bay Line of the Chesapeake*. Newport News: The Mariners Museum, 1938.

Chataigne's Peninsula Directory, 1896-7. J. H. Chataigne, Compiler. N.p.: The Chataigne Directory Company, 1896.

Curtis, Robert I., John Mitchell and Martin Copp. *Langley Field, the Early Years*. Langley Air Force Base: Office of History, 1977.

Elliott, Charles F. *Fox Hill, its people and places: a history of Fox Hill, Virginia*. N.p., 1976.

Engs, Robert Francis. *Freedom's First Generation*. Philadelphia: University of Pennsylvania Press, 1979.

Evans, Mrs. Sandidge. *Lost Landmarks of Old Hampton, Revolutionary War Port Town*. Hampton: Hamilton H. Evans, Hampton Association for The Arts and Humanities, 1976.

Hawkins, Van. *Hampton/Newport News—A Pictorial History*. Virginia Beach: The Donning Company/Publishers Inc., 1975.

Hefflefinger, Jacob. *Kecoughtan Old and New, or Three Hundred Years of Elizabeth City Parish*. Hampton: Houston Printing and Publishing House, 1910.

J. L. Hill Printing Company's Directory of Newport News, Hampton, Phoebus, and Old Point Company. Years 1900-1969. Newport News and Richmond: Hill Directory Company.

Houston, Harry R. *The Peninsula of Virginia*. Hampton: Houston Printing Company, 1933.

Jackson, Luther T. *Phoebus: A Pictorial History*. N.p., 1976.

McCabe, Gillie Cary. *The Story of an Old Town—Hampton, Virginia*. Richmond: Old Dominion Press, 1929.

Montague, E. Sclater. *A Hodgepodge of Memories of Hampton*. Hampton: Houston Printing Company, 1972.

Puryear, Bryon N. *Hampton Institute, A Pictorial Review of its First Century, 1868-1968*. Hampton: Prestige Press, Inc., 1962.

Sinclair, Margaret Munford. *In and Around Hampton—America's Oldest Continuous English Speaking Settlement*. Hampton: N.p., 1957.

Starkey, Marion L. *The First Plantation. History of Hampton and Elizabeth City County, Virginia. 1607-1887*. Hampton: Houston Printing and Publishing House, 1936.

Taylor, Donald Ransome, *Out of the Past—The Future: A History of Hampton, Virginia*. Hampton: Prestige Press, Inc., 1960.

The Industrial Edition of the Hampton Monitor, 1907. Ed. and Comp. Albert E. Walker. Hampton.

The Official Blue Book of the Jamestown Ter-Centenial Exposition. A. D. 1907. Norfolk: The Colonial Publishing Corp. Inc., 1909.

Tyler, Lyon Gardiner. *History of Hampton and Elizabeth City County, Virginia*. Hampton: The Board of Supervisors of Elizabeth City County, 1922.

Weinert, Richard P. and Robert Arthur. *Defender of the Chesapeake, the Story of Fort Monroe*. Richmond: Leeward Publications, 1978.

West, George Benjamin. *When the Yankees Came: Civil War and Reconstruction of the Virginia Peninsula*. Ed. Parke Rouse, Jr. Richmond: Dietz Press, 1977.

Whichard, Roger Dey. *The History of Lower Tidewater, Virginia*. Volumes 1 & 2. New York: Lewis Historical Publishing Co., 1959.

White, Dr. Blanche Sydnor and Mrs. Emily Lewelling Hogg. *The Hampton Baptist Church, 1791-1966*. Hampton: Houston Printing & Publishing House, 1966.

MANUSCRIPTS

Blair, Gladys A. "Northerners In The Reconstruction of Hampton, Virginia, 1865-1870." Thesis for Old Dominion University, 1975.

Brown, Thelma Robins. "Memorial Chapel. The Culmination of the Development of the Campus of Hampton Institute, Hampton, Virginia. 1867-1887." Thesis for University of Virginia, 1971.

Engs, Robert Francis. "The Development of Black Culture and Community in the Emancipation Era: Hampton Roads, Virginia, 1861-1870." Thesis for Yale University, 1972.

Garber, Ethel. "The First Free School." Thesis for University of Virginia, 1971.

Haldeman, Carolyn Louise. "National Defense Efforts and their Effect on the Growth of the Cities of Hampton and Newport News, Virginia." Thesis for University of Virginia, 1964.

Sloan, Patricia Ellen. "A History of the Establishment and Early Development of Selected Schools of Nursing for Afro-Americans, 1886-1906." PhD dissertation for Teachers College, Columbus University, 1977.

ARTICLES AND PAMPHLETS

Campbell, Helen J. "The Syms and Eaton Schools and Their Successor," *William and Mary College Quarterly*, Volume 20, Second Series, January, 1940.

NEWSPAPERS

Daily Press. Newport News, Va. 1898-1985.

Hampton Monitor. Hampton, Va. Jan. 6, 1905-Oct. 18, 1918. Aug. 11, 1972-Mar. 22, 1974.

Home Bulletin. Old Soldiers' Home. Dec. 1885-Nov. 1891.

Southern Workman. Vol. 3-68. Hampton Normal and Agricultural Institute.

Times-Herald. Newport News, Va. 1900-1985.

Additional Sources of Information

CHAPTER ONE: FROM THE SEA TO A CITY

American Beacon, 1815 Norfolk newspaper; *Virginia The Old Dominion* by Matthew Page Andrews; *Travels Through the Middle Settlements in North America in the Years 1759 and 1760* by the Rev. Andrew Burnaby; *The Three Worlds of Captain John Smith* by Phillip Barbour; *Gravestone Inscriptions from the Cemetery of St. John's Episcopal Church* by Bishop John B. Bentley; *George Wythe of Williamsburg* by Joyce Blackburn; *The First Trading Post at Kicotan (Kecoughtan), Hampton, Virginia* by Joseph Benjamin Brittingham; *Wills and Administrations of Elizabeth City County, Virginia and Other Genealogical and Historical Items 1610-1800* by Blanche Adams Chapman; The wills of Thomas Eaton and Benjamin Syms; Elizabeth City County, Virginia, *Records, Wills, Deeds, Orders 1684-1699, 1704-1723 and Record Book No. 10, 1721-1723*; *Chesapeake Bay in the American Revolution* by Ernest M. Eller; *Guardian Accounts, 1737-1748*; *Hening's Statutes, v. 1-13 plus Supplement*; *1775 Another Part of the Field* by Ivor Noel Hume; *Journal of Rear-Admiral James 1752-1821* by Bartholomew James; *Notes on the State of Virginia* by Thomas Jefferson; *The Spanish Jesuit Mission in Virginia 1570-1572* by Clifford M. Lewis and Albert J. Lewis; *Journals of the House of Burgesses of Virginia*, edited by H. R. McIlwaine; *Colonial Virginia*, vol. 1 and 2 by Richard L. Morton; *Niles Weekly Register*, vol. 4; *Norfolk Gazette and Public Ledger (1812-1816)*; *Norfolk Herald* (1812); *The British Empire in America 1673-1742* by John Oldmixon; *The Honorable George Wythe* by Oscar L. Shewmake; *Captain John Smith* by Bradford Smith; *Tidewater Towns* by John W. Reps; Royal Marines File, Correspondence; *The History of the Virginia Navy of the Revolution* by Robert Armistead Stewart; *The Secret Diary of William Byrd of Westover 1739-1741* by Louis B. Wright and Maria Tinling.

CHAPTER TWO: HAMPTON AND THE MILITARY

"Highlights of Black History at Fort Monroe" and "The Coast Artillery at Fort Monroe," Casemate Papers, Casemate Museum; "Saga of Old Fort Wool," *Periodical* (Winter 1976-1977) by Richard P. Weinert, Jr.

The numerous pamphlets in the *Tales of Old Fort Monroe* of the Casemate Museum and the *Coast Artillery Journal* also contain much interesting information on Fort Monroe.

CHAPTER THREE: RELIGION'S SPECIAL ROLE

B'nai Israel Congregation information submitted by Mrs. Lucille C. Markowitz.

Brief histories, without authors, submitted by the following churches: First Presbyterian, First United Church of Christ, First United Methodist, St. John's Episcopal and Central United Methodist Church.

Church of Jesus Christ of Latter Day Saints information submitted by Mrs. Virginia H. Rollins, Public Communications Director, Richmond Region.

The Chapel of the Centurion (A Post Publication).

Daily Press: Islamic Center information from articles by Martha Graham (3-13-84) and Virginia Riggins (4-21-84), and "The Little England Chapel" (undated article).

Much of the information contained in this chapter has come from interviews with ministers, church staff personnel and church members.

The Hampton City Assessor's Office records provided the information for the list of churches that have been organized or have owned property at any one time in Hampton.

CHAPTER FOUR: EDUCATION—IMPORTANT FROM THE ONSET

Reading, Writing and Arithmetic in Virginia by Susie M. Ames; *Men and Deeds* by Brother Julian; *Newport News 325 Years* edited by Alexander Crosby Brown; Elizabeth Buxton Hospital Nurses' School scrapbooks located at West Avenue Branch of the Newport News Public Library; "Education in Hampton" by Joseph Frankoski; "Mary S. Peake, First Teacher of the Freed Men at Fortress Monroe," by June Horsman; "History of Hampton and Elizabeth City County" by J. Luther Kibler; *A Window to the Past: 1906-1984* by Rose King; *Lee's Colonels: A Biographical Register of the Field Officers of the Army of Northern Virginia;* "A Short History of Hampton Institute" by Fritz J. Malval; *Education for Life* by Frances G. Peabody; "Local Report on Elizabeth City County Schools," June 18, 1920, by W. L. Prince; "to see justice done my children" by Hampton Association for the Arts and Humanities; "What's in a Name? Origin of the Names of Hampton City Schools" by Wendy G. Wallio; "Some Echoes from the Past," by Elizabeth Manly Hines.

CHAPTER FIVE: SEAFOOD, STEAMERS, AND STREETCARS

The Hampton Album by Frances B. Johnston; *Tobacco Coast: A Maritime History of Chesapeake Bay in the Colonial Era* by A. P. Middleton; *Hampton Guide Book* by Charles W. Betts; *Shipbuilding in Colonial Virginia* by Cerinda W. Evans; *Shipbuilding in Colonial America* by Joseph A. Goldenberg; *The Belgian Shiplover*, No. 71, Sept-Oct, 1959; *The Fish and Fisheries of Colonial Virginia* by John C. Pearson; *The Old Dominion Line Pilot* of the Old Dominion Steamship Company, 1913-14; *Norfolk Southern Railroad, Old Dominion Line and Connections* by Richard E. Prince.

CHAPTER SIX: HOSPITABLE HAMPTON

"A Citizen's Guide to Hampton City Government," by The League of Women Voters and the City of Hampton; Collected papers of Dr. Chester D. Bradley at Casemate Museum; *The Steamboat Comes to Norfolk Harbor* compiled by John C. Emmerson; "Grand Old Hotels," a slide presentation of the Casemate Museum; "Hampton" compiled by Virginia Peninsula Chamber of Commerce and the City of Hampton; *Historic Hotels of the World* by Robert B. Ludy; *The Insiders' Guide: Williamsburg, Virginia Beach, Norfolk, Hampton*, 1978; "Tourism," by Susan Tiede; the private papers of Charles H. Williams

CHAPTER SEVEN: MODERN HAMPTON 1900-1985

"Notes on Buckroe," by Jessie Skinner Anthony; *Memories of Old Hampton* by the Armstrong League of Hampton Workers; "Harrison Phoebus: From Farm to Fortune," by Chester D. Bradley; *Jamestown and Her Neighbors* by Jane E. Davis; *Back River Lighthouse* by Charles Elliott; "from Canoe...to Capsule," by Hamilton "Sis" Evans; "Hampton, Revolutionary Port Town," by Hampton Association for the Arts and Humanities; *Hampton Illustrated (1892)* by Hampton Board of Trade; *History of the Volunteer Fire Department of Hampton, Virginia 1884-1959;* "In Search of..." by Hampton Planning Department; "Hampton Redevelopment and Housing Authority, 25th Anniversary 1958-1983;" *The Civil War A Pictorial Guide to the Virginia Peninsula* by the Junior League of Hampton Roads, Inc.; "Phoebus" by Inez Knox; "Hampton, You and Tyler Too" by Irene Weston; "Uncle Sam's Eagles Save Hampton," *Richmond Times-Dispatch*, Jan. 13, 1935.

CHAPTER EIGHT:
TO THE STARS—THE DEVELOPMENT OF NASA

Frontiers of Flight: The Story of NACA Research (New York: Alfred A. Knopf, 1948), by George W. Gray; *The High Speed Frontier* (Washington, D.C., NASA, 1980), by John V. Becker; *Wind Tunnels of NASA* (Washington, D.C., NASA, 1981), by Donald D. Baals and William R. Corliss; *Model Research: The National Advisory Committee for Aeronautics, 1915-1958,* two vols. (Washington, D.C., NASA, 1985), by Alex Roland; and *Engineer In Charge: A History of the Langley Aeronautical Laboratory, 1917-1958* (Washington, D.C., NASA, forthcoming), by James R. Hansen.

ABOUT THE AUTHORS

James T. Stensvaag is a historian with the United States Army Training and Doctrine Command at Fort Monroe. He received his Ph.D. from the University of New Mexico. His primary field of interest is social and intellectual history of the American frontier (beginning with the settlement of Hampton). He is the author of numerous articles and reviews on western American history. He is married to the former Paula Lindstrom and is the father of three daughters.

Joseph Frankoski is Education Coordinator at Hampton's Syms-Eaton Museum. He retired from the United States Army with the rank of lieutenant colonel. He received his M.A. degree in history from Old Dominion University and an M.A. in communications from Norfolk State University. He is a member of numerous historical societies, for which he has published articles on history and the military. He is married to the former Chiharu Kaneko and is the father of two daughters.

Judith Milteer is a historical interpreter for the Colonial Williamsburg Foundation. She grew up in Hampton and attended the College of William and Mary. She has been active in church and community service, including membership in the Junior League of Hampton Roads. She is married to Hugh Milteer, who also grew up in Hampton, and is the mother of a son and two daughters.

Chester Brown is pastor of Hampton Baptist Church. A native of Gloucester Point, Virginia, he received his bachelor of divinity degree from Southeastern Theological Seminary. He did post-graduate work at the University of Edinburgh in history, and earned a doctor of ministry degree from Union Theological Seminary in Virginia as well as an honorary doctor of divinity degree from the University of Richmond. He is married to the former Mary Etta Mann and is the father of a son and a daughter.

Carolyn Haldeman Hawkins is a native of Hampton who attended city schools. After receiving a bachelor of arts degree in political science from Mary Baldwin College, she earned a master of arts degree in political science from the University of Virginia. A former elementary school teacher in Albemarle County and Hampton, she has served the community in many volunteer capacities as a member of the Junior League of Hampton Roads. She is married to S. Frear Hawkins, II, also a Hampton native, and is the mother of a son and a daughter.

Richard P. Weinert, Jr., is a historian with the United States Army Training and Doctrine Command at Fort Monroe. He earned his M.A. in history from American University and has done post-graduate work at Instituto Tecnologico de Monterrey, Monterrey, Mexico, as well as the University of Florida and the University of Maryland. He has served as a director of several military history societies. He is the author of more than thirty articles in historical and military journals as well as two books, *The Guns of Fort Monroe*, and *Defender of the Chesapeake: the Story of Fort Monroe*. He is married to the former Janet Bode and is the father of two sons.

Louise Watson Todd, a native of Newport News, Virginia, received her bachelor of arts degree in English from the College of William and Mary and a masters degree in education from Hampton University. She is a former teacher of English at Bethel High School who retired in 1982. She is married to Jesse E. Todd, a member of an old Elizabeth City County family. She and her husband are the parents of a son and a daughter. They also have one grandson.

Irene Bryant Weston is a Hampton native who attended city schools. She received a bachelors degree in education from Farmville State Teacher's College, now Longwood. She taught in public and private schools in Hampton and at Langley Air Force Base until her retirement in 1975. She is the author of *You, and Tyler Too* published for the dedication of John Tyler School in 1967. She and her husband, Joe, have a son and a daughter and four grandchildren.

James R. Hansen is the historian-in-residence at NASA Langley Research Center. He earned his doctor of philosophy degree from The Ohio State University. His field of special interest is the history of science. He is the author of numerous articles as well as a book, *Engineer in Charge: A History of the Langley Aeronautical Laboratory, 1917-1958*. He is married to the former Margaret Miller and is the father of a son and a daughter.

William L. Hudgins, Jr. is a native of Hampton. A mechanical engineer, he is a graduate of the University of Virginia. He has been active in community affairs and is president of the Hampton Historical Society. He is married to the former Lacey Sanford and is the father of one son.

INDEX